Microsoft® WORD For Windows™ and OS/2 Technical Reference

Written by Microsoft Corporation

Edited, produced, and distributed by Microsoft Press

Microsoft PRESS®

PUBLISHED BY
Microsoft Press
A Division of Microsoft Corporation
One Microsoft Way
Redmond, Washington 98052-6399

Library of Congress Cataloging-in-Publication Data
Microsoft Word technical reference : for Windows and OS/2

/Microsoft Corporation
p. cm.--(Application developers library)
Includes index.
ISBN 1-55615-290-6
1. Microsoft Word for Windows (Computer program) 2. Presentation Manager (Computer program) 3. Business--Data processing. 4. Business presentations--Data processing. 5. IBM Personal Computer--Programming. 6. Macroinstructions (Electronic computers) I. Microsoft. II. Series.
HF5548.4.M528M53 1990
652.5'5369--dc20 90-6211
CIP

Printed and bound in the United States of America.

3 4 5 6 7 8 9 MLML 3 2 1

Distributed to the book trade in Canada by Macmillan of Canada, a division of Canada Publishing Corporation.

Contents

Got a hot feature idea?
Call the Microsoft Word Wish Line
(206) 936-WISH
(206) 936-9474

Microsoft

FAX COVERSHEET

To: Mike Posnick
Corp:
Fax #: (612)-920-8130
Phone #: (612)-920-4344

From: Reese Manceaux — Pages: 1

NOTES:
Please understand that Macro support is not part of our standard support service. Thank You. Name this macro AutoNew:

```
Sub Main
DocMaximize(0)
width = Val(AppInfo$(6))
height = Val(AppInfo$(7))
DocMove 0, 0
DocSize width, height
End Sub
```

Fax (704) 357-1170

Chapter 1

Introduction

Microsoft Word for Windows and Microsoft Word for OS/2 are powerful word-processing applications with many advanced features that give them the flexiblilty to handle almost any word-processing need. *Microsoft Word Technical Reference* is intended for users who want to delve more deeply into these features, and for those who want to extend and customize the capabilities of Word.

HOW THIS REFERENCE IS ORGANIZED

This reference contains technical information and is intended for the advanced user. The first few chapters describe WordBASIC, Word's macro programming language. Macros are introduced in Chapter 2, "Introduction to Macros," and Word's macro editor, which you use to enter, test, and edit macros, is covered in Chapter 3, "Using the Macro Editor." If you are not a BASIC programmer and you need a gentle introduction to programming in general and to the WordBASIC macro programming language in particular, or if you are a BASIC programmer and you need an overview of the ways in which WordBASIC differs from the BASIC you know, read Chapter 4, "Interlude—WordBASIC for Beginners." For a more technical introduction to WordBASIC, read Chapter 5, "The WordBASIC Programming Language." If you want to learn about WordBASIC's more complex features, such as custom dialog boxes, error handling, and sequential file handling, read Chapter 6, "More WordBASIC Programming Concepts." For detailed information about all the WordBASIC commands, see Chapter 7, "WordBASIC Command Reference." Finally, if you want to use Dynamic Data Exchange to create links between Microsoft Word and other programs, read Chapter 8, "Dynamic Data Exchange."

Chapters 9 through 11 offer information about Word's other advanced features. If you want to automatically generate indexes and tables of contents and want Word to insert tables, charts, pictures, and text into your documents, read Chapter 9, "Fields." If you plan on writing your own file converter to use specially formatted documents with Word, read Chapter 10, "Rich Text Format" and Chapter 11, "External File Converters."

Additional information is offered in four appendixes. For hints on creating readable WordBASIC programs that are easier to use, maintain, and modify, refer to Appendix A, "Programming Style." For examples of WordBASIC programs, refer to Appendix B, "Program Examples." For information on using Windows Dynamic Link Libraries, refer to Appendix C, "Dynamic Link Libraries." And for information on translating fonts, refer to Appendix D, "Translating Fonts."

OTHER SOURCES OF INFORMATION

Users' groups are good sources of useful macros, document templates, and other information. A users' group consists of people with the same software and hardware interests. Software and hardware dealers can often tell you how to contact the users' groups in your area.

If you have a modem and telecommunications software, you can become a member of the Microsoft Applications Forum on CompuServe Information Service and the Microsoft RoundTable on GEnie. Both forums emphasize Microsoft applications software and offer user-written macros, templates, supplemental files, tips on using Word with other products, and help from other users. Membership in both forums is free and open to all CompuServe and GEnie subscribers. (You must pay normal telephone and online-service charges, however.) On CompuServe, type `go msapp` at the system prompt. On GEnie, type `microsoft` or `m 505` at the system prompt.

If you are a software developer or information system manager who needs assistance with more technical questions, Microsoft OnLine provides a direct link to qualified Microsoft support engineers. For subscription costs and more information about Microsoft OnLine, call 800–443–4672. Outside the United States, contact your local Microsoft representative for more information about available services. If you do not know who your representative is, refer to the list of Microsoft's international addresses that came with your Word package.

Unless otherwise specified, books referred to in this reference are included in the Microsoft Word documentation set. For example, "see the *Word User's Reference*" refers to the *Microsoft Word User's Reference* supplied in the Word package. If you need help learning how to program in BASIC, consult the reading list at the end of Chapter 4, "Interlude—WordBASIC for Beginners." The following books offer more information on Windows and OS/2 programming:

Petzold, Charles, *Programming Windows*, 2d ed. Redmond, WA: Microsoft Press, 1990.

Microsoft Corporation, *Microsoft OS/2 Programmer's Reference, Volume 1*. Redmond, WA: Microsoft Press, 1989.

Microsoft Corporation, *Microsoft OS/2 Programmer's Reference, Volume 2*. Redmond, WA: Microsoft Press, 1989.

Microsoft Corporation, *Microsoft OS/2 Programmer's Reference, Volume 3*. Redmond, WA: Microsoft Press, 1989.

Microsoft Corporation, *Microsoft OS/2 Programmer's Reference, Volume 4*. Redmond, WA: Microsoft Press, 1990.

TYPOGRAPHIC CONVENTIONS

In this reference, the following typographic conventions are used:

- The names used for keyboard commands are shown in small capitals. For example:

  The INSERT FIELD key is Ctrl+F9.

- Rich Text Format control words and symbols, WordBASIC statement and function keywords, field types, and field switches and their arguments are shown in bold. The following is an example of a Rich Text Format control word:

  {\colortbl}

- WordBASIC statement and function arguments and other parameters that take variable input are shown in italic. For example:

  InsertBreak *Type*
  \pich*n*

- DOS and OS/2 file names and field names are shown in all capital letters. For example:

  You can change this entry in your WIN.INI file.
  The AUTONUM field is an automatic result field.

- Program listings, user input, and program output are shown in monospace type. Examples are sometimes truncated due to space constraints, and ellipses are used when only a portion of the program code is shown. For example:

```
Sub MAIN
   Dim dlgrec As FormatDocument
   GetCurValues dlgrec
   .
   .
   .
```

- Brackets ([ ]) enclose optional items in syntax lines. For example:

  SmallCaps *[On]*
  {include *Filename [PlaceReference]***}**

Chapter 2

Introduction to Macros

Microsoft Word is a feature-packed document-processing system. However, features alone cannot solve all common document-processing problems. Situations are bound to arise that present problems the program designer could not possibly have anticipated—problems whose solutions seem to involve time-consuming and repetitive work. For example, a design change might require that all headings in a 200-page proposal be modified from bold, left-justified, 12-point Times Roman to italic, centered, 14-point Courier, except for the first heading of the first page of each section. Or a weekly company newsletter might require that dozens of messages received through an electronic-mail system undergo complicated reformatting to be included in the newsletter document. Or a large number of form letters and contracts prepared with an obsolete or obscure word-processing program might need to be reformatted for use with Microsoft Word.

Fortunately, the designers of Microsoft Word have anticipated the unanticipatable, by incorporating into Word a macro capability that allows you to configure and customize Word for many situations.

Word offers a powerful macro-recorder function with which you can combine a series of Word commands and actions to create a macro—in effect a custom command—suited to the special needs of your problem. Whenever you frequently repeat the same steps in Word, you are likely to find that creating a macro to perform the task can save you some time and effort. Having created the macro, you run it either by choosing the Macro Run command, by adding the macro to a

Word menu and choosing it from there, or by assigning the macro to a specific key combination.

WHAT IS WORDBASIC?

When you record a macro in Word, you are actually creating a program in a special programming language called WordBASIC. WordBASIC is based on a subset of Microsoft QuickBASIC, with many special word-processing functions added. You can use Word's macro editor to modify, extend, or combine WordBASIC programs created with the macro recorder. You can even create a macro totally from scratch by typing commands and statements into the macro editor.

You don't have to be a programmer or computer expert to program in WordBASIC. Like any "dialect" of BASIC, WordBASIC is easy to learn. Besides, the macro recorder allows you to create useful programs without ever having to look at the WordBASIC programs themselves.

USES FOR WORDBASIC

At first glance, WordBASIC might seem to have a daunting number of commands and statements. However, most of them are WordBASIC terms for Microsoft Word commands with which you may already be familiar. For example, the WordBASIC term for the Copy command on the Edit menu is **EditCopy**. Word uses terms like this one for the macros you create with the macro recorder, but WordBASIC has capabilities that go far beyond the basic Word commands.

Most important of these additional capabilities are WordBASIC's mechanisms for branching and control of program flow. Using the extended control capabilities of WordBASIC, you can repeat a macro or a portion of a macro a specified number of times, or you can repeat an action until a specified condition, such as searching to the end of a document, has been satisfied. Using WordBASIC's branching capabilities, a macro can perform different actions depending on the conditions encountered. For example, a macro might convert occurrences of a company name in a document to all capitals only when they occur in a chapter or section heading.

With WordBASIC, you can create macros that use printed prompts and custom dialog boxes to communicate with the user. WordBasic programs can create and store their own files on disk, and they can intercept error messages and attempt to handle problems without your intervention.

WordBASIC provides all of the advanced document-manipulation capabilities of Word with the flexibility and control of a programming language. WordBASIC allows you to customize Word for special tasks, and it allows Word to perform complex and repetitive tasks without your constant attention. Using macros, fields (see Chapter 9, "Fields"), and templates, you can create a complete document-processing system that meets your specific needs.

IF YOU ARE NOT A BASIC PROGRAMMER

This book is not intended as a BASIC tutorial. Most sections assume some familiarity with the fundamentals of BASIC programming. If you have never programmed in BASIC before, it is recommended that you proceed to Chapter 4, "Interlude—WordBASIC for Beginners." That chapter provides an introduction to WordBASIC programs and how they work. A list of books that give a more complete introduction to BASIC is provided at the end of that chapter.

IF YOU ARE A BASIC PROGRAMMER

If you have experience programming in a more conventional dialect of BASIC, such as IBM BASICA, Microsoft GWBASIC, or Microsoft QuickBASIC, you will find many aspects of WordBASIC familiar, but you will also find many differences. A few issues are of special interest to BASIC programmers.

Word Approach vs. BASIC Approach

No matter how much it may look like a stand-alone programming language, WordBASIC is a function of Microsoft Word. Consequently, when solving any problem with WordBASIC, you will often have a choice between two ways of doing things: the BASIC-oriented way (using common BASIC statements and functions) and the Word-oriented way (using WordBASIC's access to Word features). As a BASIC programmer, you may have a preference for the BASIC approach, but the Word approach is often faster, involves less code, and is easier to write. For example, if you needed to search a block of text for *Data Marketing* and replace it with *Data Marketing, Inc.*, the BASIC approach would have you:

- Set up a loop to break the text into a series of strings.
- Search each string with the **MID$** function.
- Replace occurrences of *Data Marketing* using other string functions.

Additional steps would be required to convert document text into BASIC strings and back again after you had completed the replacement. The Word approach would require only a single command: **EditReplace**.

WordBASIC programs also differ from programs written in other versions of BASIC in the way they interact with the user. Although WordBASIC supports **Print** and **Input**, these functions operate only in the single-line status bar at the bottom of the Word window. In most instances, it is better to take advantage of Word's graphical interface by using dialog, input, and message boxes for communication between the macro and the user. A variety of new commands have been added to WordBASIC to make possible the use of the graphic interface, and every BASIC programmer should become familiar with them.

Line Numbers

The version of BASIC you are familiar with may use line numbers. WordBASIC does not. Inserting line numbers in WordBASIC programs generates an error. Instead of using line numbers, WordBASIC calls functions and subroutines by name. You can insert labels in the program for reference by the **Goto** command. These labels can be text, numbers, or a combination of the two.

Recording vs. Typing of Programs

Simply because you have the skills to write programs from scratch is no reason to avoid the macro recorder. No matter how great your programming skills, the macro recorder can save you time and effort. You will find that you can record many WordBASIC functions and commands much faster than you can type them. In particular, Word's formatting and editing commands lend themselves to recording. You can then use the WordBASIC programs you have recorded as the basis for your custom programming.

Macros as a Subroutine of Microsoft Word

With a standard programming language, each program stands alone. With WordBASIC, each macro program acts as a subroutine of Word. For this reason, when you use the macro editor to start a new macro, Word has already inserted the following lines:

```
Sub MAIN

End Sub
```

With only a few exceptions, you must put everything in your program between those two statements. The exceptions are other subroutine definitions, function definitions, and statements that define global variables. You cannot define subroutines, functions, or global variables within a subroutine. Instead, you define and name them outside the subroutine and then call them inside the subroutine simply by referencing their names. Failure to follow this rule will cause your macro to generate an error.

WordBASIC as a Batch Language

Thinking of WordBASIC as a programming language may cause you to overlook some of its many applications. You can also use WordBASIC as a batch language, much like the batch language in DOS or OS/2. To facilitate this use, Word includes a special class of macros, called *auto macros*, that execute whenever certain conditions occur. For example, the AutoExec macro runs each time you start Word. AutoClose runs each time you close a file. See Chapter 6, "More WordBASIC Programming Concepts," for details of several other auto macros.

WordBasic programs are like batch programs in one other important way. Word processes commands in a specific order. For example, when you select Format Paragraph from a menu, Word searches for a Format Paragraph function in three levels of program. First, it searches template macros; second, it searches global macros; and finally, it searches Word's built-in functions (see Chapter 5, "The WordBASIC Programming Language," for more information on this hierarchy). This method of processing commands means that if you write your own Format Paragraph global macro, Word will run it rather than its own built-in function. Such a macro might present a menu of paragraph formats that you use often. You could add an option for calling the built-in Format Paragraph function if none of the paragraph formats on the menu is appropriate. In this way, you can customize the functionality of Word to your specifications.

Chapter 3

Using the Macro Editor

A macro is a set of WordBASIC instructions that use the features of Microsoft Word to perform a specific task. This task can be simple, such as changing a paragraph indent, or complex, such as converting a Word document to the format required by a proprietary typesetting system.

As mentioned in Chapter 2, "Introduction to Macros," there are three ways to create a macro in Word. First, you can use the Macro Record feature to record a macro consisting of a series of keystrokes and commands. Second, you can use the Macro Edit feature to write a macro consisting of the statements of WordBASIC, the Word programming language. And third, you can combine the first two methods, recording part of the macro and then adding to its functionality using the macro editor.

This chapter introduces you to the macro editor and shows you how to create a macro using the macro recorder, the macro editor, or a combination of the two. For information about specific WordBASIC statements and functions, see Chapter 7, "WordBASIC Command Reference."

The macro editor offers a subset of the functions available in the regular Word document editor. Like the document editor, the macro editor lets you place your insertion point anywhere in the document and select a block of text. You can cut, copy, or paste selected text elsewhere within the macro or into a different macro or file. The macro editor also incorporates Word's powerful Find and Change commands.

Because the macro editor is not designed to produce a printed document or a stand-alone file, many of the document editor's functions are unnecessary and are therefore disabled. For example, character-formatting and paragraph-formatting functions are disabled. If you paste text with special formatting into a macro, the formatting is automatically removed when the macro is executed.

In addition to providing an environment where you can write macros, the macro editor also provides a laboratory for testing, refining, and debugging any WordBASIC macros you write. Special features allow you to execute a macro a step at a time, to inspect and modify the contents of variables, and to observe the order in which Word performs the steps of the macro.

MACRO STORAGE

Word stores macro programs differently from documents, and so many of the commands on the File menu are unavailable. Rather than storing each macro as a separate file, Word stores macros as part of a document template. If you choose the Global option when saving a macro, Word stores the macro in the default template file (NORMAL.DOT). Macros stored this way are available in any document any time that you use Word.

If you choose the Template option when saving a macro, Word stores the macro in a specific document template file (*filename*.DOT). Macros stored this way are available only within that particular template or in documents created from that template.

It might seem reasonable, given the limitations of the Template option, to store all your macros with the Global option. There are good reasons for not doing this, however. You will find, as you incorporate more of Word's advanced features into your macros, that many macros are closely associated with a particular type of document and have no application to other types of documents. As a result, your NORMAL.DOT file can soon become cluttered with macros that are useless in most documents. The NORMAL.DOT file itself can become so large that it is burdensome, wasting disk space and taking up memory required for other purposes. It is better to create a separate template for each of the tasks you perform on a regular basis and store the pertinent macros in each template. Store a macro with the Global option only when you will use it often and when the macro is of general utility, rather than being associated with a particular type of document.

USING THE MACRO RECORDER TO RECORD A MACRO

To record a macro, you turn on the recorder, and Word stores all the actions you take until you turn off the recorder. The macro recorder cannot record mouse movements, so you cannot select or manipulate text with the mouse while the recorder is turned on. You must select and manipulate text from the keyboard. However, you can use the mouse to control windows and to select commands from menus.

To record a macro:

1. Choose Macro Record (Alt,M,C).

   The Macro Record dialog box appears on the screen.
2. Type the name you want to give the macro or accept the proposed name.
3. If you want, type a description of the macro in the Description box.
4. When you are ready to begin recording, choose OK. Word records any subsequent steps you perform.
5. To stop the macro recorder, choose Macro Stop Recorder (Alt,M,C).

USING THE MACRO EDITOR TO WRITE A MACRO

To write a macro, you invoke the macro editor by choosing the Macro Edit command. When you choose Macro Edit, the Edit Macro dialog box is displayed. When creating a new macro, you should first select the macro's context. Select Global if you want the macro to be stored in your NORMAL.DOT file and be available to all your documents. Select Template if you want the macro to be stored in a document template. The Template option will be unavailable if a template file is not open (that is, the current document window contains a document template or a document created from one).

If you have already created a macro, its name is displayed in the dialog box's list box. If you check Show All, the macro list includes the names of WordBASIC's built-in commands. Selecting one of these names creates a new macro with the same name as the built-in function. As mentioned in Chapter 2, "Introduction to Macros," if a macro and a built-in WordBASIC command both have the same name, Word executes the macro. If a global and a template macro both have the same name, Word executes the template macro. By creating global macros that override built-in Word commands and template macros that override global macros, you can customize Word functions to meet your needs.

If you select an existing macro from the list, you can delete or rename the macro by choosing the appropriate buttons. The Delete and Rename options are unavailable if you select one of the built-in commands.

To create a new macro with a new name, type the name in the text box. Macro names can be up to 40 characters long and can include uppercase and lowercase letters. Only macro names that fit in the text box appear in their entirety on the macro list or on menus.

You can use the text box at the bottom of the dialog box to add an optional description of the macro. Including descriptions is good practice, because even a few words can serve as a reminder of the macro's purpose. If you add a macro to one of Word's menus, the description appears in the status bar whenever you highlight the macro's name on its assigned macro. When you add or edit a macro description, use the Set button to save the new description.

To write a macro:

1. Choose Macro Edit (Alt,M,E), type a name for the macro, and then choose OK.

   The macro-editing icon bar appears below the menu bar.

2. Type the desired macro statements and functions.

3. Close the macro-editing window (Alt,F,C).

4. Choose Yes when you see a message box asking if you want to save the changes.

The Macro-Editing Icon Bar

The macro-editing icon bar includes a number of functions that can help you find and correct errors in your macro programs. These icons include:

Start/Continue. Runs the active macro; changes from Start to Continue when the macro stops (such as after a step in step mode, or when the macro contains a **Stop** command).

Step. Runs a single macro instruction and then stops. If the instruction is a subroutine, Word treats each instruction in the subroutine as a single step.

Step SUBs. Runs a single macro instruction and then stops. If the instruction is a subroutine, Word treats the entire subroutine as a single step.

Trace. Runs the active macro, highlighting each instruction as Word carries it out.

Vars. Displays the variables the macro uses. Also allows you to modify the contents of a variable.

Global/(Template name). Displays the context (global or template) of the active macro. If the context is template, the template name is displayed.

(Name). Displays the name of the active macro.

RUNNING A MACRO

> NOTE: *Because an untested macro can create errors or alter a file, always make backup copies of your files before you test a new macro. You may also want to develop macros in a special test template. After you have written and tested the macro, you can copy it onto the Clipboard and then paste it into a working template.*

After you have written your macro, you run it by doing the following:

1. Choose Macro Run (Alt,M,R).
2. Type the name of the macro you want to run or select the name from the list in the Macro Run Name box.
3. Choose OK.

A SAMPLE MACRO

The following procedures create a macro that automatically sets formatting properties for a document:

1. Be sure you are in draft view or normal document view.
2. If the status bar is not displayed, choose View Status Bar (Alt,V,S).
3. Choose Macro Record (Alt,M,C).
4. In the Macro Record Name box, type `PageSetup` as the name for the macro.

   Note that the Global Context option is selected, meaning the macro can be used in any document you open.

5. Choose OK.

   The letters *REC* appear at the right end of the status bar, indicating that Word is now recording any keystrokes you make.

Now choose the commands and options you want Word to record in the PageSetup macro:

1. Choose Format Document (Alt,T,D).
2. Change the default tab stops to 0.25".
3. Change the left margin to 1".
4. Change the right margin to 0.5".
5. Choose OK to accept these changes.
6. Choose Format Character (Alt,T,C).
7. Change the font to Tms Rmn.
8. Change the font size to 12.
9. Choose OK to accept these changes.
10. Choose Edit Header/Footer (Alt,E,H).
11. Select Footer and choose OK to open the header/footer window.
12. Choose the page icon to insert a page number at the left side of the footer.
13. Press Tab twice and then choose the date icon to insert the date at the right side of the footer.
14. Choose Close.
15. To stop recording, choose Macro Stop Recorder (Alt,M,C).

    The letters *REC* disappear from the status bar.

To test the macro you have just recorded:

1. Choose Macro Run (Alt,M,R).
2. Select PageSetup and choose OK.

   If you made any mistakes while recording the macro, messages appear on the screen.

You can add the macro to the Macro menu for easier access. To add the PageSetup macro to the Macro menu:

1. Choose Macro Assign To Menu (Alt,M,M).
2. In the Assign Macro Name list box, select PageSetup.
3. In the Menu box, select &Macro.
4. Choose Assign, and then choose Close.

   The PageSetup macro now appears on the Macro menu with the name PageSetup.

To run this macro, press Alt,M,P. If you want to remove the macro from the Macro menu, choose Macro Assign To Menu, select PageSetup, and choose Unassign.

You can use the Macro Edit command to look at the WordBASIC commands that Word inserts when you record a macro. To look at the PageSetup macro:

1. Choose Macro Edit (Alt,M,E).
2. Type or select PageSetup and choose OK.
3. The PageSetup macro appears in the macro-editing window. The statements and functions that make up the PageSetup macro correspond with the actions you recorded.

Other example macros are available in the EXAMPLES.DOT file that came on your Word disks.

Chapter 4

Interlude—

WordBASIC for Beginners

This chapter introduces the general principles of programming in Microsoft WordBASIC. It focuses on the fundamentals so that you can start programming as quickly as possible. The chapter emphasizes the control and numeric functions of WordBASIC, because these aspects of WordBASIC may be unfamiliar to beginners.

If you have never programmed before, you should read this chapter carefully. When you have finished this chapter, you will be able to write simple WordBASIC programs. Later chapters will show you how to use the Word-related features of WordBASIC.

If you have programmed in BASIC before, you may want to skim this chapter to get a general idea of the differences between WordBASIC and the BASIC dialect you know. Or you may want to go straight to Chapter 5, "The WordBASIC Programming Language," referring to this chapter only if you come across something you don't understand. Remember that WordBASIC is a subset of QuickBASIC and does not contain a number of BASIC commands with which you might be familiar. Remember also that such features as recursion and error checking are limited in WordBASIC.

This chapter offers many brief program examples that show how each element of WordBASIC works. The quickest way to learn WordBASIC is to enter and run these examples as you read, so take the time to study each example to understand why it works the way it does. Be sure you grasp the material in one section before going on to the next.

When you have completed this chapter, you will understand how to do the following:

- Display words and numbers in the status bar and in dialog boxes.
- Define and use variables.
- Perform calculations and use WordBASIC's math functions.
- Use arrays of variables.
- Execute sections of your program selectively.
- Repeat a group of instructions a specific number of times or until a condition is met.

WHAT IS A PROGRAM?

A *program* is a sequence of instructions to the computer, written in a language both you and the computer understand. Each instruction is called a *statement* and usually takes up one line in the program. The goal of any program is to perform some useful job. The goal of a WordBASIC program might be, for example, to reformat a document, merge elements from several documents into a new document, or insert a chart into a weekly report.

Programming is the process of deciding what you want the program to do and then selecting and arranging statements to accomplish the individual tasks needed to reach the overall goal. This process is part science and part art. You learn the science from books; the art comes gradually, from writing your own programs and analyzing programs written by others.

THE ELEMENTS OF A WORDBASIC STATEMENT

Before you can write a WordBASIC program, you need to be familiar with the elements of a WordBASIC statement and understand how they fit together. The first part of this chapter introduces the elements. Many WordBASIC statements have features that are not described in this chapter. If you want more information about a particular statement or language feature, refer to Chapter 7, "WordBASIC Command Reference."

In this section, concepts are illustrated with the **Print** statement. The **Print** statement is WordBASIC's simplest command for writing on the screen. Although **Print** is very easy to use, WordBASIC can display only a single line in the status bar at the bottom of the Word window. You will use it in early examples. Later, you will learn how to produce message boxes that overlay the Word window and ask for confirmation before the program continues.

To do the exercises in this section, you should load Word and then open a test template:

1. Choose File New.
2. Select the Template button.
3. Choose OK.

Because WordBASIC programs can modify your documents and other programs, it is best to make a backup of all your files and then write and test a new program in its own template file. If you want to add a tested program to your NORMAL.DOT or to another template, you can use the Clipboard to cut and paste the program between templates.

Next, you need to display the macro-editing window:

1. Select Macro Edit.
2. Select Template in the Context group box.
3. In the Edit Macro Name text box, type `Print1`. Choose OK. The macro-editing window is displayed.

Notice that the lines

```
Sub MAIN

End Sub
```

are already displayed on the screen. These lines begin and end the main part of all WordBASIC programs. The statements that make up your program will appear between these two lines.

Statements and Functions

A statement is one or more WordBASIC keywords, sometimes combined with strings, numbers, variables, and operators. (A *keyword* is the name of a particular statement or function. Strings, numbers, variables, and operators will be explained in subsequent sections of this chapter.) WordBASIC treats a statement as a single unit—an instruction to carry out a particular task. The term *statement* can refer to one-line instructions such as **Beep**, as well as to multiline, compound instructions such as **If...Then** and **While...Wend** loops (discussed later in this chapter).

A function also consists of a WordBASIC keyword, often combined with variables and sometimes combined with variables and operators. A function carries out a procedure and produces a value that can be used elsewhere in the program. WordBASIC has many built-in functions for carrying out common procedures, such as **Window( )**, which fetches (returns) the number of the active window, and **Date$( )**, which returns today's date. Notice the parentheses following the function's keyword. If the function has variables and operators, they are placed between the opening and closing parentheses.

Strings and Numbers

A *string* is any group of characters (letters, numbers, or symbols) enclosed in quotation marks. The following example program shows how the **Print** statement displays a string:

1. Type the following line:

   ```
   Print "Hello, World"
   ```

2. Choose Start from the macro-editing icon bar.

The output in the status bar at the bottom of the Word window appears as follows:

```
Hello, World
```

The quotation marks that surround a string are not part of the string, so they do not appear in the display.

> **NOTE:** *WordBASIC is not case sensitive; that is, you don't have to enter the examples with uppercase and lowercase letters exactly as shown. WordBASIC recognizes keywords and automatically capitalizes their first letters, leaving everything else just as you entered it. The examples are shown the way WordBASIC formats them.*

You can also use the **Print** statement to display numbers, as in the following example:

1. Select the text `"Hello, World"`, including the quotation marks.

2. Select Edit Cut.
3. Type the following:

```
63 + 1
```

4. Choose Start from the macro-editing icon bar.

The output in the status bar at the bottom of the Word window appears as follows:

```
64
```

To see more clearly the difference between strings and numbers, do the following:

1. Insert quotation marks before `63` and after `1`.
2. Choose Start from the macro-editing icon bar.

This time the output appears as follows:

```
63 + 1
```

Variables

Programs take data from the outside world (input) and process it to produce useful information (output). The input and output data are stored in the computer's memory. You don't have to know where the data is stored or how. WordBASIC keeps track of that for you. You do need a method of telling WordBASIC which piece of data you want to work with, however. You specify the data by means of *variables*.

Variables are names for locations in memory where data is stored. You decide what these names should be. For example, the first time you use a particular piece of data in a program, you might tell WordBASIC to store the data in a location called `Sales`. WordBASIC automatically assigns the name `Sales` to a storage location in memory, and each time you want to use the data stored in `Sales`, all you have to do is refer to the data by the name under which it is stored.

If you include in a program a word that is not a WordBASIC keyword, a string, or a number, WordBASIC assumes that the word is a variable and automatically assigns the variable name to a storage location. Here is an example:

1. Select the text `63 + 1`.
2. Select Edit Cut.

3. Type the following:

   ```
   Hello, World
   ```

   Do not enclose these words in quotation marks.

4. Choose Start from the macro-editing icon bar.

The output in the status bar at the bottom of the Word window appears as follows:

```
0         0
```

When WordBASIC encounters `Hello` and `World`, it has to figure out what these words are. They aren't keywords (that is, they aren't part of the WordBASIC language, as **Print** is). They aren't strings, because they aren't enclosed in quotation marks. They are definitely not numbers. Therefore, `Hello` and `World` must be variables.

After making this decision, WordBASIC sets aside storage space with the names `Hello` and `World`. No data has yet been stored in these spaces, so they contain initial values of zero, and the **Print** statement displays two zeros.

Variable names

Variable names can contain digits, but you cannot begin a variable name with a digit, because WordBASIC interprets any word starting with a digit as a number. Variable names allowed by WordBASIC include:

```
gerbils
birthdate
Kroyl
NAME3
ep451p33
```

These are illegal names:

```
5remove
4.3less
```

Variable types

Because the data you use in your programs might be string data or numeric data, WordBASIC has two categories of variables: string and floating point.

String Variable. Holds a string of characters. The name of a string variable ends in $. Initially, a string variable contains no data at all, not even blank spaces, and is assigned a length of zero. For example, if the string variable `blank$` has not previously been given a value, the statement `Print blank$` displays an empty line.

Floating-Point Variable. Holds a floating-point number. A floating-point number can have a fractional part (though it doesn't have to). For example, 0.123, 78.26, 7.0, and 1922.001234 are all floating-point numbers. Any variable name ending in a letter or digit is a double-precision floating-point variable and can have values from about -1.7×10^{308} to 1.7×10^{308} (that's 17 followed by 307 zeros). A double-precision floating-point variable is accurate to about 15 decimal places.

Assigning values to variables

You assign data—a value—to a particular storage location—a variable—with an *assignment statement.* An assignment statement has three components: the variable that is to receive the new value; an equal sign (=); and the value itself. The value can be a string, a number, or an expression that produces a string or value. (Expressions are explained later in the chapter.)

These are all valid assignment statements:

```
age = 41

myname$ = "Willie"

result = result3 + leftval + rightval
```

Try assigning values to variables. In the following example, you combine two strings to make a longer string and then assign the result to a third string:

1. Select the text.

   ```
   Print Hello, World
   ```

2. Select Edit Cut.

3. Type the following program lines:

   ```
   String1$ = "Hello,"
   String2$ = " there!"
   BigString$ = String1$ + String2$
   Print BigString$
   ```

4. Choose Start from the macro-editing icon bar.

The output in the status bar at the bottom of the Word window appears as follows:

```
Hello, there!
```

Although you use the equal sign in assignment statements, in this case the equal sign does not signify algebraic equality. To WordBASIC, the assignment statement means: "Perform all the calculations and data manipulations on the right side of the equal sign and then give the result to the variable on the left side of the equal sign."

You can use the same variable name on both sides of the equal sign—for example, when you want to change the variable's value. Try the following example program:

1. Select the following text:

```
String1$ = "Hello,"
String2$ = " there!"
BigString$ = String1$ + String2$
Print BigString$
```

2. Select Edit Cut.

3. Type the following program lines:

```
Counter = 6
Counter = Counter - 1
Print Counter
```

4. Choose Start from the macro-editing icon bar.

The output in the status bar at the bottom of the Word window appears as follows:

```
5
```

You cannot assign numeric values to string variables (or vice versa), so the following statements are illegal:

```
Strg$ = 3.14159
Number= "hi, there"
```

Either one of these statements halts execution and causes WordBASIC to display the error message *Type mismatch.*

A string variable accepts whatever you type, because all entries—even numbers—are actually strings. When you type 42, you are not typing the number 42, but rather the characters 4 and 2. If the variable is numeric, WordBASIC converts the string to a number before assigning it. If the variable is a string, WordBASIC simply assigns the character sequence 42 to the variable.

A numeric variable, however, can only be assigned to a number. If you type `dog` when you should enter a number, WordBASIC assigns a value of 0 (zero) to the variable. Unlike some other versions of BASIC, WordBASIC does not generate an error in this situation.

Expressions

An *expression* is what most people would call a *formula*. An expression is any combination of numbers, strings, variables, functions, and operators that can be evaluated. For example, `2 + 2` is a simple expression that evaluates to 4. Here are some other examples of valid expressions:

```
Code$ = Zip$ + PlusFour$

WrdCount = DocCount + AppdxCount

Pages = Pages - 1

Retail = Cost + (Cost * .23) + (Cost * TaxPercent)
```

The expression `Animals = Dog$ + Cats` is illegal. If you include this expression in a program, WordBASIC displays the error message *Type mismatch* when you run the program. You cannot add a number (or floating-point variable) to a string (or string variable). Nor can you assign the value of a number (or floating-point variable) to a string (or string variable). You must first use a WordBASIC function to convert the number into a string or the string into a number (see Chapter 7, "WordBASIC Command Reference," for more information about conversion functions).

Expressions can be quite complex; for example, the results of one expression might be passed to a function, and the value returned by the function might then be combined with other expressions to yield the final value. You can use a numeric or string expression (no matter how complex) that evaluates to a number or a string almost anywhere you would use a simple number or string, including in WordBASIC's assignment statements.

Another kind of expression called a *Boolean expression* or *relational expression* is discussed later in this chapter.

Mathematical Calculations

One type of expression you might need to use frequently is mathematical calculations. In WordBASIC, the mathematical operations of addition, subtraction, multiplication, and division are represented by + , – , * (the asterisk), and / (the forward slash), respectively. Here are some examples:

Operation	Result
`Print 2 + 3`	`5`
`Print 2 - 3`	`-1`
`Print 2 * 3`	`6`
`Print 2 / 3`	`.6666667`

In addition, WordBASIC has one mathematical operator you may not have seen before: **MOD**, the remainder operator. **MOD** performs a special type of division in which the whole-number part of the division result is discarded and the remainder is returned. For example:

Operation	Result
`Print 7 MOD 3`	`1`
`Print 11 MOD 4`	`3`

MOD truncates the numbers to be divided before performing the calculation. Thus, the number 9.6 becomes 9 and 2.4 becomes 2.

Precedence of operations

WordBASIC evaluates mathematical expressions from left to right, following the rules of algebraic precedence: Exponentiation is performed first, then multiplication and division, and then addition and subtraction. The following example illustrates algebraic precedence:

1. Select all the program lines between, but not including, the **Sub MAIN** and **End Sub** lines.
2. Select Edit Cut.
3. Type the following program line:

   ```
   Print 2 * 3 + 3 - 2 / 3
   ```

4. Choose Start from the macro-editing icon bar.

The output in the status bar at the bottom of the Word window appears as follows:

```
8.3333333333
```

You can use parentheses to confirm or override normal precedence. Try this example:

1. Select the following text:

   ```
   Print 2 * 3 + 3 - 2 / 3
   ```

2. Select Edit Cut.
3. Type the following program line:

   ```
   Print (2 * 3) + 3 - (2 / 3)
   ```

4. Choose Start from the macro-editing icon bar.

The output appears as follows:

```
8.3333333333
```

The result is the same as in the previous example because the precedence of operations dictated by the parentheses is no different from the usual order. However, the next example program produces a different result:

1. Select the following text:

   ```
   Print (2 * 3) + 3 - (2 / 3)
   ```

2. Select Edit Cut.
3. Type the following program line:

   ```
   Print (2 * 3) + (3 - 2)/ 3
   ```

4. Choose Start from the macro-editing icon bar.

The output appears as follows:

```
6.3333333333
```

The result here is different because WordBASIC performs the calculations within parentheses first.

Within parentheses, the usual precedence applies. The expression `(3 - 2 / 3)` evaluates as `(3 - .6666667)`, not `(1 / 3)`.

You might want to use parentheses to control the order of calculations, rather than depending on precedence. Even when the usual precedence of operations meets your needs, using parentheses prevents errors and makes your programs easier to understand.

Mathematical functions

Along with the addition, subtraction, multiplication, division, and **MOD** operators, WordBASIC provides the following mathematical functions for performing common calculations:

Function	Description
ABS	Returns the absolute value of the expression.
SGN	Returns –1 if the expression is less than 0; 0 if it is 0; +1 if it is greater than 0.
INT	Returns the integer form of the number.

To use a function, you insert the variable or expression on which you want WordBASIC to perform the function in the parentheses following the function name. The expression may be any valid combination of variables, numbers, and math functions.

The following example shows a use of the **INT( )** function:

1. Select the following text:

```
Print (2 * 3) + (3 - 2)/ 3
```

2. Select Edit Cut.
3. Type the following program lines:

```
NumWords = 19
Middle = Int(NumWords / 2)
Print "The middle word is" ; Middle; " words from the left."
```

4. Choose Start from the macro-editing icon bar.

The output appears as follows:

```
The middle word is 9 words from the left.
```

COMMENTS

Comments are an important part of programming. They explain the program to others and remind you why you wrote it the way you did. Comments begin with an apostrophe, as follows:

```
'This is a comment
Beep          'The Beep statement causes the speaker to beep
```

When WordBASIC encounters an apostrophe, it ignores everything between the apostrophe and the end of the line. Use of comments is one way of making your programs clear and easy to understand. Another method of including comments in your programs and other techniques for writing clear, readable programs are discussed in Appendix A, "Programming Style."

DISPLAYING VARIABLES AND EXPRESSIONS

In the previous examples, you used the **Print** statement to display numbers and strings. As some of the examples have shown, you can also use the **Print** statement to display the values of variables and expressions. In fact, the **Print** statement is quite flexible; it can display any combination of strings, numbers, variables, and expressions. You separate the items to be displayed by semicolons (;) or commas (,). When you use a semicolon to separate two items, WordBASIC displays the second item immediately after the first, as shown in the example below:

1. Select the following text:

   ```
   NumWords = 19
   Middle = Int(NumWords / 2)
   Print "The middle word is" ; Middle; " words from the left."
   ```

2. Select Edit Cut.
3. Type the following program line:

   ```
   Print "Sum of 5.29 and"; 2.79; " is"; 5.29 + 2.79
   ```

4. Choose Start from the macro-editing icon bar.

The output appears as follows:

```
Sum of 5.29 and 2.79 is 8.08
```

When you use a comma to separate two items in a **Print** statement, WordBASIC positions the second item at the next preset tab location. (The tab stops are 4 columns apart.) Note the difference between the output of the following example and that of the preceding one:

1. Change the following program line:

```
Print "Sum of 5.29 and"; 2.79; " is"; 5.29 + 2.79
```

   to

```
Print "Sum of 5.29 and", 2.79, " is", 5.29 + 2.79
```

2. Choose Start from the macro-editing icon bar.

The output appears as follows:

```
Sum of 5.29 and        2.79        is        8.08
```

You can use commas and semicolons in the same **Print** statement to position the items any way you want.

CREATING A MESSAGE BOX

Although the **Print** statement has many uses, it does have two major shortcomings: It can print only in the status bar, where its output may go unnoticed, and it has no way of verifying that the user has seen the output. If you need to communicate an important message to your program's user, you might want to use a message box instead of relying on the **Print** statement. To create a message box, you use the **MsgBox** command. **MsgBox** creates a message box with the title you specify at the top and your message inside. You can give the message box one or more buttons to allow the user to respond to or acknowledge the message, and you can also display an icon that indicates the nature of the message. Try the following example:

1. Select the following text:

```
Print "Sum of 5.29 and", 2.79, " is", 5.29 + 2.79
```

2. Select Edit Cut.
3. Type the following program line:

```
MsgBox "Unable to find that phone number.","Possible Problem", 16
```

4. Choose Start from the macro-editing icon bar.
5. Choose OK in the Possible Problem message box.

The first string in the **MsgBox** statement is the message, the second string is the message-box title, and the number `16` indicates the message-box type. This number controls such items as the type of icon displayed (if any), the number and type of buttons, and which button is the default. For more information on **MsgBox**, see Chapter 7, "WordBASIC Command Reference."

Like **Print**, the **MsgBox** statement has its limitations. The message and title of a message box must each be a single string. You cannot display a number or a numeric variable, nor can you display more than one string as the message or message-box title. You can overcome these limitations with a few tricks, however. In the next example, you convert a number into a string and combine that string with another one to create a single string variable that **MsgBox** can handle:

1. Select the following text:

```
MsgBox "Unable to find that phone number.","Possible Problem", 16
```

2. Select Edit Cut.
3. Type the following program lines:

```
Num$ = Str$(34)
Mess$ = "Bad paragraph format found on page" + Num$
MsgBox Mess$, "FormatMaster", 16
```

4. Choose Start from the macro-editing icon bar.
5. Choose OK in the FormatMaster message box.

In the first line, the **Str$** function converts the number `34` into the string `"34"` and assigns this number to the variable `Num$`. (The **Str$** function can also convert numeric variables and numeric expressions into strings.) Note that when **Str$** returns the number in string form, the string is preceded by a space.

In the second line of the example, two strings are combined in a process called *concatenation*. Although concatenation uses the + operator, the process differs greatly from addition, as the following examples demonstrate:

Operation	**Result**
`"Space " + "Station"`	`Space Station`
`"20" + "10"`	`2010`
`"NCC" + "-" + "170" + "1"`	`NCC-1701`

ENTERING DATA WITH THE INPUT STATEMENT

The **Input** statement displays a prompt that you specify in the status bar and then waits for the user to enter a value. The value entered in response to the prompt is assigned to a variable that you also specify in the **Input** statement. Here's an example:

1. Select the following text:

   ```
   Num$ = Str$(34)
   Mess$ = "Bad paragraph format found on page" + Num$
   MsgBox Mess$, "FormatMaster", 16
   ```

2. Select Edit Cut.
3. Type the following program lines:

   ```
   Input "What is your age", Age
   Print Age
   ```

4. Choose Start from the macro-editing icon bar.

The **Input** statement displays the prompt `What is your age?` in the status bar. If you typed `39` in response to the prompt, the value 39 would be assigned to the variable `Age`. That value is then displayed in the status bar by the following `Print Age` statement.

Input also accepts strings; for example:

```
Input "What is your name", YourName$
Print YourName$
```

ENTERING STRINGS WITH INPUTBOX$

Just as **Print** has **MsgBox** as its dialog-box equivalent, **Input** has **InputBox$**. Like **MsgBox**, **InputBox$** can deal only with strings. **InputBox$** accepts three strings as arguments. The first is the message to be printed in the input box, and the second is the input-box title. The third string, unique to **InputBox$**, is an optional default input string. If you include this string in the **InputBox$** statement, it appears in the text area of the input box. The user can accept this default input, edit it, or replace it with new text. Try this example to see how **InputBox** works:

1. Select the following text:

```
Input "What is your age", Age
Print Age
```

2. Select Edit Cut.
3. Type the following program lines:

```
Any$ = InputBox$("Enter headline","Make Headline","Blank")
Print Any$
```

4. Choose Start from the macro-editing icon bar.
5. Enter `WordBASIC Makes Programming Easy.`
6. Choose OK.

The output appears as follows:

```
WordBASIC Makes Programming Easy
```

You may have noticed that the input box has a Cancel button in addition to an OK button. Try this:

1. Choose Start from the macro-editing icon bar.
2. Choose Cancel. WordBASIC displays an error-message box.
3. Choose OK.

Selecting the Cancel button interrupts the program. In Chapter 6, "More WordBASIC Programming Concepts," you'll learn that it is possible to intercept, or trap, the error and have WordBASIC take some action other than displaying the message box. For example, WordBASIC might allow the program to continue without creating a headline.

ARRAYS OF VARIABLES

If you wanted to keep track of the high temperature for each day in February, 1990, you could use 28 floating-point variables named `February1`, `February2`, `February3`, and so on through `February28`. However, a group of related but individually named variables is clumsy to work with; each variable has to be handled separately. For example, if you wanted to prompt the user to enter temperatures for each day in February, you would have to write 28 individual prompt statements, like these:

```
Input "What was the high temperature on February 1", February1
    .
    .
    .
Input "What was the high temperature on February 28", February28
```

An analogous problem occurs when you're trying to write a program to retrieve the stored data. You wouldn't want the program to display all 28 variable names when you want to retrieve the value for only one (for example, the value for `February4`—the high temperature for February 4). It would be much more convenient if you could specify the date (the number 4) and the computer would select the correct variable and therefore the correct value.

Another problem with using many similarly named variables is that this approach is inflexible. It can't be used for a leap year, when February has 29 days, and it can't be used for the month of July, which has 31 days. The program is specifically for use with data for the month of February in nonleap years.

The solution to these problems is to give the entire set of values the same name (`February`, in this example) and distinguish the individual values by a numeric index called a *subscript*. A group of identically named variables distinguished by their subscript values is called an *array*. Arrays are especially powerful when used in conjunction with loops (see the section entitled "Repeating Program Operations," later in this chapter).

Declaring Arrays

An array of variables must first be "declared" with a **DIM** (dimension) statement, which establishes the size of the array. You have to include a **DIM** statement in a program before you can use the array of variables.

You include in the **DIM** statement the collective name of the variables and a value that specifies the maximum number of variables that will appear in the array. For example, the following statement declares an array of 29 floating-point variables named `February`, whose subscripts run from 0 through 28:

```
DIM February(28)
```

Note that array subscripts always start at zero. For convenience, you can ignore the `February(0)` element in the high-temperature array, but it exists nonetheless.

Because the first element in an array always has the subscript 0, `February(4)` is actually the fifth element in the array.

DIM also works with string variables:

```
DIM StringVar$(250)
```

You can even use a variable as the value in a **DIM** statement, leaving it to WordBASIC to create an array that is the size needed for a particular task:

```
DIM Month(Days)
```

After declaring the number of variables in an array, you need to assign values to each variable. You can do this with simple assignment statements, with **Input** statements that request input from the user, or with more sophisticated statements such as the **For...Next** loop. (**For...Next** loops are explained in the section entitled "Repeating Program Operations," later in this chapter.)

Specifying Array Elements

You can tell WordBASIC to use a particular element of an array for a certain operation simply by following the variable name with that element's subscript or an expression that evaluates to that element's subscript. For example, you can tell WordBASIC to use the high temperature value for February 4 by specifying `February(4)` or even `February(Abs(-4))` as the variable.

The following program fragment prompts the user for a date in February and then prints the high temperature for that day (assuming that all the temperatures have been assigned to the `February` array):

```
DIM February(28)
.
.   [Assignment statements]
.
Input "Enter February date: ", Date
Print "High temperature for February"; Date; " was"; February(Date)
```

DECISION-MAKING

WordBASIC can evaluate whether or not two numbers or strings are the same. On the basis of such an evaluation, WordBASIC can then execute or not execute a group of program statements, or it can repeat a group of statements until the evaluation changes.

For example, suppose the standard income-tax deduction is $2,500. If your itemized deductions are less than $2,500, you deduct the standard amount. But if your itemized deductions are greater than $2,500, you deduct the itemized amount. An income-tax program can decide which amount is greater and can then execute either the part of the program that performs itemized deductions or the part that takes the standard deduction. You don't have to tell the program which to do.

The following sections explain how WordBASIC makes logical decisions that you can use in your programs.

Relational Operators

WordBASIC compares numbers and strings by using *relational operators*. Six possible relationships are defined by the following operators:

Relational operator	Meaning
=	Equal to
<>	Not equal to
>	Greater than
<	Less than
>=	Greater than or equal to
<=	Less than or equal to

NOTE: *WordBASIC uses the equal sign (=) both to assign a value to a variable and to indicate logical equality. WordBASIC knows which usage is intended from the context of the statement containing the equal sign.*

Boolean Expressions

When you want WordBASIC to compare two values, you use relational operators in logical assertions called *Boolean expressions* (named for George Boole, who formulated some of the rules of mathematical logic). Boolean expressions are concerned with only one thing: Is the expression true or false? Unlike mathematical expressions, which WordBASIC evaluates to numbers, WordBASIC evaluates Boolean expressions to one of two values: True or False.

To see how WordBASIC represents True and False, try the following example:

1. Select any program lines between, but not including, the **Sub MAIN** and **End Sub** lines.

2. Select Edit Cut.
3. Type the following program line:

```
Print 5 > 6, 6 > 5
```

4. Choose Start from the macro-editing icon bar.

The output in the status bar at the bottom of the Word window appears as follows:

```
0           -1
```

The number 5 is not greater than 6, so WordBASIC prints `0`, its value for False. But the number 6 is greater than 5, so WordBASIC prints `-1`, its value for True.

The following table shows a few examples of Boolean expressions:

Expression	**Evaluation**
`7 = 35`	False
`7 <> 6`	True
`6 > 1`	True
`4 < 3`	False
`7 <= 7`	True
`8 >= 7`	True
`apples = oranges`	Depends on the values of the variables

In the last statement, apples obviously aren't oranges. But if `apples` and `oranges` are variable names, the truth or falsity of the statement depends on the values of these variables.

The following Boolean expressions compare strings. Are they True or False?

```
"Tarzan" <> "Jane"
"Y" = "Y"
"Y" = "y"
"miss" > "misty"
```

The first three expressions are straightforward. `Tarzan` and `Jane` are different strings, so the first expression is True. `Y` and `Y` are the same character, so the second expression is True. However, `Y` and `y` are not the same character, so the third expression is False.

The fourth expression may seem confusing at first. How can one string be "larger" or "smaller" than another? Here's how WordBASIC makes this decision.

First, WordBASIC compares the strings character by character, until it finds characters that don't match. In this example, the fourth characters are the first nonmatching characters. WordBASIC then decides which character is "larger" or "smaller" by comparing the numeric value of the character. It can do this because, within the computer, each character is represented by a number. Letters that occur later in the alphabet have numeric values larger than those that occur earlier. Since *t* follows *s* in the alphabet, *t* is "larger" than *s*, and the expression `"miss" > "misty"` is False, because `misty` is "larger" than `miss`. WordBASIC's ability to determine the relative value of strings makes it easy to write programs to alphabetize a list of words or names.

In these examples, WordBASIC compared numbers with numbers and strings with strings. But WordBASIC can compare any combination of numbers and numerical variables, and any combination of strings and string variables. However, it cannot compare numerical values with string values, because the comparison is logically meaningless.

Compound Expressions

In WordBASIC, you can create compound Boolean expressions by connecting two Boolean expressions with a *logical operator*. The two most commonly used logical operators are **And** and **Or**. The **And** operator requires both expressions to be True in order for the compound expression to be True. The **Or** operator requires only one of the expressions to be True for the compound expression to be True.

The following compound expressions combine two simple expressions by using **And** or **Or**:

Expression	Evaluation
`10 > 5 And 100 < 200`	True
`3 < 6 And 7 > 10`	False
`8 < 7 Or 90 > 80`	True
`2 < 1 Or 3 > 60`	False
`"Y" > "N" And "yes" <> "no"`	True
`"Y" < "N" Or 4 <> 4`	False

The **Not** logical operator reverses the truth or falsity of an expression:

Expression	Evaluation
`Not (5 > 10)`	True
`Not (8 < 7 Or 90 > 80)`	False
`Not (3 < 6 And 7 > 10)`	True
`Not (0)`	True

The logic of the last example may not be immediately obvious. In WordBASIC, False is 0. Therefore, `Not (0)` means "not (False)," or True. You can use combinations of **And**, **Or**, and **Not** to build up very complex expressions. There is no practical limit to their complexity, except that, obviously, the more complex the expression, the more difficult it is to read.

When WordBASIC evaluates Boolean expressions, it follows a precedence of operations just as it does when evaluating mathematical expressions. Evaluation goes from left to right, with all the simple expressions evaluated first, then all **And**-connected expressions, and finally all **Or**-connected expressions. As with mathematical expressions, you can use parentheses to control the order of evaluation, rather than relying on the rules of precedence.

CONTROLLING PROGRAM FLOW

You are constantly deciding what to do next, by evaluating your needs and wants and asking yourself which is most important. Similarly, WordBASIC can decide which part of a program should be executed next.

The mechanism WordBASIC uses to make program-flow decisions is the **If...Then...Else** statement, which has this syntax:

If *BooleanExpression* **Then**
    Statements to execute if BooleanExpression is True
Else
    Statements to execute if BooleanExpression is False
End If

If the Boolean expression is True, WordBASIC executes the statements following **Then**. If the expression is False, WordBASIC instead executes the statements following **Else**. The Boolean expression must be either True or False, so WordBASIC has to execute one or the other group of statements; it cannot execute both. The process of selecting among two or more possible groups of statements is called *branching*. Branching decisions in programming are like deciding which direction to take when you reach a fork in a road.

Try the following simple example of the **If...Then...Else** statement, which requires WordBASIC to decide whether the number entered is greater than, less than, or equal to 100:

1. Select any program lines between, but not including, the **Sub MAIN** and **End Sub** lines.
2. Select Edit Cut.
3. Type the following program lines:

```
Input "Enter a number: ", n             'Assign entered value to n
If n > 100 Then                         'Is value greater than 100?
   Print n; " is greater than 100"      'Display value with string
Else
   Print n; " is less than or equal to 100"
End If
```

4. Choose Start from the macro-editing icon bar.

Notice that the logical opposite of *greater than* is *less than or equal to* (not *less than*). Run this example with several values for *n*, including a value of 100 to verify that WordBASIC displays the `is less than or equal to 100` statement.

REPEATING PROGRAM OPERATIONS

Suppose you want to raise a number *N* to the power *P*; do you have to write out all the statements for *N* to be multiplied by itself *P* times? Or suppose you want to enter the data for a 10-element array; do you have to prompt the user for input ten times? Fortunately not. WordBASIC offers several mechanisms for executing a group of program statements repeatedly. You can specify that WordBASIC repeat them a fixed number of times or until a particular logical condition is met. If you want to execute a block of statements 100 times, you type them only once; WordBASIC's control mechanisms then take care of the repetitions.

The For...Next Loop

One mechanism for repeating a group of statements is the **For...Next** loop. WordBASIC executes the statements between the **For** and **Next** keywords the number of times you specify.

Try the following:

1. Select any program lines between, but not including, the **Sub MAIN** and **End Sub** lines.
2. Select Edit Cut.
3. Type the following program lines:

```
For Count = 1 To 5
   Print "This program beeps five times:";Count
   Beep
Next Count
```

4. Choose Start from the macro-editing icon bar.

In this example, the variable `Count` is called the *loop variable* or *loop counter*. The two numbers after the equal sign (separated by the keyword **To**) are the start and end values for the loop counter. In this case, 1 is the start value, and 5 is the end value.

Before WordBASIC executes the statements in the **For...Next** loop for the first time, it gives the loop counter the start value specified in the **For** statement (in this case, 1). After each execution of the statements in the loop, WordBASIC automatically increments `Count` by one. This cycle continues until `Count` is larger than the end value specified in the **For** statement (in this case, 5). WordBASIC therefore executes the statements between the **For** and **Next** keywords in this example five times.

To repeat a **For...Next** loop *n* times, where *n* is any number you choose, you normally specify a start value of 1 and an end value of *n*. You don't have to specify 1 and *n*, though. You can use any two values that differ by $n - 1$. For example, using –2 and 2 also causes five repetitions.

As already mentioned, entering each element in an array is a common use for a **For...Next** loop. The counter is then the subscript for each array variable. The next example prompts the user for the high temperature on each day in February:

```
DIM February(28)
For Date = 1 To 28
   February(Date) = Val(InputBox$("Enter Temperature")
Next Date
```

Neither the start nor the end value has to be a constant; either or both can be a variable. The following example requests start and end values and then prints out every value in that range:

```
Input "Starting value", StartVal
Input "Ending value", EndVal
For Count = StartVal To EndVal
   Print "Current value is "; Count
Next Count
```

The amount by which WordBASIC increments the counter defaults to a value of 1 if you don't specify a different increment. You use the **Step** statement to specify a different increment value, as shown in the following example program:

1. Select any program lines between, but not including, the **Sub MAIN** and **End Sub** lines.
2. Select Edit Cut.
3. Type the following program lines:

```
Sub MAIN
   Print "Prepare for launch."    'Print message in status bar
   For Delay = 1 To 1000          'Loop 1000 times to create pause
   Next Delay
   For Count = 5 To 0 Step -1     'Set up countdown from 5 to 0
      Print Count;                'Print current number in status bar
      For Delay= 1 To 200         'Loop 200 times to pause about
                                  '1 second between numbers
      Next Delay
   Next Count
   Print "Lift off";              'Print message in status bar
End Sub
```

4. Choose Start from the macro-editing icon bar.

The step value must be consistent with the start and end values. If the end value is larger than the start value, the step must be positive. If the end value is smaller than the start value, the step must be negative. If the step has the wrong sign, WordBASIC doesn't execute the **For...Next** loop; it skips over it because the counter has already reached the end value in the specified step direction.

The preceding example also illustrates another use for **For...Next** loops. The two loops that use the variable `Delay` are *timer loops* or *delay loops*. Even though WordBASIC may do nothing inside a timer loop, the program is delayed for a measured amount of time before continuing. The example program uses this mechanism both to allow time for the user to read the `Prepare for launch` message and to slow the count down to simulate that of a real launch. Although this technique can be useful, the exact delay created by a timer loop can vary depending on the speed of the computer on which the program is running and other factors, so it is best not to use a timer loop when accurate timing is necessary.

The While...Wend Loop

This is the syntax of the **While...Wend** loop:

> **While** *BooleanExpression*
> *Statements to be repeated*
> **Wend**

If the Boolean expression following the **While** statement evaluates to True, WordBASIC executes the group of statements between **While** and **Wend**. After executing the statements, WordBASIC loops back to the **While** statement and again evaluates the expression. If the expression is still True, WordBASIC repeats the group of statements. If the expression is False, WordBASIC stops looping and executes any statements that follow **Wend**.

This simple **While...Wend** loop that demonstrates how such a loop operates:

```
Big = 256
Little = 1
While Big <> Little
   Big = Big / 2
   Little = Little * 2
   Print "Big ="; Big; " Little ="; Little
Wend
```

The loop continues as long as `Big` is not equal to `Little`.Initial values are assigned to the two variables outside the loop. Within the loop, Word-BASIC first prints the values and then divides `Big` by 2 and multiplies `Little` by 2. This process is repeated until both variables are equal to 16. Because the expression is then False, the loop terminates. For this example, the starting values of `Big` and `Little` were chosen to guarantee that they would eventually become equal. If you use random numbers that can never become equal, the loop repeats indefinitely. (In practice, the program eventually stops regardless of the values chosen. WordBASIC repeatedly doubles the variable `Little` until the variable ultimately becomes so large that its value cannot be represented by a WordBASIC floating-point variable. The program then halts, displaying an overflow error message.)

Note that for WordBASIC to execute a **While** loop at least once, the Boolean expression must be True. If the `Big` and `Little` variables start with the same value, the expression `Big <> Little` is False, and WordBASIC does not execute the loop at all; it skips over it. Always be sure the variables used in the Boolean expression have values that evaluate to True when WordBASIC enters the loop.

WRITING A SIMPLE WORDBASIC PROGRAM

If you've worked through the examples given so far in this chapter, you should now know the fundamentals of programming in WordBASIC. To test your understanding, try writing a simple program that computes the average of several numbers. Here's one sequence of programming steps you might use:

1. Prompt the user to enter how many numbers are to be averaged.
2. If the user enters 0 or a negative quantity, print a warning message and do nothing else.
3. If the user enters a positive quantity, pick a variable name for the running total and set it equal to 0.
4. Prompt the user for the numbers, one at a time.
5. When the user has entered all the numbers, compute and print the average value.

To write this program, you need only the WordBASIC language elements that have been explained in this chapter. If you get stuck, simply reread the relevant parts of the chapter to remind yourself of how to use the statements you need.

There are many ways to write a program. If your program works, it's correct, even if it differs from the program given here:

```
Sub MAIN
   Input "How many numbers do you want to average", HowMany
   If HowMany <= 0 Then
      MsgBox "Not a valid quantity; must be greater than 0."
   Else
      Total = 0                          'Set running total to zero
      For Count = 1 To HowMany
         Input "Value to average", Value
         Total = Total + Value           'Add next value to total
      Next Count
      Print "The average value is"; Total / HowMany
   End If
End Sub
```

FOR MORE INFORMATION

Now you know how to write simple programs in WordBASIC. As you might suspect, however, there is a great deal more to programming than the simple concepts presented in this chapter.

This book and Microsoft Word's on-line help feature provide complete information on programming in the WordBASIC environment and using each of WordBASIC's statements and functions. However, this book does not set out to provide a complete introduction to BASIC and does not teach the general principles of programming. The following books contain more information on those subjects. They are listed for your convenience only. With the exception of its own publications, Microsoft Corporation neither endorses these books nor recommends them over others on the same subjects.

Craig, John Clark, *Microsoft QuickBASIC Programmer's Toolbox*. Redmond, WA: Microsoft Press, 1988.

Dwyer, Thomas A., and Margot Critchfield, *BASIC and the Personal Computer*. Reading, MA: Addison-Wesley Publishing Co., 1978.

Enders, Bernd, and Bob Petersen, *BASIC Primer for the IBM PC & XT*. New York, NY: New American Library, 1984.

Feldman, Phil, and Tom Rugg, *Using QuickBASIC 4*. Carmel, IN: Que Corporation, 1988.

Hergert, Douglas, *Microsoft QuickBASIC*. 3d ed. Redmond, WA: Microsoft Press, 1989.

Inman, Don, and Bob Albrecht, *Using QuickBASIC*. Berkeley, CA: Osborne McGraw-Hill, 1988.

Rygmyr, David, and Michael Halvorson, *Learn BASIC Now*. Redmond, WA: Microsoft Press, 1989.

Waite Group, The, *The Waite Group's Microsoft QuickBASIC Bible*. Redmond, WA: Microsoft Press, 1990.

Chapter 5

The WordBASIC Programming Language

As we've discussed, WordBASIC is a programming language rather than merely a macro language. Many applications have macro languages that allow you to record and repeat a series of actions within the application. WordBASIC performs the functions of a macro language, but recording macros is only the beginning of its capabilities. WordBASIC also lets you combine and extend existing Word features to create totally new ones. You can assign these new features to keystroke combinations and menus, just as you can assign built-in Word commands. The casual user cannot distinguish the features you create with WordBASIC from the features that are built into Word.

It is possible to take this capability one step farther. WordBASIC contains commands that enable you to redefine Word itself by changing the program's menus and features. You can add or remove menu items or replace them with new features with the same name. And you can modify built-in commands to change or extend their function.

Here are some examples of ways in which you can customize Word:

- You could create a newsletter template containing a macro that intercepts the Format Section command and presents a menu of section formats commonly used in the newsletter.
- You could add a new Answers menu to the menu bar. The menu items would give the answers to the ten questions most often asked of a customer service department. Selecting an item from the menu would cause Word to insert the answer in the current document.
- In a template designed to convert Windows Write files to Word, you could modify the File Open command to load files that have the .WRI extension as the default rather than files that have the .DOC extension.

Each of these examples requires only small changes to Word. You can also use WordBASIC, templates, and fields to change Word into a totally new application that handles specialized text- and document-handling tasks.

STATEMENTS AND FUNCTIONS

Like other types of BASIC, WordBASIC is raised above the level of a complex calculator by its statements and functions. Statements and functions give WordBASIC its control capabilities, whereby it can repeat an action a specified number of times or perform different tasks depending on the conditions encountered. They also allow WordBASIC to access the various capabilities of Word itself.

Statements are to WordBASIC as verbs are to English; they are concerned only with action. They may accept arguments that modify the nature of their actions, but they do not return information to the program. Here are some examples of WordBASIC statements:

Statement	Action
`Print "Hello"`	Prints the word `Hello` in the status bar at the bottom of the Word window.
`EditCut`	Places the currently selected text on the Clipboard.
`Insert Item$`	Inserts the text contained in the string variable `Item$` into a document at the current insertion point.

Functions may also perform actions, but the primary purpose of functions is to calculate numeric values or produce strings of characters. You therefore use functions as expressions or as part of expressions. For example, you might use the following functions to assign values to variables:

```
Tag = FontSize()

Value = Rnd()
```

In WordBASIC, a function is always followed by parentheses. For some functions, the parentheses may contain arguments that are passed to the function. Other functions, such as the **Rnd** (random number) function in the previous example, do not accept arguments, but you still use the parentheses to clearly identify it as a function.

If a function's name ends with a letter, it is a numeric function and returns a numeric value. If a function's name ends with a $, it is a string function and returns a string of characters. The following are examples of string functions:

```
FirstInitial$ = Left$(FirstName,1)

Current$ = Selection$()
```

You can use functions as part of more complex expressions, as in the following examples:

```
Result$ = Left$((Chr$(KeyVal) + Buffer$),10)

FontSize = FontSize() + Int(FontUp) - Int(FontDown)
```

Notice the two different usages of **FontSize** in the preceding example. Many WordBASIC keywords have both a statement and a function form. **FontSize** is a statement that sets the font size of the selected text. **FontSize( )** is a function that returns the font size of the currently selected text.

WordBASIC also allows you to define your own functions and use them just as you would built-in functions. User-defined functions are discussed later in this chapter.

For a complete list of WordBASIC commands and functions, as well as detailed information on their syntaxes and usages, see Chapter 7, "WordBASIC Command Reference."

VARIABLES AND CONSTANTS

Variables are temporary storage locations for information, such as numbers or strings of text. WordBASIC programs can place information in variables and then retrieve it for later use. Information is stored only while the program is running. Once the program ends, the information is lost, unless the program has stored the information in a Word document or a sequential disk file.

Constants are values that are fixed in your program and are not changed by either the program or external conditions.

Variables and constants in WordBASIC have two forms: numeric and string.

Numeric Variables and Constants

In WordBASIC, any variable name that ends with a letter or number is a numeric variable. All numeric variables in WordBASIC are double-precision, floating-point variables. This means that they accept decimal values and are accurate to about 15 decimal places.

Numeric constants are numbers that you use as part of an expression. The following are valid examples of numeric constants:

```
ShortPi = 3.14

Feet = Inches * 12

Dozens = (Gross * 144) / 12
```

String Variables and Constants

Any variable name that ends with a $ is a string variable. A string variable can contain any sequence of characters, such as letters, numbers, spaces, and punctuation marks. A string variable may also contain unprintable control characters. The number of characters is limited to 32,767 or to the amount of available memory, whichever is less. The combined length of all the string variables in a program cannot exceed 65,535 characters.

String constants must always be surrounded by double quotation marks, as in the following examples:

```
Name$ = "Harry Mudd"

ProductName$ = "Microsoft " + ProgramName$

Banner$ = "Greetings Dr. " + Name$ + ", you may have already won!"
```

TALKING WITH THE USER

WordBASIC differs from other versions of BASIC in the features it provides for communications with the user. The familiar **Print** and **Input** statements are available, but with some limitations. More powerful and useful are the **MsgBox** (message box) and **InputBox$** statements, which allow WordBASIC programs to use dialog boxes, buttons, and icons as easily as other BASIC programs use **Print** and **Input**.

For more complex interaction, WordBASIC lets you use any of Word's built-in dialog boxes or even create your own using check boxes, buttons, list boxes, and other features. These capabilities are discussed in Chapter 6, "More WordBASIC Programming Concepts."

Print

The biggest difference between the WordBASIC **Print** statement and that of other versions of BASIC lies in where it places text or numbers on the screen. **Print** operates only in the single-line status bar at the bottom of the Word window. If you have not turned on the View Status Bar option, running a **Print** statement creates a special one-line bar at the bottom of the window. The text displayed by the **Print** statement remains on the screen until the next action that causes Word to update the status bar. At that time, if you have turned on the View Status Bar command, Word replaces the text with the updated status information. If you have not turned on View Status Bar, the special **Print** status bar disappears.

Here is an example:

```
SUB Main
   Print "Greetings. This is a test"
End Sub
```

WordBASIC does not support special forms of **Print**, such as **Print@**, **Print Tab**, and **Print Using**. You can use **Print** to display string or numeric variables, string or numeric constants, and expressions in any combination. The following are all valid uses of **Print**:

```
Print Name$

Print Total

Print "Hello"

Print 365.25
```

```
Print Abs(WordCount / 3)
Print "Cost is ";Item + Tax;" as supplied by: ";Vendor$
Print FirstCount,SecondCount,ThirdCount
```

When you use commas as delimiters between multiple items in a **Print** statement, the next printed item starts at the next print tab position. When you use semicolons as delimiters between items, the next item starts immediately following the previous one.

Unlike in some BASICs, in WordBASIC ending a **Print** statement with a trailing semicolon does not cause the output of the next **Print** statement to appear on the same line. Instead, the next **Print** statement clears the status bar and overwrites the output of the previous **Print** statement.

Even with these new limitations, **Print** remains an effective command. It is useful when a program must update information on a frequent basis or when the information must be presented in an accessible but unobtrusive way.

MsgBox

In many cases, you will need your programs to display a message that you don't want the user to overlook. For example, you may want the user to verify something before proceeding with an irreversible change to a document. This is the sort of task for which the **MsgBox** statement was created.

Message boxes have four elements:

A Message. A string that appears in the message box.

A Title. A string that appears at the top of the message box. This is optional. If no title is provided, Microsoft Word is used.

Buttons. At a minimum, a message box has an OK button. Other possible buttons are Cancel, Abort, Retry, Ignore, Yes, and No.

An icon. The default is no icon, but you can display one of four icons to reinforce the purpose of the message string.

In its simplest form, a **MsgBox** statement consists of the command and a message string, as in these examples:

```
MsgBox "Macro complete"
MsgBox Note$
```

In each of these cases, the title of the message box is `Microsoft Word`, and the box has an OK button and no icon. Adding a title string is simple:

```
MsgBox "Macro complete", "Salutation 1"
```

A numeric *Type* argument controls which icon and buttons are displayed, and which button is the default. Here is an example:

```
MsgBox "OK to reformat?", "Make Two Column", 292
```

This statement creates a message box with a message of `OK to reformat`, a title of `Make Two Column`, Yes and No buttons with No as the default, and a question-mark icon. The number for the *Type* argument, `292`, is the sum of three values. A table of these values and their meanings, along with instructions for their use, can be found in Chapter 7, "WordBASIC Command Reference," in the section entitled "MsgBox."

Input

You can use **Input** to prompt the user to provide values for variables. These variables can be string, numeric, or a combination of the two. Prompts created by WordBASIC's **Input** statement appear only in the status bar.

For example, to prompt the user for a value for a single variable, use **Input** statements like these:

```
Input Length
Input Address$
```

To prompt for a list of variables, use statements like these:

```
Input Height, Width
Input UserID$, Password$
```

To provide values for a list of variables, the user must respond with the appropriate values separated by commas, as in these examples:

```
6,3
JamesK, Tribble
```

No matter how many variables you use in an **Input** statement, **Input** always attempts to divide the user's response at a comma. If you want to allow responses that contain commas, use a **Line Input** statement. **Line Input** works exactly the same as **Input** with one important difference; you can specify only a single string variable. Here's an example:

```
Line Input Address$
```

If Word encounters a comma in the response, it returns the comma as part of the string. With some imagination and the use of WordBASIC's string functions, you can use **Line Input** to accept almost any kind of value—numeric or string. An example of creative **Line Input** usage can be found later in this section, in the discussion of **InputBox$( )**.

To request a value for a variable by using a customized prompt, use a statement like this one:

```
Input "What point size of type for headline";Size
```

Note that you don't have to include a question mark in the prompt string, because the prompt created by **Input** is a question mark. The prompt displayed by this statement is

```
What point size of type for headline?
```

If you include a question mark in the prompt string, as in

```
Input "What point size of type for headline?";size
```

then the prompt that users see in the status bar is

```
What point size of type for headline??
```

InputBox$( )

Although the unobtrusive way in which **Input** prompts in the status bar is sometimes desirable, you may want a prompt that halts the program until the user supplies input to draw more attention to itself. The prompt created by an **Input** statement can easily be overlooked, but there is no missing the result of the **InputBox$( )** function. Even if Word is minimized to an icon while the macro is running, the **InputBox$( )** prompt appears in the middle of the screen, demanding attention.

Even though **MsgBox** is a statement and **InputBox$( )** is a function, their syntaxes are similar. Like **MsgBox**, **InputBox$( )** takes three arguments. The first two arguments are strings, the first of which is the prompt string and the second the title string. The title string is again optional. Examples of valid usage are

```
File$ = InputBox$("Name of the file to load?")
Search$ = InputBox$("Type search string:", "Search for Last")
MsgBox InputBox$("What is your message?")
```

The last of these examples may seem strange, but remember that **InputBox$( )** is a function and you can use it anywhere you might use a string expression. In this case, Word displays the input box first to prompt the user for a string. The string that the user enters then appears in the message box.

The following examples are also valid:

```
Print InputBox$("String to print?","Print")
Sort$ = Left$(InputBox$("Sort key (first four letters used)"),4)
```

Although the **InputBox$( )** function can return only a string, you can convert the string with WordBASIC's **Val( )** function to input a numeric variable, as in the following example:

```
Number = Val(InputBox$("Input a number from 1 to 10"))
```

The **Val( )** function returns the numeric value, if any, of a string. If in response to the prompt created by the above statement the user typed `10`, then **Val( )** would assign the value 10 to `Number`. If, however, the user typed `Ten` or `Microsoft`, **Val( )** would assign the value 0 to `Number`, because `Ten` and `Microsoft` contain no digits (the only things **Val( )** can detect).

You use the **InputBox$( )** function's optional third argument to insert a default string into the text area. For example:

```
Name$ = InputBox$("Find what name?", "File Search", "No name selected")
```

Here, `No name selected` appears in the text area as the default. The user can replace the default, edit it, or accept it as is.

EXPRESSIONS

Word can evaluate complex numeric and string expressions. An expression is any valid combination of variables, numbers or strings, and functions that evaluate down to a single result. This result can be a number, a string, or, in the case of logical expressions, a True or False condition. (In WordBASIC, all logical expressions return –1 if True and 0 (zero) if False.)

At its very simplest, an expression is only one of the above items. The following are examples of simple expressions:

```
Heading$

LineCount

80486

"Word"

Rnd()
```

More often, an expression consists of several elements in combination, as in the following:

```
Page1Lines + Page2Lines

"The " + CarName$ + "automobile is the best seller this week"

(2 * Pi) * Radius

(Rain Or Snow) And (Hail Or Sleet)

Int((365 - Days) / 7)

FirstQtr + SecondQtr + ThirdQtr + FourthQtr > LastYear
```

You can use an expression anywhere that a constant or a variable can be used, as in these examples:

```
Print Left$(FirstName$,1) + ". " + LastName$

LineDown ParaLong + 1, Switch

If Profit > 0 and Month$ = "Jan" Then Print "Good Year!"
```

Numeric Expressions

Bitwise operators (**Not**, **And**, and **Or**) convert numbers to 16-bit integers and then process the individual bits of the number in binary format.

> **NOTE:** **Not** *of –1 is False.* **Not** *of any other number, including 0 (zero), is True. Therefore, be careful when using bitwise operators with non-Boolean functions.*

When Word evaluates numeric expressions, it performs multiplication and division before addition and subtraction. To have Word perform operations in a different order, use parentheses, as shown in the second example that follows:

Expression	Effect
`14 * 5 - 6`	Multiplies 14 by 5 and then subtracts 6 from the result.
`14 * (5 - 6)`	Subtracts 6 from 5 and then multiplies 14 by the result.

The following table lists the numeric and logical operators, describes the operations and the order in which they are performed, and gives examples and their results. The examples assume `Sales = 300`. Because of space constraints, some of the statements in the third column of the table fall on more than one line. In a real program, all of these examples would be one-line statements.

Operator	Description	Example	Result
–	Negates the number.	`Print -Sales`	-300
*	Multiplies the numbers.	`Print Sales * 12`	3600
/	Divides the first number by the second number.	`Print Sales / 10`	30
Mod	Rounds the numbers to integers, divides the first number by the second number, and returns the remainder.	`Print 19 Mod 12`	7
+	Adds the numbers	`Print Sales + 10`	310
–	Subtracts the second number from the first number.	`Print Sales - 10`	290
+	Appends the second string to the first string.	`Print "concat" + "enation"`	concatenation
=	Tests for equality.	`If Sales = 300 Then Print "three hundred"`	three hundred
<>	Tests for inequality.	`If Sales <> 27 Then Print "not 27"`	not 27
>	Tests whether the first number is greater than the second number.	`If Sales > 200 Then Print "greater than 200"`	greater than 200
<	Tests whether the first number is less than the second number.	`If Sales < 400 Then Print "less than 400"`	less than 400

(continued)

Continued

Operator	Description	Example	Result
<=	Tests whether the first number is less than or equal to the second number.	`If Sales <= 300 Then Print "<= 300"`	`<= 300`
>=	Tests whether the first number is greater than or equal to the second number.	`If Sales >= 300 Then Print ">= 300"`	`>= 300`
Not	Performs the bitwise complement of the number; also toggles the state of the expression between True and False.	`If Not Sales > 300 Then Print "not > 300"`	`not > 300`
		`Print Not -1`	`0`
		`Print Not 1`	`-2`
And	Performs a comparison that returns True if both of the conditions are met.	`If Sales > 200 And Sales < 400 Then Print "Average"`	`Average`
		`Print 2 And 6`	`2` (bitwise And)
Or	Performs a comparison that returns True if either of the conditions are met.	`If Sales < 310 Or Sales > 400 Then Print "Wild!"`	`Wild!`
		`Print 1 Or 6`	`7` (bitwise Or)

String Expressions

If you compare strings using logical operators, Word first converts the strings to ASCII values and then uses the resulting values in the comparison. For example, when Word evaluates the expression

```
If "Apple" < "Orange" Then Print "Apple is less than Orange."
```

Word first converts the relational expression into a value that represents True or False. It then evaluates the **If** statement using that value and performs the print operation accordingly.

STRING FUNCTIONS

WordBASIC includes most of the string-manipulation functions available in QuickBASIC, GWBASIC, and IBM BASICA. With these functions, you can create a string using ANSI character values, disassemble an existing string into its component parts, or shuffle the characters in a string like cards in a deck.

The following table lists WordBASIC's string functions. For individual descriptions, see Chapter 7, "WordBASIC Command Reference."

Function	Description	Example	Result
Asc( )	Returns the ANSI code for the first character in the specified string.	`Asc("ABC")`	65
Chr$( )	Returns a one-character string based on the specified ANSI code.	`Chr$(67)`	C
InStr( )	Returns a number representing the location of a specified search string in a target string. Can also specify an index point.	`InStr("Television","v")`	5
LCase$( )	Converts a string into lowercase characters.	`LCase$("HELLO")`	hello
Left$( )	Returns a specified number of characters from the left of a target string.	`Left$("Automobile",4)`	Auto
Len( )	Returns a numeric value indicating the length in characters of a target string.	`Len("Elephant")`	8
Mid$( )	Returns a specified number of characters from a target string starting at a specified index point.	`Mid$("ABCDEFGH",4,3)`	DEF
Right$( )	Returns a specified number of characters from the right of a target string.	`Right$("Microsoft",4)`	soft
Str$( )	Returns a string representation of the specified numeric value.	`Str$(10)`	"10"
String$( )	Returns the first character of a target string repeated a specified number of times.	`String$("*",3)`	***
UCase$( )	Converts a string into uppercase letters.	`UCase$("hello")`	HELLO
Val( )	Returns the numeric value of the target string.	`Val("1234")`	1234

Some of WordBASIC's string functions duplicate or approximate Word command equivalents. You can duplicate other command equivalents by using a combination of WordBASIC commands and string and other functions. The approach to use for text-manipulation tasks is best dictated by the nature of the individual task. In general, command equivalents are usually faster, more compact and, when it comes to manipulating document text, easier to program; however, string functions offer more flexibility.

Beyond this, the major difference between the use of string functions and the use of Word command equivalents is that the command equivalents work on text in an open document, and string functions work on string variables. The goal of using WordBASIC is to modify or enhance Word's word-processing features, which involves manipulating text in Word documents, not simply manipulating string variables. WordBASIC provides ways to work around this fundamental incompatibility.

Converting Document Text to String Variables

You can use the **Selection$( )** function to load text from an open Word document into a string variable. **Selection$( )** loads either the currently selected text or, if no text is selected, the first character following the insertion point. You must work within the standard limitations on WordBASIC string variables when using **Selection$( )**. You cannot load more than 32,767 characters into one string variable, and you cannot store more than a total of 65,535 characters in all the variables in a program. If you select more than 32,767 characters, only the first 32,767 characters are loaded into the variable and an error is generated. All formatting is stripped from the text when it is placed in the variable. **Selection$( )** does not delete the selected text from the document or change its formatting. In this respect, it is much like the Edit Copy command. The syntax for **Selection$( )** is as follows:

*Text$* = **Selection$( )**

The following are all valid uses of **Selection$( )**:

```
Cut$ = Selection$()
Big$ = Selection$() + OldText$
Print Selection$()
First$ = Left$(Selection$(),1)
```

Converting String Variables to Document Text

You use the **Insert** command to insert strings from a WordBASIC program into a Word document at the insertion point. **Insert** is the WordBASIC statement for typing at the keyboard. When you record typing, the macro recorder records **Insert** statements. Consequently, the actions Word takes when you run **Insert** are the same as those Word takes when you type. If Typing Replace Selection is turned off in the Utilities Customize dialog box and document text is selected when **Insert** is run, Word inserts the string before the selection. If Typing Replace Selection is turned on, Word replaces the selection with the string. After the **Insert** operation, Word moves the insertion point to the end of the inserted text. Word assigns the current style attributes to the inserted text.

The syntax for **Insert** is as follows:

Insert *Text$*

The following are all valid uses of **Insert**:

```
Insert Name$

Insert "To our valued customers:"

Insert "Dr. "+ Name$

Insert Chr$(9)
```

The last example illustrates how the **Chr$( )** function can be used with **Insert** to insert nonprinting characters into a document. (**Chr$(9)** is a tab character.)

CONTROL STRUCTURES

This section discusses the control structures you can use in your WordBASIC programs. These structures have characteristics similar to equivalent structures in Microsoft QuickBASIC.

For...Next

For *CounterVariable* = *Start* **To** *End* [**Step** *Increment*]
Statement(s)
Next *[CounterVariable]*

Word executes the statements between **For** and **Next** as many times as it takes for the *CounterVariable* to increment from the *Start* value to the *End* value. The *Increment* is the value (usually 1) by which Word increments the counter.

For names the *CounterVariable* and specifies the *Start* and *End* values that constitute the range of the *CounterVariable*. These values can be expressed as constants, as variables derived before the start of the loop, or as expressions from which Word can compute a range of values for the *CounterVariable*.

The *Increment* can be a positive or a negative number; positive numbers increase the counter, and negative numbers decrease the counter. If *Increment* is omitted, the default of 1 is used. An example follows:

```
For Month = 1 To 12
   Print Month
Next Month
```

Here are some other valid beginnings of **For...Next** loops and their resulting operations:

Example	Result
`For DayMonth = 1 To 31`	The variable `DayMonth` increments from 1 to 31 in steps of 1.
`For Dozens = 0 To 144 Step 12`	The variable `Dozens` increments from 0 to 144 in steps of 12.
`For CountDown = 10 To 1 Step -1`	The variable `CountDown` decrements from 10 to 1 in steps of -1.
`For Loop = Start To Finish Step Size`	The variable `Loop` is incremented or decremented from the value of the variable `Start` to the value of the variable `Finish` in steps equal to the variable `Size`.
`For Count = Count To Count + 10`	The initial value of the variable `Count` is increased by 10 in steps of 1.

Note that *Start* and *End* values, as well as the *Increment* value are only checked once. Changing them once the loop has started does not affect the progress of the loop. The *CounterVariable* itself, however, should not be altered until the loop is completed, or problems such as those produced by the following example can result:

```
For Count = 1 To 10
   Count = 5
Next Count
```

This example creates an endless loop. The value of `Count` never reaches 10 because the statement `Count = 5` resets the value to 5 each time Word repeats the loop.

The following are not valid **For** statements:

Invalid statement	**Remarks**
`For 10 = 1 To 10`	Counter variable needed
`For Count = 300 To 50`	Negative *Step* value needed
`For Count = 1 To 100 Step -1`	Positive *Step* value needed
`For Count = 1000 To 0 Step 5`	Negative *Step* value needed

The **Next** statement can be used with or without the variable name that identifies the loop with which the statement is associated. The **Next** statement always attempts to associate itself with the nearest preceding **For** statement. If you don't specify a *CounterVariable* after **Next**, Word completes the loop without generating an error. If you do specify a *CounterVariable* after **Next** and the variable does not match the *CounterVariable* of the previous **For** statement, an error is generated. Although it is easier to omit the *CounterVariable*, use of the *Counter-Variable* can serve as a good test of your program's logic. If an error is generated, it may indicate that you have omitted a **Next** statement somewhere else in the program, that you have incorrectly spelled a variable name, or that you have made some other error that would otherwise be difficult to detect. This safeguard is most important in large programs that may have multiple loops and many variables.

Goto

Goto *Label*

In response to this command, Word branches unconditionally to the line in the program that starts with the label. The syntax for the label is simply

Label: [Statement]

where *Label* is text or a number. Lines beginning with labels cannot be indented with the Tab character, because the label must be the first character in the line.

Here is an example:

```
Goto Bye
   Print "Hello"
Bye:
```

In this case, the statement `Print "Hello"` is not performed. The program jumps directly from the `Goto Bye` statement to the `Bye` label without executing the statement between them.

The label can also occur before the **Goto** statement, as in this example:

```
Bye:
   Print "Hello"
Goto Bye
```

This program creates another endless loop, because the `Goto Bye` statement always returns to the `Bye:` label. There are situations in which endless loops can be useful, but you usually need to include some sort of switch in the program to enable Word to exit the loop when desired. One way of exiting is with an **If** statement, which is discussed next.

If...ElseIf...Else...End If

If *Condition* **Then** *Statement(s)* [**Else** *Statement(s)*]

If *Condition1* **Then**
    Statement(s)
[**ElseIf** *Condition2* **Then**
    Statement(s)]
[**Else**
    Statement(s)]
End If

The **If...Then** control structure performs conditional execution or branching, depending on its component expressions. The conditions stipulated in an **If...ElseIf...Else...End If** block can be any logical expressions that WordBASIC can evaluate as True or False. To build conditional expressions, you use the relational operators (=, <>, <, >, >=, and <=) and the Boolean operators (**And**, **Or**, and **Not**). Each **If...Then** control structure has only one **If** *Condition* **Then** statement. However, each **If** control structure can have as many **ElseIf** *Condition* **Then** statements as needed. WordBASIC evaluates the expressions in the order in which they appear and executes the statements corresponding to the first condition that results in a True (nonzero) value.

If tests for a specified condition. If the condition is True, Word executes the operations following the **Then** statement. The operations following **Else** are performed if none of the **If** or **ElseIf** conditions evaluate to True. **Else** is optional; if you do not include it and all previous conditions are False, Word takes no action.

Here is an example of the **If...Then** control structure:

```
If Sales > 300 Then Print "Sales were more than 300"
```

and here is an example of the **If...ElseIf...Else...End If** control structure:

```
If Sales > 300 Then
   Print "Sales were more than 300!"
ElseIf Sales > 280 Then
   Print "Sales were OK"
Else
   Print "Another year goes by"
End If
```

Select Case

Select Case *Expression*
Case *CaseExpression*
    Statement(s)
[**Case Else**
    Statement(s)]
End Select

This control structure is similar to a multiline **If** statement, in that Word executes a statement or group of statements based on the result of some expression. With **Select Case**, however, statements following only one *CaseExpression* are evaluated, even though there may be several groups of statements. The result of the *Expression* is compared with the *CaseExpression* that follows the keyword **Case**. The *CaseExpression* may be a single value, a list of values separated by commas, a range of values separated by the keyword **To**, or a relational expression beginning with the keyword **Is**, followed by a relational operator (=, <>, <, >, <=, >=) and an expression.

Word compares the *Expression* with all the values in each *CaseExpression* until a match is found. If a match is found, Word executes the *Statement(s)* following that particular *CaseExpression*. If there is no match and there is a **Case Else** statement, Word executes the *Statement(s)* following **Case Else**.

Here is an example:

```
Select Case Int(Rnd() * 10) - 5
Case 1,3
   Print "1 or 3"
Case Is > 3
   Print "Greater than 3"
Case -5 to 0
   Print "Between -5 and 0 (inclusive)"
Case Else
   Print "Must be 2"
End Select
```

Stop

Stop

The **Stop** statement stops a running macro and displays a message that the macro has been interrupted. You can use **Stop** when testing and debugging a program. **Stop** leaves the contents of variables intact so that you can examine them with the Vars... button in the macro-editing icon bar. After Word executes a **Stop** instruction, the Start button in the macro-editing icon bar is replaced by a Continue button. Selecting Continue continues the program from the point where the last **Stop** was encountered with all variable values intact.

While...Wend

While *Condition*
    Statement(s)
Wend

The **While...Wend** loop repeats the statements between the **While** and **Wend** as long as the *Condition* is True. If the *Condition* is initially False, the loop is never executed.

A **While...Wend** loop uses a conditional expression to determine the number of times the *Statement(s)* are executed. WordBASIC evaluates the *Condition* each time the *Statement(s)* are executed and, as long as the *Condition* evaluates as True, continues executing the *Statement(s)*. When the *Condition* evaluates as False, WordBASIC stops executing the *Statement(s)* and exits the loop.

The *Condition* can be any numeric expression. To build conditional expressions, use the relational operators (=, <>, <, >, >=, and <=) and the Boolean operators (**And**, **Or**, and **Not**). The evaluation results are either –1 for True or 0 for False.

In the following example, WordBASIC searches the document for the string "macro" until the function **EditSearchFound( )** returns a zero, indicating that the end of the document has been reached. The example illustrates the major distinction between **For...Next** and **While...Wend** loops. **For...Next** loops are most useful when instructions must be repeated a fixed number of times and that number is known or can be calculated in advance. **While...Wend** loops are most useful when the number of repetitions necessary to satisfy the *Condition* is not known and cannot be calculated in advance. In the latter case, the document could be of any length and the string "macro" could occur any number of times.

```
Sub MAIN
   Count = 0
   StartOfDocument
   EditSearch "macro", 0, 0, 2
   While EditSearchFound()
      Count = Count + 1
      EditSearch "macro", 0, 0, 2
   Wend
   Print "macro was found ";Count; " times"
End Sub
```

SUBROUTINES: TOOLS YOU CAN REUSE

A subroutine is a group of statements that performs a specific task. Every WordBASIC macro program is a Word subroutine that must begin with a **Sub MAIN** statement and end with an **End Sub** statement. You cannot nest subroutines; that is, you cannot insert one subroutine within another subroutine. The syntax of the **Sub** and **End Sub** statements is as follows:

> **Sub** *Name [ParameterList]*
>
>   *Statement(s)*
>
> **End Sub**

The simplest macro programs consist of only one subroutine. As programs get more complicated, they are usually broken down into small units and written as separate modules. If you want to perform the same action in different parts of your program, it makes sense to write the statements that carry out that particular action as a separate subroutine. For example, suppose you want the computer to beep before displaying a message. One way to do this is shown in the following program listing:

```
Sub MAIN
   BeepMsg "Are you sure you want to quit?", 0
   BeepMsg "Don't you want to save your work first?", 0
   BeepMsg "This is your last chance. Choose OK to quit.", 65
End Sub
'*** SubRoutine begins here
Sub BeepMsg (msg$, type)
   Beep
   MsgBox msg$, type
End Sub
```

USER-DEFINED FUNCTIONS

User-defined functions are similar to subroutines in that they are modular units of program code that can be called from elsewhere in the program. They differ from subroutines in that they return a value or string and must be used as part of an expression. You define new functions in a manner similar to subroutines, except that instead of using the **Sub** keyword, you use the **Function** keyword. The syntax is as follows:

> **Function** *Name [ParameterList]*
>
> *Statement(s)*
>
> **End Function**

The *ParameterList* is a list of the variables, separated by commas, that are being passed as arguments to the function. The statements between **Function** and **End Function** are used to produce a value that is returned to the subroutine that called the function. An example follows:

```
Sub MAIN
   Print RndInt(100)
   Print RndInt(200)
End Sub
Function RndInt(n)
   RndInt = Int(Rnd() * n)
End Function
```

The **Rnd( )** function is a built-in WordBASIC function that returns a fractional value between 0 and 1. The user-defined **RndInt( )** function generates a random integer between 0 and some specific value. The `Function RndInt(n)` statement tells Word that a new function is being defined and that the function takes a single numeric parameter called `n`. The next line indicates that the value of the function is the formula `Int(Rnd() * n)`.

Every user-defined function includes an implied variable with the same name as the function. Assigning a value to that variable defines the value that is to be returned from the function. In the example, the formula `Int(Rnd() * n` is assigned to the variable `RndInt`, which has the same name as the **RndInt( )** function. A function can contain statements above and/or below the assignment, just as if it were a subroutine.

The following are also valid ways to call the user-defined **RndInt( )** function:

```
NewValue = RndInt(OldValue)

Print RndInt(Number) + 100

If RndInt(50) > 25 Then TailsMsg
```

A user-defined function returns a numeric value unless the function name is terminated with a dollar sign ($), in which case the function returns a string.

THE HIERARCHY OF WORD

If you are an experienced DOS user, you know that DOS executes files in the following order: *filename.com*, next *filename.exe*, and then *filename.bat*. You can therefore have three files with the same file name—but with different extensions—and DOS will run them according to this convention.

Word also has three layers: the template layer, the global layer, and the built-in command layer. These layers are described in the following table:

Layer	Description
Template	Includes only the macros stored in the document template file.
Global	Includes all the macros stored in the NORMAL.DOT file, which is available to all documents.
Built-in command	Includes all the commands that are on all the default Word menus and that are assigned to default key combinations. These commands are part of the Word program.

When you run a macro or command, Word searches the layers for it in the following order: the template layer, next the global layer, and then the built-in command layer. So, if you create a macro with the same name as a built-in command, Word executes your macro instead of its original command. If Word cannot find the macro you specify, it displays a message to that effect.

Remember the order of macro execution when naming macros. Suppose you have a template macro and a global macro with the same name. If you want Word to execute the global macro, you must either rename one of the macros or precede the macro name with the **Super** prefix statement. Using the **Super** prefix forces Word to ignore the current layer and search the next layer for the macro you specify. For example, the following macro, called FormatDocument, disables mirror margins when the Format Document command is chosen:

```
Sub MAIN
   Dim dlgrec As FormatDocument    'Create dialog record called dlgrec
   GetCurValues dlgrec             'Move dialog record values to dialog box
   Again:
   Dialog dlgrec                   'Display dialog box
   If dlgrec.MirrorMargins = 1 Then    'Check MirrorMargins
                                       'check box for True
      Beep
      MsgBox "Mirror Margins have been disabled by this macro"
      dlgrec.MirrorMargins = 0     'Set check box to False
      Goto Again                   'Branch back to Again to redisplay
                                   'dialog box
   End If
   Super FormatDocument dlgrec     'Format document per contents of dlgrec
End Sub
```

Chapter 6

More WordBASIC Programming Concepts

Some of WordBASIC's most powerful elements rely not on a single statement or function, but on a group of related commands, functions, and features that work in concert to perform a single task. To understand how one of these elements works, you must understand the other elements involved and know how they all relate both to one another and to the WordBASIC programming environment. This chapter introduces you to the following features:

- Custom dialog boxes
- Error handling
- Auto macros
- Sequential file access
- Special bookmarks
- Macro debugging

CREATING CUSTOM DIALOG BOXES

You can use WordBASIC macro programs to create your own dialog box as a means of communicating with the user while the macro runs. The dialog box allows the user to make choices by entering specific values, as well as by clicking selections, option buttons, and checkboxes. You can preset the dialog box so that it contains default values which the user can change as necessary to perform the task at hand. When the user selects OK to close the dialog box, the macro examines the dialog record (described later), created by Word to determine what selections and choices were made by the user, and takes the appropriate action. The following sections describe how to create a custom dialog box that suits the needs of your macro and how to use the selections and entries made by the user to perform subsequent operations.

The Dialog Record

For every dialog box displayed to the user, Word creates a dialog record in memory. The dialog record defines a data field for each of the dialog-box elements. The field contains the value of that particular element. The value is a number in some cases and a string in others.

For example, if you select the Replace command on the Edit menu, the following dialog box appears:

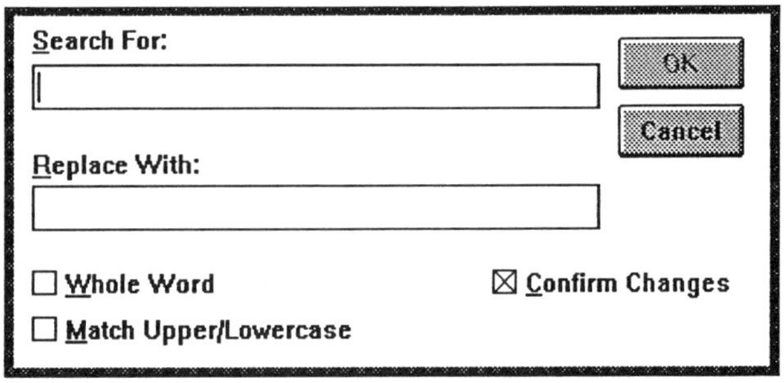

When Word displays this dialog box, it creates a corresponding dialog record. In the case of the Edit Replace dialog box, this dialog record contains the following five data fields:

Field name	Contents
.Search	The Search For text
.Replace	The Replace With text
.WholeWord	1 or 0 for the Whole Word checkbox
.MatchCase	1 or 0 for the Match Upper/Lowercase checkbox
.Confirm	1 or 0 for the Confirm checkbox

When the user closes the Edit Replace dialog box by selecting the OK button, Word records the text entries and checkbox selections in their respective fields in the dialog record. Word then carries out the Edit Replace operation, taking the search/replace parameters from the dialog record to complete the task according to the user's selections.

Some dialog-record fields can accept either a number or a string. In these cases, Word converts a string such as `"1 in"` to the equivalent number of typesetter's points (a typesetter's point is approximately 1/72 inch). This flexibility is available for only some dialog-record fields. Fields that can accept either numbers or strings are followed by a dollar sign enclosed in brackets (**[$]**) in the statement syntaxes given later in this chapter. This convention is used for your information only. Do not include the [$] when you create dialog records in macros.

To create a dialog record in a WordBASIC program, you use the **Dim** (dimension) statement. The syntax is as follows:

Dim *DialogRecord* **As** *DialogBox*

Essentially, **Dim** allocates to *DialogRecord* the storage space and associated field types for *DialogBox.*

To copy the current values of all the elements of a dialog box into the corresponding fields of the dialog record, you use the **GetCurValues** statement. (For more information on the **GetCurValues** statement, see Chapter 7, "Word-BASIC Command Reference.") You can set or read a specific field of a dialog record by specifying the field name, preceded by a period (.).

```
Sub MAIN
   Dim dlg As FormatDocument   'Create Format Document type dialog record
   GetCurValues dlg            'Place current values of Format Document
                               'command into record

   If dlg.MirrorMargins = 0 Then
      dlg.MirrorMargins = 1 Else
      dlg.MirrorMargins = 0    'Toggle mirror margins field of record
                               '(this represents one line of code; lines
                               'have been broken here due to space
                               'constraints)
   FormatDocument dlg          'Perform action using values specified in
                               'dialog record "dlg"
End Sub
```

You use the **Dialog** statement to display a dialog box with the elements described by the values in the fields of the specified dialog record. (For more information on the **Dialog** statement, see Chapter 7, "WordBASIC Command Reference.")

A Simple Dialog-Box Macro

When you create a custom dialog box, you define the field names in which Word will record the user-entered data and checkbox/button selections, and you create the dialog record that will contain the fields. At an absolute minimum, a dialog box must contain an **OKButton** statement; otherwise, the user cannot close the dialog box and continue the execution of the macro. To illustrate, the following statements create a simple dialog box that contains a text field (a prompt), a text box in which the user can enter a string, and an OK button that the user selects to close the box:

```
Begin Dialog UserDialog 350, 75        'Define type and size
                                       'of dialog box
   Text 7, 10, 200, 18, "&Name of File to Edit:"
                                       'Define and position field of text
   TextBox 210, 8, 120, 18, .FileText  'Define text box for user entry of
                                       'text
   OKButton 155, 50, 40, 18            'Allow user to close dialog box
End Dialog                             'End dialog-box definition
Dim FileDlg As Dialog UserDialog       'Create dialog record as FileDlg
FileDlg.FileText = "*.DOC"             'Supply default value to TextBox
Dialog FileDlg                         'Display dialog box
```

The first five statements in this example define the look of the dialog box. (These statements are described under their respective headings in the sections that follow.) The last three statements do not define any portion of the box itself, but they do form a part of any dialog-box macro.

As already mentioned, a dialog box must have a dialog record so that Word can store in memory the selections and entries made by the user. In the example, the dialog record is created immediately after the definition of the dialog box, with a **Dim** statement:

```
Dim FileDlg As Dialog UserDialog
```

This **Dim** statement tells Word to create a dialog record named `FileDlg` of the correct format for the dialog box defined in the preceding statements, which in this case is a User Dialog type of dialog box. If you follow the **Dim** statement with:

```
Dialog FileDlg
```

Word displays your custom dialog box, and when the user closes the dialog box by selecting the OK button, Word writes the user-entered/selected parameters in the dialog record named `dlg`. In this example, any text entered by the user is stored in the field named `.FileText` of the dialog record named `FileDlg`. Between the **Dim** and **Dialog** statements, you can include statements that define default values for any of the dialog fields. You define these values by using the record and field name in an assignment statement, as in the seventh line of the example:

```
FileDlg.FileText = "*.DOC"
```

The string `*.DOC` will appear in the text box when the custom dialog box is displayed. If the user edits or replaces the string, Word stores the new string in the `FileDlg.FileText` field. If you don't provide a default, the text box will be empty.

Note that the combination of the dialog record and field name (in this example, `FileDlg.FileText`) can be used with WordBASIC statements just like any other expression, as in the following examples:

```
Print FileDlg.FileText
Exten$ = Right$(FileDlg.FileText, 3)
```

Positioning of Dialog-Box Elements

Most of the dialog-box definition statements contain position and size information for the particular element they describe. The table on the next page lists the horizontal and vertical positions and sizes expressed as fractions of the system-font character width (the system-font character is approximately 12-point bold).

Position	Meaning
x	Horizontal position of the item in 1/8 system-font character-width units
y	Vertical position of the item in 1/12 system-font character-width units
dx	Width of the item in 1/8 system-font character-width units
dy	Height of the item in 1/12 system-font character-width units

Dialog Box Definition Statements

The following sections describe the statements that you can use to define a dialog box. If you use the Word macro editor to enter the statements given at the end of each description, you will create the example custom dialog box shown at the end of each section.

Begin Dialog

Begin Dialog UserDialog *[x, y,] dx, dy*

Use this statement to start the dialog-box declaration for a custom dialog box. The *x* and *y* arguments are the coordinates for the upper left corner of the dialog box relative to the upper left corner of the screen. If you do not supply *x* and *y*, Word positions the dialog box in the usual location near the center of the screen. The *dx* and *dy* arguments are the width and height of the dialog box (relative to the given *x* and *y* coordinates).

The **Begin Dialog** statement must be followed by at least one other dialog-box definition statement and the **End Dialog** statement; otherwise, an error will result. The other statements must include an **OKButton** statement; otherwise, the user will be unable to close the dialog box, and the macro will not be able to continue executing.

The following statement starts a dialog-box definition and specifies a box width of 50 (400/8) characters and a height of 14 (168/12) characters:

```
Begin Dialog UserDialog 400, 168
```

When Word processes a **Begin Dialog** statement, it assumes that if only two arguments are given, they are *dx* and *dy*. So, in the absence of *x* and *y* arguments, Word positions the dialog box in the center of the display. You can include *x* and *y* in the **Begin Dialog** statement to position the dialog box elsewhere on the screen.

By defining *x* and *y* as 10, the following statement creates a dialog box that occupies the upper left quadrant of the screen:

```
Begin Dialog UserDialog 10, 10, 320, 200
```

End Dialog

End Dialog

This statement ends the definition of the dialog box. You must include an **End Dialog** statement; otherwise, an error results.

CheckBox

CheckBox *x, y, dx, dy, Text$, .Field*

This statement creates a check box with an accompanying text field. The *x* and *y* arguments are the position of the upper left corner of the check box relative to the upper left corner of the dialog box.

The *dx* argument is the combined width of the check box and the *Text$* field. In determining the value of *dx*, a good rule of thumb is to multiply the number of characters in the text (including spaces and punctuation) by 10. Since the system font is proportionally spaced, the exact width varies depending on the characters used. Some experimentation may be necessary to arrive at the proper value.

The *dy* argument is the vertical height allowed for the *Text$* field. A *dy* value of 18 is typical for the default system font; the value should be increased as necessary to accommodate larger fonts. An increase in the value of *dy* causes the check box (and its text) to move downward within the dialog box, effectively altering the value of *y*.

Text$ is the title that appears to the right of the check box. If the width of *Text$* exceeds *dx*, the trailing characters of the text string are truncated. To include an underlined character in the text string so that the user can select the check box from the keyboard, precede the desired character with an ampersand (&).

The *.Field* argument is the name of the dialog-record field that will contain the current setting of the check box. If the value of *.Field* is 0, the box is not checked; any other value in *.Field* displays the box as checked.

The following statements create a check box that is positioned the equivalent of 20 text characters from the left side of the dialog box and approximately 12 text lines from the top. The size of the entire check box and text area is approximately 21 characters wide and 1 line high. The name of the field established in the dialog record for the setting of the checkbox is .CB1 (`.Field - .CB1`). The identifying text displayed to the right of the check box is `Display Status Bar`.

The dialog box generated by the following statements is shown below:

```
Begin Dialog UserDialog 400, 168
   CheckBox 110, 84, 180, 18, "Display Status &Bar", .CB1
   OKButton 180, 28, 40, 18      'Provide way of closing dialog box
End Dialog                       'End dialog-box definition
Dim Foo As Dialog UserDialog     'Create dialog record
Dialog Foo                       'Display dialog box
```

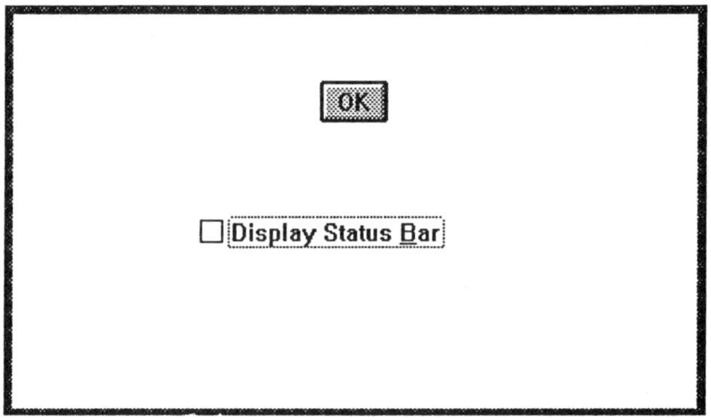

ComboBox

ComboBox *x, y, dx, dy, ArrayVariable$, .Field*

This statement creates a combination text box/list box. When a combination box is displayed in the dialog box, the user can enter a text string in the associated text box or select from entries that have been placed in the list box from the *ArrayVariable$* argument. (Refer to Chapter 4, "Interlude—WordBASIC for Beginners," and Chapter 5, "The WordBASIC Programming Language," for information on creating an array of variables.)

The *x* and *y* arguments are the position of the upper left corner of the list box relative to the upper left corner of the dialog box. The *dx* and *dy* arguments are the width and height of the combo box in which the user enters or selects the text.

The *.Field* argument is the name of the dialog-record field that will contain the text string entered in the text box or selected from the list box. When the user selects the OK button, the string in the text box will be recorded in the *.Field* field.

The following array and **ComboBox** statements generate the dialog box shown after the statements:

```
Dim TypeArr$(5)
TypeArr$(0) = "Draft"
TypeArr$(1) = "Letter"
TypeArr$(2) = "Legal"
TypeArr$(3) = "A4"
TypeArr$(4) = "B5"
TypeArr$(5) = "Custom"
Begin Dialog UserDialog 200, 112
   Text 6, 10, 130, 18, "Document Type:"
   ComboBox 6, 25, 100, 85, TypeArr$(), .DocType
   OKButton 130, 80, 40, 18        'Provide way of closing dialog box
End Dialog                         'End dialog-box definition
Dim WhatDoc As Dialog UserDialog   'Create dialog record
Dialog WhatDoc                     'Display dialog box
```

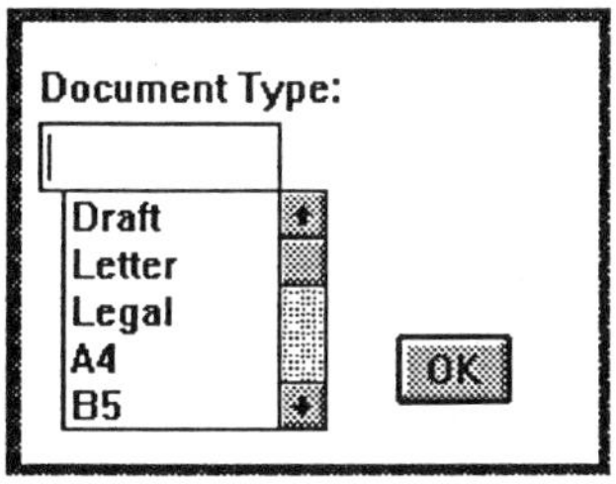

NOTE: *Combination boxes and list boxes are defined in the same way. However, they differ in the type of values they pass to and from the fields in their dialog records. Combination boxes pass literal text strings (because the user is not limited to the selections that appear in the list box), whereas list boxes pass numeric values that correspond to positions in the defined array. If you use a combination box, your macro may need to evaluate text strings in order to control the flow of the program.*

GroupBox

GroupBox *x, y, dx, dy, Text$*

This statement creates a box-shaped graphic image that can include a title in its top border. You can use a group box to enclose sets of option buttons or check boxes, or any other items that need to be grouped together in the dialog box. The group box does not return any values to the dialog record.

The *x* and *y* arguments are the position of the upper left corner of the group box relative to the upper left corner of the dialog box. The *dx* and *dy* arguments are the width and height of the box. *Text$* is the title embedded in the top border of the box. If the width of *Text$* exceeds *dx*, the trailing characters of the text string are truncated. If you specify an empty string ("") as *Text$*, the top border of the box is a solid line.

The following **GroupBox** and accompanying statements generate the group box shown after the statements:

```
Begin Dialog UserDialog 200, 112
   GroupBox 6, 25, 120, 70, "Printer Type"
   OKButton 140, 80, 40, 18          'Provide way of closing dialog box
End Dialog                           'End dialog-box definition
Dim WhatPrinter As Dialog UserDialog 'Create dialog record
Dialog WhatPrinter                   'Display dialog box
```

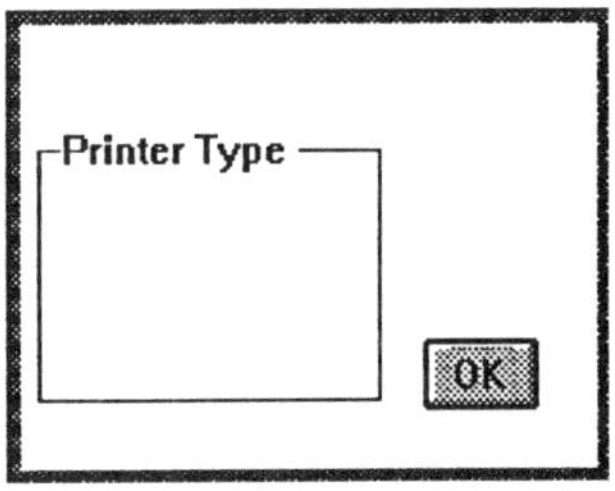

ListBox

ListBox *x, y, dx, dy, ArrayVariable$, .Field*

This statement creates a list box containing the strings from the *ArrayVariable$* argument. The *x* and *y* arguments are the position of the upper left corner of the list box relative to the upper left corner of the dialog box. The *dx* and *dy* arguments are the width and height of the list box.

The *.Field* argument is the name of the dialog-record field that will contain the selection made from the list box. When the user selects the OK button, the string's number in the array (defined in the corresponding *ArrayVariable$* statement) is recorded in the *.Field* field.

The **ListBox** statement operates in a manner similar to the **ComboBox** statement. Refer to the **ComboBox** statement description for additional details and an example.

> **NOTE:** *Although list boxes and combination boxes are defined in the same way, they differ in the type of values they pass to and from their dialog-record fields. Combination boxes pass literal text strings, whereas list boxes pass numeric values that correspond to positions in the defined array.*

OKButton and CancelButton

OKButton *x, y, dx, dy*

CancelButton *x, y, dx, dy*

These statements define the position and size of the OK and Cancel buttons. You must specify both the location and size of the buttons. The *x* and *y* arguments are the position of the upper left corner of the button relative to the upper left corner of the dialog box. The *dx* and *dy* arguments are the width and height of the button. Typical values for *dx* and *dy* are 40 and 18, respectively.

If the user chooses the OK button, the macro continues. But if the user chooses the Cancel button, an error is generated. This error can be trapped with **On Error** (see "Error Handling," later in this chapter for additional information).

The following **OKButton** and **CancelButton** statements generate the buttons in the dialog box shown after the statements:

```
Begin Dialog UserDialog 400, 160
   OKButton 180, 28, 40, 18
   CancelButton 160, 48, 80, 18
End Dialog                        'End dialog-box definition
Dim GoNoGo As Dialog UserDialog   'Create dialog record
Dialog GoNoGo                     'Display dialog box
```

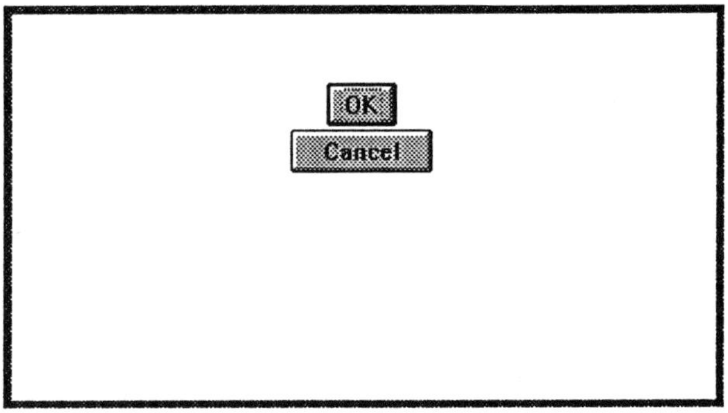

OptionGroup and OptionButton

OptionGroup *.Field*

OptionButton *x, y, dx, dy, Text$*

These statements are used together to define a series of related, but mutually exclusive, option buttons. The **OptionGroup** statement begins the definition of the option buttons and defines the dialog-record field that will contain the result of the user's selection. The **OptionButton** statements (there are always at least two) define the position and text associated with each button.

The *.Field* argument is the name of the dialog-record field that will contain the current option-button selection. If the value of *.Field* is 0, the option button associated with the first **OptionButton** statement is selected. If the value of *.Field* is 1, the option button associated with the second **OptionButton** statement is selected, and so on.

The *x* and *y* arguments are the position of the upper left corner of the button relative to the upper left corner of the dialog box. The *dx* and *dy* arguments are the width and height of the button. A typical value for *dy* is 18, which accommodates text in the system font.

Text$* is the title that appears to the right of the option-button icon. If the width of *Text$ exceeds *dx*, the trailing characters of the text string are truncated. To include an underlined character in the text string so that the user can select the option button from the keyboard, precede the character with an ampersand (&).

The following **OptionGroup** and **OptionButton** statements generate the group of option buttons in the dialog box shown after the statements:

```
Begin Dialog UserDialog 200, 112
   OptionGroup .PrinterType
      OptionButton 20, 35, 60, 18, "&Laser"
      OptionButton 20, 55, 50, 18, "L&ine"
      OptionButton 20, 75, 100, 18, "Dot &Matrix"
   OKButton 140, 35, 40, 18          'Provide way of closing dialog box
End Dialog                           'End dialog-box definition
Dim WhatPrinter As Dialog UserDialog 'Create dialog record
Dialog WhatPrinter                   'Display dialog box
```

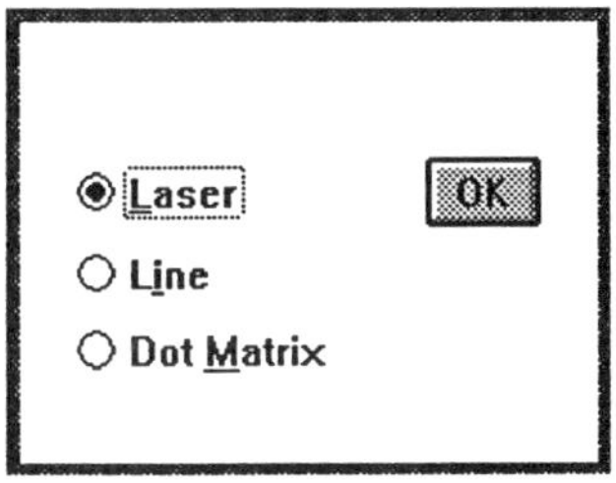

Text

Text *x, y, dx, dy, Text$*

This statement creates one or more lines of static text depending on the length of the text string and the dimensions specified by *dx* and *dy*. The **Text** statement does not return any values to the dialog record.

The *x* and *y* arguments are the position of the upper left corner of the text area relative to the upper left corner of the dialog box. The *dx* and *dy* arguments are the width and height of the area reserved for *$Text.*

Text$* is the text string that appears to the right of the position specified by x and y. If the width of *Text$ exceeds *dx*, the excess characters are wrapped to the next line, filling as many lines as required, as long as the height of the text area specified by *dy* is not exceeded. If the height exceeds *dy*, the excess characters are truncated. You can specify an underlined character in *Text$* by preceding the character with an ampersand (&). Pressing the underlined character on the keyboard allows the user to position the cursor in the combination box or text box defined in the statement immediately following the **Text** statement. (Note that if the width of *Text$* exceeds *dx*, the underlined character may not appear in the correct position.)

For examples of uses of **Text**, see the example for **ComboBox** earlier in this section, and the example for **TextBox** that follows.

TextBox

TextBox *x, y, dx, dy, .Field*

This statement creates a text box in which the user can enter and edit text. The *x* and *y* arguments are the position of the upper left corner of the text box relative to the upper left corner of the dialog box. The *dx* and *dy* arguments are the width and height of the text box in which the user will enter the text. A typical value for *dy* is 18, which accommodates text in the system font.

The *.Field* argument is the name of the dialog-record field that will contain any text entered in the text box. When the user selects the OK button, Word records the text string entered in the text box in the *.Field* field.

The following statements create a text box that is positioned the equivalent of 24 text characters from the left side of the dialog box and 1 text line from the top. The text box is 20 characters wide by about 1 line high. The name of the field established in the dialog record for the text is `.FileName`. Note that, because the **Text** statement immediately precedes the **TextBox** statement, the underlined `N` of the **Text** statement allows the user to place the cursor in the text box by simply pressing Alt+N.

```
Begin Dialog UserDialog 200, 112
   Text 7, 10, 190, 18, "&Name of File to Edit:"
   TextBox 10, 35, 120, 18, .FileName
   OKButton 160, 28, 34, 14      'Provide way of closing dialog box
End Dialog                        'End dialog-box definition
Dim dlg As Dialog UserDialog      'Create dialog record
Dialog dlg                        'Display dialog box
```

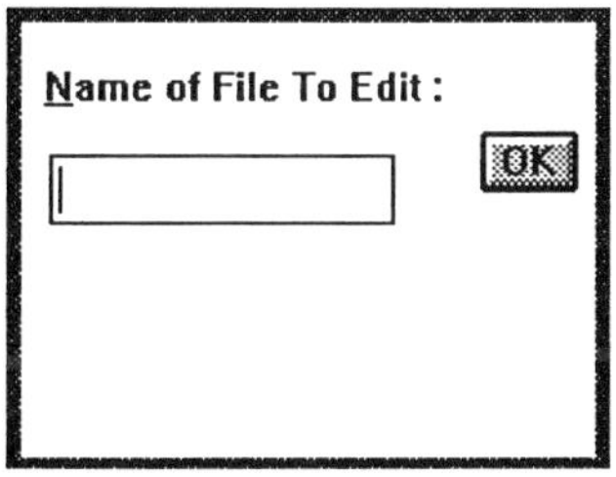

An Example Dialog-Box Macro

The following sample program illustrates the use of the various dialog-box statements to build the custom dialog box shown after the listing:

```
Sub MAIN
   DisableInput
   Dim TypeArr$(5)
   TypeArr$(0) = "Draft"
   TypeArr$(1) = "Letter"
   TypeArr$(2) = "Legal"
   TypeArr$(3) = "A4"
   TypeArr$(4) = "B5"
   TypeArr$(5) = "Custom"
   Begin Dialog UserDialog 509, 160
      Text 8, 10, 254, 18, "&Name of File to Edit:"
      TextBox 204, 10, 280, 18, .FileName
      Text 8, 30, 191, 10, "&Document Type:"
      ComboBox 8, 50, 172, 85, TypeArr$(), .DocType
      GroupBox 204, 42, 165, 87, "Printer Type"
      OptionGroup .PrintType
         OptionButton 210, 59, 127, 18, "&Laser"
         OptionButton 210, 79, 127, 18, "L&ine"
         OptionButton 210, 99, 146, 18, "Dot &Matrix"
```

(continued)

Continued
```
      CheckBox 8, 135, 165, 18, "&Show Styles", .StyleCheck
      CheckBox 204, 135, 306, 18, "Display Status&Bar", .StatCheck
      OKButton 382, 48, 102, 18
      CancelButton 382, 78, 102, 18
   End Dialog

   Dim WhatPrinter As Dialog UserDialog
   WhatPrinter.Doctype = "Draft"
   WhatPrinter.StyleCheck = 1
   On Error Goto bye
   Dialog WhatPrinter
bye:
End Sub
```

This macro produces the following dialog box:

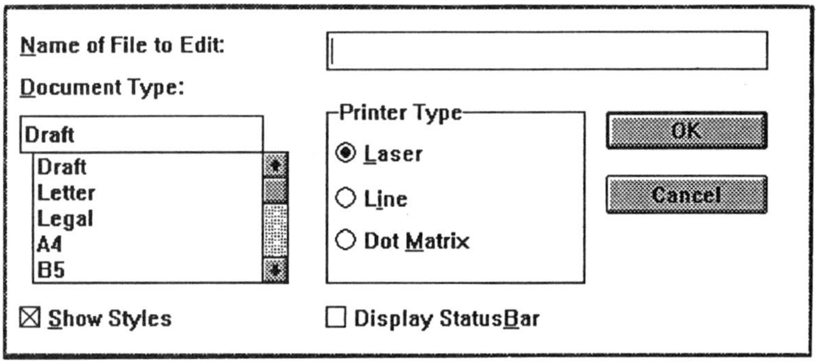

Loading Default Values into the Dialog Box

When users will often make the same selections and you know ahead of time what those selections are, you can "preload" the selections into the custom dialog box so that when the dialog box is opened, the most likely selections appear as the defaults. Note that the dialog box produced by the preceding example has two default selections when the box is opened: The document type is set to Draft, and the Show Styles check box is turned on. The following sections describe how to make this example dialog box appear with specific selections already made, thereby eliminating the need for the user to select commonly used functions.

Selecting a check box

The following statement causes an X to be placed in the Show Styles check box when the user opens the example dialog box:

```
WhatPrinter.StyleCheck = 1
```

In this statement, WhatPrinter is the name assigned to the dialog record by the **Dim** statement following the **End Dialog** statement. .StyleCheck is the declared name of the field within the dialog record that indicates whether the check box is selected.

```
.
.
.
End Dialog                           'End dialog-box definition
Dim WhatPrinter As Dialog UserDialog 'Create dialog record
WhatPrinter.StyleCheck = 1           'Load 1 into .StyleCheck field
Dialog WhatPrinter                   'Display dialog box
```

Placing an item in a combination box

The following statement causes the text string "Legal" to be placed in the text-box portion of the combination box shown in the example dialog box:

```
WhatPrinter.DocType = "Legal"
```

Again, WhatPrinter is the name assigned to the dialog record by the **Dim** statement, and .DocType is the declared name of the field in the dialog record that indicates which item in the combination box is selected. Because the field associated with the combination box is defined as containing the string "Draft", the text-box portion of the combination box contains the word Draft when the user opens the dialog box.

```
.
.
.
End Dialog                      'End dialog-box definition
Dim dlg As Dialog UserDialog    'Create dialog record
WhatPrinter.DocType = "Draft"   'Load "Draft" into .DocType field
Dialog dlg                      'Display dialog box
```

Selecting an item in a list box

If the combination box of the example dialog box is redefined to be a list box (by simply changing the **ComboBox** statement to **ListBox** and leaving all other parameters as they are), the following statement:

```
WhatPrinter.DocType = 2
```

causes `"Legal"` to be selected when the user opens the dialog box.

As for the previous examples, `WhatPrinter` is the name assigned to the dialog record by a **Dim** statement, and `.DocType` is the declared name of the field in the dialog record that indicates which item in the list box is selected. The numbers of the items in the list box correspond to their numbers in the dimensioned array. In this case, `"Legal"` is defined as `TypeArr$(2)`, so `WhatPrinter.DocType = 2` indicates that `"Legal"` is to be selected.

```
.
.
.
End Dialog                           'End dialog-box definition
Dim WhatPrinter As Dialog UserDialog 'Create dialog record
WhatPrinter.DocType = 2              'Set .DocType field to 2
Dialog WhatPrinter                   'Display dialog box
```

Selecting an option button

The following statement causes the option button associated with the `Dot Matrix` selection of the example dialog box to be selected:

```
WhatPrinter.PrintType = 2
```

As for the previous examples, `WhatPrinter` is the name assigned to the dialog record by the **Dim** statement, and `.PrintType` is the declared name of the field in the dialog record that indicates which option button in the group of buttons (defined by the **OptionGroup** statement) is selected. The numbers of the option buttons correspond to the order of their definition statements. In the example dialog box, the option-button numbers placed in the `.PrintType` field are 0, 1, and 2 for `"Laser"`, `"Line"`, and `"Dot Matrix"`, respectively.

```
.
.
.
End Dialog                   'End dialog-box definition
Dim dlg As Dialog UserDialog 'Create dialog record
WhatPrinter.PrintType = 2    'Set .PrintType field to 2
Dialog dlg                   'Display dialog box
```

Placing text in a text box

The following statement causes the text "C:\FORECAST\SALES" to be placed in the text box of the example dialog box:

```
WhatPrinter.FileName = "C:\FORECAST\SALES"
```

As for the previous examples, WhatPrinter is the name assigned to the dialog record by the **Dim** statement. .FileName is the declared name of the field in the dialog record that contains the text string to be placed in the text box. If the dialog box has more than one text box, each is assigned a different dialog-record field, as the two check boxes are in the example.

```
.
.
.
End Dialog                                'End dialog-box definition
Dim WhatPrinter As Dialog UserDialog      'Create dialog record
WhatPrinter.FileName = "C:\FORECAST\SALES"  'Insert path into .FileName
                                          'field
Dialog WhatPrinter                        'Display dialog box
```

An example of loading default values

The following program listing is a continuation of the earlier example and illustrates the various methods of loading default selections and text into the dialog box, which is shown after the listing:

```
End Dialog
Dim dlg As Dialog UserDialog    'Create dialog record Style CheckBox
WhatPrinter.StyleCheck = 1      'Load 1 into .StyleCheck ComboBox
WhatPrinter.DocType = "Normal"  'Set .DocType to "Normal" OptionButtons
WhatPrinter.PrintType = 2       'Set selection to Dot Matrix TextBox
WhatPrinter.FileName = "C:\FORECAST\SALES"  'Insert path into .FileName
Dialog dlg                      'Display dialog box
End Sub
```

Evaluating the Contents of a Dialog Box

To evaluate the selections made by the user in a custom dialog box, you have to evaluate the contents of the dialog record created by the **Dim** *RecordName* **As Dialog UserDialog** statement. This **Dim** statement should follow the **End Dialog** statement as soon as practical, because the dialog box created as **UserDialog** is volatile and is overwritten each time a new **Begin Dialog UserDialog** statement is executed. See the preceding descriptions of the dialog-box definition statements for information on how the **Begin Dialog UserDialog** statement is used.

Evaluating a check box

A check box places either a 0 (zero) or a 1 in the dialog-record field that is defined by the corresponding **CheckBox** statement. A 0 indicates that the check box is not selected, while a 1 indicates that it is selected. One way to evaluate the condition (selected or not selected) of a check box is to use an **If...Then** control statement, as in the following example:

```
If WhatPrinter.StyleCheck = 1 Then
   ViewStatusBar 1
Else
   ViewStatusBar 0
End If
```

In the above example, if the value of `WhatPrinter.StyleCheck` evaluates to 1, `ViewStatusBar 1` is executed to turn on the status bar at the bottom of the display; otherwise, `ViewStatusBar 0` is executed to ensure that the status bar is turned off.

Determining what text is in a combination box

The user of a combination box can choose from specific selections, which are made to appear in a predetermined order in the list-box portion, or enter a text string in the text-box portion. Consequently, the corresponding dialog-record field for a particular combination box contains either one of several known text strings or an unknown text string. The macro can examine the dialog-record field and determine whether one of the known selections is present; if so, the macro can take the appropriate action. If the macro finds none of the known text strings in the dialog-record field, it can assume that the field contains an unknown, user-entered text string that will require further evaluation.

One method of determining whether one of the known selections is present is to evaluate the combination-box field of the dialog record for each selection. The following example shows a way of making this evaluation:

```
Select Case WhatPrinter.DocType
   Case "Draft"
      MsgBox "Draft is selected"
   Case "Letter"
      MsgBox "Letter is selected"
   Case "Legal"
      MsgBox "Legal is selected"
   Case "A4"
      MsgBox "A4 is selected"
   Case "B5"
```

```
      MsgBox "B5 is selected"
   Case "Custom"
      MsgBox "Custom is selected"
   Case Else
      Call UserType
End Select
```

This listing is just an example, so it does not branch to another part of the macro and continue execution. Instead, it simply displays a message box to verify that the evaluation of the combination-box field has taken place. If the user enters an unknown text string, the `Call UserType` statement branches to a subroutine in the macro that processes the text contained in `WhatPrinter.DocType`.

Evaluating an item in a list box

In a list box, the user has to choose from specific selections that appear in the order determined by the array that contains the selections. Consequently, the field in the dialog record for a particular list box contains one number from a range of known numbers. The macro can examine the dialog record, determine which number is present in the list-box field, and take the appropriate action.

A simple method of determining which choice the user has made is to evaluate the list-box field of the dialog record for each selection by checking for each possible numeric value. The following statements show a way of making this evaluation. (These statements assume that the combination box from the example dialog box has been redefined as a list box by simply changing the **ComboBox** statement to a **ListBox** statement and leaving all other parameters as they are.)

```
Select Case WhatPrinter.DocType
   Case 0
      MsgBox "Draft is selected"
   Case 1
      MsgBox "Letter is selected"
   Case 2
      MsgBox "Legal is selected"
   Case 3
      MsgBox "A4 is selected"
   Case 4
      MsgBox "B5 is selected"
   Case 5
      MsgBox "Custom is selected"
   Case Else
End Select
```

As for the combination-box evaluation, this example does not branch to another part of the macro and continue execution. Instead, it simply displays a message box verifying that the evaluation of the list-box field has taken place. In a real macro, you would replace the **MsgBox** statement with a **Goto** statement, a subroutine **Call**, or whatever statements were required to complete the operation.

Evaluating an option button

As with a list box, selecting an option button involves choosing from specific selections that appear in a predetermined order within the option group box. Consequently, the corresponding field in the dialog record contains a number from a range of known numbers. The macro can examine the dialog-record field to determine which number is present and take the appropriate action.

The following example, similar to that given for evaluation of a list box, shows one method of identifying the number:

```
Case WhatPrinter.PrintType
   Case 0
      MsgBox "Laser is selected"
   Case 1
      MsgBox "Line is selected"
   Case 2
      MsgBox "Dot Matrix is selected"
   Case Else
End Select
```

As for the list-box evaluation, this example does nothing other than display a message box verifying that the evaluation of the option-group field has taken place. In a real macro, you would replace the **MsgBox** statement with a **Goto** statement, a subroutine **Call**, or whatever statements were required to complete the operation.

Using text in a text box

When the user enters an unknown text string in a text box, the string is usually passed on to some other operation in the macro. The string might be a file name, a search string, a user name, a date, a revision number, and so on. The macro simply passes the text string as an argument to the appropriate statement for further action. For example, the macro might assign a file name to a string variable for use by a **FileOpen** statement or pass a search string to an **EditSearch** statement.

The dialog-record field that contains the text-box string is defined in the **TextBox** statement. In the example dialog box, the field corresponding to the Name of File to Edit: text box is `.FileName`. The macro expects the text string that is entered in this text box to be the name of a file to be opened for a subsequent operation. To open the file, the macro could include the following statements:

```
WhatPrinter.FileName = FileName$
MsgBox "Opening File: " + FileName$
FileOpen FileName$
```

These statements move the contents of the dialog record's `.FileName` field to the variable `FileName$` and then open the designated file using a **FileOpen** statement.

ERROR HANDLING

Normally, when WordBASIC encounters an error in a program, it displays a message explaining the error and terminates the program. WordBASIC provides a number of tools that allow macros to intercept and (with certain limitations) correct errors without any intervention on the part of the user or interruption of the macro's operation.

The most fundamental error-handling tool is the **On Error** statement. An **On Error** statement can be thought of as a trap, waiting quietly until an error triggers its operation. What action the statement takes after being triggered depends on which of the three forms of **On Error** are used. These forms are as follows:

On Error Goto *Label*

On Error Resume Next

On Error Goto 0

The first form, **On Error Goto**, causes the program to branch to the specified *Label* whenever an error occurs. This form is most often used to transfer control of the program to a specific error-handling routine, which attempts to identify the error and take action to correct or bypass it.

Before exiting an error-handling routine, you should always use the statement `Err = 0`. Like a real trap, the **On Error Goto** statement must be reset before it can be used again. However, it is best not to reset the error trap until the error-handling routine is complete, because if you place an `Err = 0` statement at the beginning of an error-handling routine and an error occurs before the routine is complete, you create an endless loop. Thc **On Error Goto** statement causes a jump from the middle to the start of the error-handling routine, where the trap is reset and the error in the error-handling routine occurs again. This sequence continues until the macro is interrupted by the user.

The *Err* variable also serves another important function in dealing with errors because it contains the value of the last error in the current context. Using the value in *Err*, an error-handling routine can determine which of many possible errors has occurred and take the appropriate action. A list of the error values and their associated error messages can be found at the end of Chapter 7, "WordBASIC Command Reference."

On Error Resume Next is a simpler approach to dealing with errors. When an error occurs, **On Error Resume Next** passes control to the line in the macro after the one in which the error occurred. Be cautious when using **On Error Resume Next**; the error is ignored and the problem that caused the error may not have been corrected. If the statement that caused the error has performed some, but not all, of its actions, other statements that rely on those actions may fail. Because **On Error Resume Next** generates no error message, the user may not be aware that an error has occurred or that the program could malfunction and produce incorrect results.

The last form of **On Error** is **On Error Goto 0**. This statement disables an earlier **On Error Goto** *Label* or **On Error Resume Next** statement. Following an **On Error Goto 0** statement, errors are not trapped, and the occurrence of an error causes an error message to be generated and the macro to halt.

WordBASIC provides one other tool for error handling: the **Error** *Num* statement. **Error** *Num* causes WordBASIC to believe that the error specified by *Num* has occurred. This statement can be valuable in two ways. First, you can use it to simulate a particular error in order to test an error-handling routine. Executing an **Error** statement when an **On Error** statement is in effect causes the action specified by the **On Error** to be performed. If an error routine uses *Err* to test for particular errors, different values of **Error** can be used to easily test all parts of the routine.

Because there are so many possible errors, it is not practical for an error-handling routine to deal with them all. You must anticipate which errors are likely to occur in a given situation and develop ways for dealing with each of them. Unanticipated errors are always a possibility, and some errors can be anticipated but are impossible for a macro to correct. In these cases, it is often best to inform the user about the problem and halt the macro.

It is valuable to include an **Error** statement in an error-handling routine. If the error-handling routine is unable to deal with a particular error, it can fall back on the statement **Error Err**. This statement generates an error message using the error number stored in the special variable *Err* and halts the macro.

For more information on error handling and some program examples, see the entries for **Err**, **Error**, and **On Error** in Chapter 7, "WordBASIC Command Reference."

Errors and Subroutines

It is important to understand that **On Error**, **Err**, and **Error** are not global in their operation. If you include an **On Error** statement at the beginning of the main macro and an error occurs in a subroutine or user-defined function, the error is not trapped by that statement. Each subroutine and user-defined function should have its own **On Error** statement and error-handling routine because each error trap operates independently of the others. Note, however, that if an **On Error** statement occurs before a subroutine is called and the subroutine has its own **On Error** statement, you don't have to repeat the main **On Error** statement when control is returned to the main program.

Use the localized nature of WordBASIC error trapping to your advantage. For example, local error trapping makes it possible to trap an error created by a **CancelButton** without disturbing the more general-purpose error checking you may already have in place. It also makes it easier to anticipate all the errors that are likely to occur in a given situation and to install error-handling mechanisms for them all.

Word Errors vs. WordBASIC Errors

Errors with numbers less than 1000 are generated internally by WordBASIC and can be trapped and handled as described above. Errors with numbers of 1000 or greater are generated outside WordBASIC by Word itself and behave somewhat differently. An untrapped Word error behaves exactly like an untrapped WordBASIC error; an error message is displayed and the macro halts. If the Word error is trapped, however, an error message box is still displayed and the macro pauses until the user selects OK in the message box; then error trapping continues. The fact that trapped Word errors require user input is an important consideration when designing macros to operate unattended.

AUTO MACROS

When Word performs certain operations, such as opening or closing a document, it routinely checks to see if an appropriate auto macro exists. If an auto macro does exist, Word executes the macro after completing the operation. For example, if you want to create a backup copy of every file you open, you could write a macro called AutoOpen to perform the backup operation. Whenever you open any file, Word checks for the presence of an AutoOpen macro and, if available, runs it. If an AutoOpen macro is not available, Word opens the file in the normal manner.

You can create five different auto macros, each triggered by a different Word operation. You can prevent the auto macro from running by holding down the Shift key when you perform the operation that triggers the macro.

AutoNew

The AutoNew macro runs after you create a new document. You can include an AutoNew macro in a template so that the macro is run each time you create a new document based on that template, or you can save the macro in a global context so that it is run each time you create a document, regardless of which template you are using.

Word runs only one AutoNew macro, and the template AutoNew always has priority over the global AutoNew. In other words, if you create a document that is based on a template containing an AutoNew macro and the NORMAL.DOT template also contains an AutoNew macro, Word runs only the template AutoNew macro and ignores the global AutoNew macro.

The following is an example of an AutoNew macro:

```
Sub MAIN
   Edit SelectAll
   UpdateFields
End Sub
```

AutoOpen

The AutoOpen macro runs after you open a file with File Open or File Find, or from the list of documents at the bottom of the File menu.

The following is an example of an AutoOpen macro:

```
Sub MAIN
   Dim dlg As EditSummaryInfo
   GetCurValues dlg
   Print FileName$(0) + "last worked on by " + dlg.LastSavedBy
End Sub
```

AutoExec

The AutoExec macro runs when you start Word. With this macro, you can easily instruct Word to automatically configure its menus and options the way you like them. For example, you might use an AutoExec macro to reconfigure Word's menus and command keys in order to create a custom application, based on Word, that you can run from DOS or Program Manager just like any other application.

You can prevent AutoExec from running by using the **/m** switch when you start Word (`winword /m` or `pmword /m`).

The following is an example of an AutoExec macro:

```
Sub MAIN
   MacroAssignToMenu "Bold", Forma&t", "&Bold", .Assign
End Sub
```

AutoClose

The AutoClose macro runs when you close a document by using File Close, document Control Close, or File Exit, or by closing Windows or shutting down OS/2.

The following is an example of an AutoClose macro:

```
Sub MAIN
   Dim dlg As EditSummaryInfo
   GetCurValues dlg
   MsgBox "Total editing time for this document is: " + dlg.EditTime
End Sub
```

AutoExit

The AutoExit macro runs when you quit Word. The following is an example of an AutoExit macro:

```
Sub MAIN
   MsgBox "Remember to back up your files", "Reminder"
End Sub
```

FILE INPUT/OUTPUT

WordBASIC supports sequential file input and output. Record-based (random-access) files are not supported. You use sequential files to store data from WordBASIC programs on disk. You can also use sequential-file input to load unformatted or nontext files, as in the example later in this section.

You can have up to four files open at one time. Each file is assigned a "stream" number from 1 through 4 that identifies the file to Word's macro processor. You precede the number with a # symbol to indicate that it is a stream number. For example:

```
Open "RBOW.TXT" For Input As #1
```

opens the specified file for input and assigns it the stream number 1. Using the number with other file statements identifies which stream to access.

Accessing a disk file in WordBASIC is a three-step process:

1. Open the file using the **Open** statement. You can open a file for **Input**, **Output**, or **Append**.
2. Perform the transaction. You can write to the file using the **Write** or **Print** statements. You can read from the file using **Line Input**, **Input**, or **Read**.
3. Close the file using the **Close** statement. Closing the file ensures that all data has been transferred from the computer's memory to disk and frees the stream number for other use.

Opening a File

The statement

```
Open "PHONE.TXT" For Output As #1
```

opens the file PHONE.TXT and assigns it stream number 1. If the file does not exist, opening the file in the **Output** mode creates an empty file with that name. If the file does exist, any existing data in the file is deleted and replaced with any new data.

The statement

```
Open "PHONE.TXT" For Append As #1
```

does the same thing, except that any new data is appended to the end of any existing data in the file. Because **Append** also creates a new file if one does not exist, it is always safer to use **Append** rather than **Output**, unless you specifically want to overwrite data in an existing file.

File Transactions

After you have opened a file for **Append** or **Output**, data can be written to that file. Data cannot be written to a file that has been opened for **Input**. Any attempt to do so generates an error.

Data can be written in two ways. You can use a special form of the **Print** statement to send data to a file exactly as it would appear if you "printed" the data in the status bar. The difference between **Print** for the status bar and **Print** for file output is the stream number. Without the number, the output appears in the status bar. **Print** is useful for producing ASCII text files or files with special delimiters needed for data exchange with other applications.

The **Write** statement works much like **Print** except that it stores variables with delimiters that allow the **Read** statement to process it correctly. To create a file with **Print** that can later be recalled with **Read**, you must insert these delimiters yourself before saving the data. You should use **Write** when you know the file will be recalled with either WordBASIC's **Read** statement or another application that uses the same data delimiters as WordBASIC.

The following examples show how WordBASIC statements store information on disk. Not shown are two special characters: the carriage-return character, which marks the end of each record (line) in the file, and the end-of-file (EOF) character, which follows the last record in the file.

Example	Result
`Write #1, 300`	`300`
`Write #1, "Testing"`	`"Testing"`
`Write #1, "Testing",123,"Testing"`	`"Testing",123,"Testing"`
`Print #1, 300`	`300`
`Print #1, "Testing"`	`Testing`
`Print #1, "Testing",123,"Testing"`	`Testing    123    Testing`

Three WordBASIC statements and one function are available for reading data files. As already mentioned, the **Read** statement is most commonly used to read data files created with the **Write** statement or files created by other applications that use the same delimiters. **Read** automatically strips quotation marks from strings in files created with **Write**. It can also load data into a variable or a series of variables. These variables can be numeric, string, or a combination, but they must correspond with the type of data that exists in the file. Lack of correspondence creates a *Type Mismatch* error.

You can use a special form of the **Input** statement to read data from a sequential file into a variable or a series of variables. The difference between **Input** from the status bar and **Input** from a file is the stream number. Without the number, the input prompt appears in the status bar. **Input** works much the same as **Read**, except that it does not strip quotation marks from around strings.

The other two file-input methods—one function and one statement—are suitable for reading unformatted data, such as ASCII text files, or for reading data files from applications that store records in ways incompatible with **Read**.

The **Input$( )** function takes an argument that specifies how many characters are to be read from a file. The result must always be returned to a single string variable. This function is useful when an unformatted data file must be processed in small chunks or when records in the file are of fixed length.

The **Line Input** statement reads an entire line from a file into a string variable. This statement is similar to **Input**, except that **Line Input** does not break the line into separate values at commas, and you cannot use it to read data from a file into a numeric variable.

Detecting the End of the File

Any attempt to read beyond the end of a sequential file results in an error. Because a macro often does not know how long a file is or how many records it contains, WordBASIC has an **Eof( )** function with which you can detect when the last record in a sequential file has been reached. The **Eof( )** function returns a –1 when the last record in the specified stream number has been read. By testing for the end of the file after each read, you can avoid the *Input Past End of File* error.

Closing a File

After a macro has finished with a file, you must close the file with the **Close** statement. Closing a file ensures that all data output from **Print** or **Write** statements is written from memory to disk. It also frees the current stream number for other use.

If you have opened a file for **input** and you now need to output data or append data to the file, you must first close the file and then reopen it in the appropriate mode. This is also the case when you need to input data from a file opened for **Output** or **Append**.

You can use the **Close** statement in two ways. If you invoke **Close** with a stream number, the statement closes only the file that is currently open with the specified stream number. If you don't include a stream number, the statement closes all currently open files. As a precaution, you may want to include a **Close** statement before exiting any program that uses disk files. If no files are open, an error does not occur, but if files are open, using the **Close** statement can prevent the loss of any data remaining in memory that has not yet been written to disk.

File Input/Output Programming

As you have seen, a number of statements and functions must work in concert for a WordBASIC program that uses file input/output to run correctly. For a better understanding of how these statements and functions work, read their individual discussions in Chapter 7, "WordBASIC Command Reference." You might also find it helpful to study the working program examples in Appendix B, "Program Examples." The StringSearch program shows an example of using **Line Input** to read an unformatted text file. The ListManager program shows an example of creating data files with the **Write** statement and recalling them with the **Read** statement.

SPECIAL BOOKMARKS

As described in the *Microsoft Word User's Reference*, the user can set bookmarks anywhere within a document for use as quick access points, references to selected portions of text, and so on. In addition to maintaining any user-defined bookmarks, Word maintains several reserved bookmarks, which it places in documents and automatically updates. You can use these special bookmarks just like those that you place in documents, except that you don't have to set them.

These special bookmarks are listed in the following table:

Bookmark	Definition
\Sel	Current selection
\PrevSel1	Previous selection 1 where editing occurred (nil at the start)
\PrevSel2	Previous selection 2 where editing occurred (nil at the start)

(continued)

Continued

Bookmark	Definition
\StartOfSel	Start of the selection
\EndOfSel	End of the selection
\Line	Current line (first of the selection)
\Char	Current character (first of the selection)
\Para	Current paragraph (first of the selection)
\Section	Current section (first of the selection)
\Doc	Entire document
\Page	Current page
\StartOfDoc	Beginning of the document
\EndOfDoc	End of the document
\Cell	Cell
\Table	Table
\HeadingLevel	A heading level

Like user-defined bookmarks, special bookmarks can be used with several WordBASIC statements. These statements are:

CompBookmarks( )	**EndofBookmark( )**
CopyBookmark( )	**Existing Bookmark( )**
EditGoTo	**GetBookmark$( )**
EmptyBookmark( )	**StartofBookmark( )**

The following sections describe the special bookmarks, with some examples of how they are used.

The \Sel Bookmark

The **\Sel** bookmark is assigned to the current selection or the insertion point. When this bookmark is used as an argument in a statement, direct reference is made to the current selection. As an example, you can use the **\Sel** bookmark in conjunction with the **\EndOfDoc** bookmark and the **CmpBookmarks( )** function to determine whether the cursor is at the end of the document.

The following macro moves line-by-line through a document from the current selection or insertion point and removes any leading spaces from the lines. The

`While CmpBookmarks("\Sel", "\EndOfDoc")` statement uses the **\Sel** (current selection) bookmark to determine whether the selection is at the end of the document. When the end of the document is reached, Word displays a message box to alert the user.

```
Sub MAIN
   While CmpBookmarks("\Sel", "\EndOfDoc")
      LineDown
      StartOfLine                  'Move selection to start of line
      A$ = GetBookmark$("\Line")   'Assign selection to A$
      B = Asc(A$)                  'Assign character code of A$ to
                                   'variable B
      If B = 32 Then DeleteWord    'Delete any space character(s)
                                   '(32 is Chr code for space)
      EndOfLine                    'Move selection to end of line
   Wend                            'If not at end of document, start over
   MsgBox "End of document"        'Otherwise, display message
End Sub                            'End program
```

The \PrevSel1 and \PrevSel2 Bookmarks

The **\PrevSel1** and **\PrevSel2** bookmarks mark the previous two selections that were made in the document. An **EditGoTo** statement with **\PrevSel1** as its argument is equivalent to executing the **GoBack** statement once; an **EditGoTo** with **\PrevSel2** as its argument is equivalent to executing the **GoBack** statement two times.

The \StartOfSel and \EndOfSel Bookmarks

The **\StartOfSel** bookmark is assigned to the beginning point of any amount of selected text, whereas the **\EndOfSel** bookmark is assigned to the ending point of any amount of selected text.

The \Line Bookmark

The **\Line** bookmark includes the entire contents of the current line (the line containing the insertion point). However, if the insertion point is at the end of a line that is not the last line in the paragraph, the bookmark includes the entire contents of the next line. If the current selection contains several lines, the **\Line** bookmark is the first line of the selection.

The \Char Bookmark

The **\Char** bookmark is assigned to the character immediately following the insertion point. If the current selection contains several characters, the **\Char** bookmark is the first character in the selection.

The \Para Bookmark

The **\Para** bookmark includes the entire contents of the current paragraph (the paragraph containing the insertion point). If the current selection encompasses several paragraphs, the **\Para** bookmark is the first paragraph of the selection. (A paragraph is defined as all the text that exists between two paragraph marks.)

The \Section Bookmark

The **\Section** bookmark includes the entire contents of the current section (the section containing the insertion point). If the current selection contains more than one section, the **\Section** bookmark is the first section of the selection. (A section is defined as all the text that exists between two section breaks.)

The \Doc Bookmark

The **\Doc** bookmark includes the entire contents of the active document.

The \Page Bookmark

The **\Page** bookmark includes the entire contents of the current page (the page containing the insertion point). If the current selection contains more than one page, the **\Page** bookmark is the first page of the selection. (A page is defined as all the text that exists between two page breaks.)

The \StartOfDoc and \EndOfDoc Bookmarks

The **\StartOfDoc** bookmark is the beginning of the document, and the **\EndOfDoc** bookmark is the end of the document.

The \Cell Bookmark

The **\Cell** bookmark includes the entire contents of the current cell (the cell containing the insertion point) in a table. If one or more cells of a table are included in the current selection, the **\Cell** bookmark is the first cell.

The \Table Bookmark

The **\Table** bookmark includes the entire contents of the current table (the table containing the selection or insertion point). If the selection includes more than one table, the **\Table** bookmark is the entire first table of the selection, even if the entire table is not selected.

The \HeadingLevel Bookmark

The **\HeadingLevel** bookmark includes the text associated with the current heading, plus any subordinate headings and text. If the current selection is body text, the **\HeadingLevel** bookmark includes the preceding heading, plus any subordinate headings and text. If Word is in outline mode, the **\HeadingLevel** bookmark includes the current heading and all subordinate headings that are visible in the outline mode.

MACRO DEBUGGING TIPS

As you write a macro program, you will find it easiest to test and debug the macro while in the macro editor. The macro editor provides a number of tools to assist you in finding and correcting errors. You can run programs while editing them and quickly correct errors as they occur. The following sections offer a few hints to help you create trouble-free macros.

Finding Where Errors Occur

When the macro-editing window is open and an error occurs in the macro, Word highlights the line in the program where the error occurred. Even if you run the macro with the macro-editing window obscured, Word highlights the program line where the error was detected, and when you activate the macro-editing window, the offending line will be highlighted. Usually, you'll find the statement that is the source of the problem on the highlighted line, but sometimes the statements on the highlighted line may have only detected a problem whose actual cause lies elsewhere in the program.

As an example, suppose the following line appears in a program:

```
File$ = "3JULY<>LETTERS.DOC"
```

This line assigns the text "`3JULY<>LETTERS.DOC`" to a string variable called `File$`. The line is perfectly legal as far as WordBASIC is concerned and does not create an error. However, suppose it is followed by this line:

```
FileOpen File$
```

An error occurs and the latter line is highlighted, even though this line is also perfectly legal. All it does is open a file with the name stored in the variable called `File$`.

If both statements are legal, what is causing the error? The problem is that `3JULY<>LETTERS.DOC` is not a legal file name. When the FileOpen command tries to open a file using that name, an error results.

When you can find no errors of syntax or usage in a line where an error has occurred, look for statements outside the line that might somehow be connected. Also check the values of any variables used in that line.

Checking Variable Contents

As already mentioned, it is often useful to inspect the contents of macro variables while the macro is running. There are two ways to do this.

The first method is to insert in the macro at various points **Print** statements that print the values of selected variables. In most macros, these statements do not interfere with the operation of the program and allow the macro to continue running while you observe its progress. For example, you could insert a **Print** statement before the line where the error occurred in the previous example:

```
.
.
.
File$ = "3JULY<>LETTERS.DOC"
.
.
.
Print File$
FileOpen File$
.
.
.
```

This technique is helpful when the line that assigns a value to a variable and the line that uses the value are not located close enough to each other in the program for their relationship to be obvious.

A second method allows inspection of all the variables in a program. With this method, you insert a **Stop** statement in the macro instead of a **Print** statement, as in this example:

```
.
.
.
File$ = "3JULY<>LETTERS.DOC"
.
.
.
Stop
FileOpen File$
.
.
.
```

WordBASIC stops execution of the program when it encounters the **Stop** statement and displays the message *Macro Interrupted.* If you are running the program with the macro-editing window open, the Vars... icon is now available. Selecting this icon opens a dialog box containing a list of all the variable names and their values. For example, the `File$` variable might appear as:

```
MAIN#!File$=3JULY<>LETTERS.DOC
```

The `MAIN#` in front of the variable name is the name of the subroutine where the variable is declared (assigned its value). The exclamation point is a separator character. If a variable is declared global (with a **Dim Shared** statement), no subroutine name appears in front of the variable name, only the exclamation point.

If you select the Set button, you can change the contents of any variable. Making changes can be useful in some kinds of program testing. When you select the Close button, you are returned to the macro editor. You can then select the Continue icon, and the program continues from the point where it was interrupted.

You can also press the Esc key to interrupt a running macro so that you can inspect its variable contents, but this method is usually much less precise than using **Stop**.

Using Trace

Clicking the Trace icon on the macro-editing icon bar causes Word to highlight program lines in the macro-editing window as they are executed. You may experience some difficulty in using this feature (or while using the Start, Step, or Step SUBs icons) because many commands are not available in the macro-editing window. For example, many formatting commands are unavailable because macros don't have character or paragraph formatting. Other commands are disabled because they are only relevant to printed documents. As a safety measure, some commands are disabled to prevent a macro from accidentally modifying itself. If any of these commands is included in your macro and you run the macro while the macro-editing window is active, an error occurs and your macro may display the message *Command is Unavailable.*

To use Trace to follow the operation of a program that includes unavailable commands, select the Window Arrange All command to split the screen between the macro-editing window and the document window. Be sure that the document window is active and then choose the Trace icon. This time, the error will not occur, and you can observe the operation of the macro on the document while tracing its operation in the macro-editing window.

Chapter 7

WordBASIC Command Reference

This chapter is your guide to the tools that WordBASIC provides for constructing macros. This chapter has three sections: "Word BASIC Cross Reference," "Alphabetic Listing of WordBASIC Statements and Functions," and "Macro Error Messages."

The section entitled "Word BASIC Cross Reference" lists WordBASIC keywords (the names of commands or functions) by purpose. Some keywords are listed in multiple categories. The following functional categories are listed:

BASIC Statements and Functions
Bookmark Statements and Functions
Environment Statements and Functions
DDE (Dynamic Data Exchange) Statements and Functions
Dialog Definition and Control Statements and Functions
Editing Commands and Functions
Field Statements and Functions
File Statements and Functions
Formatting Statements and Functions
Glossary Statements and Functions

Help Statements
Macro Control, Creation, and Editing Statements and Functions
Mode Statements and Functions
Outlining Statements and Functions
Selection and Insertion Point Definition and Control Statements and Functions
Table Creation and Editing Statements and Functions
Utility Statements and Functions
View Control Statements and Functions
Window Control Statements and Functions

Within each category, keywords are listed alphabetically. Refer to the section entitled "WordBASIC Cross Reference" when you know what you want to do, but not which commands you need to accomplish the task.

The section entitled "Alphabetic Listing of WordBASIC Statements and Functions" lists all WordBASIC keywords in alphabetic order and gives the syntax and a description of each statement and function. Some keywords also include syntax examples, program examples, or other notes on usage. Refer to the section entitled "Alphabetic Listing of WordBASIC Statements and Functions" to look up individual keywords from "WordBASIC Cross Reference" or when you know the command or function for your application and need details about usage.

The section entitled "Macro Error Messages" provides a list of Microsoft Word's macro error messages and their corresponding error codes. It is included for use in error trapping using WordBASIC's **On Error Goto**, **Err**, and **Error** statements. This list is located at the end of the chapter and is divided into two parts: macro error messages and Word error messages.

Notes on WordBASIC

The WordBASIC language consists of statements and functions. A statement performs an action; **Bold 1**, for example, makes the selection bold. A function produces, or "returns," a number or string of characters that represents information. Most functions do not perform any action, but some do. Those that do perform an action usually return a value that indicates the success or failure of that action. A function is always followed by parentheses. For example, **Overtype( )** is a function; **Overtype 1** is a statement. If a function ends with a dollar sign ($), it returns a string of characters. For example, the **StyleName$( )** function returns a string of characters that represent the style name of the selection.

For Boolean operators, if a function returns 0 (zero), False is implied. Any other value implies True. If a function can be nothing but True or False, –1 is returned for True.

Measurements for statements can be entered in points, or as a string value (for example, `"1in"` or `"2.5cm"`). Measurements in recorded macros appear as strings. When the quotation mark character (") is used to designate inches, it appears in recorded macros as the statement **Chr$(34)**, as follows:

Value in recorded dialog	Recorded result
`1"`	`"1" + Chr$(34)`

Macro programs have access to system information such as free memory and software version numbers. Be aware that free memory changes constantly. Values returned may be only an approximation of free memory.

Statements can take arguments. In this chapter, a dollar sign ($) follows arguments that accept a string of characters. Some arguments take a value or a string. The string can be Auto, in the case of certain measurements, or a string such as *1 in*, *2 cm*, and so on. Word converts these measurements to points. In this chapter, these arguments are followed by a dollar sign in brackets ([$]). Note that this is a convention adopted for your information only; do not use the dollar sign when you supply the arguments for actual macros.

Dialog Control Definition Statements

You can create your own dialog boxes and customized menus using Word macros. The control statements used in dialog box construction are described in this section. For more information on dialog box construction, see Chapter 6, "More WordBASIC Programming Concepts."

In the syntax lines for these statements, the following arguments are used:

Argument	Description
x	Horizontal position of the item in ⅛ system font character width units.
y	Vertical position of the item in 1⁄12 system font character width units.
dx	Width of the item in ⅛ system font character width units.
dy	Height of the item in 1⁄12 system font character width units.

Dialog-Box Equivalents

Some statements are dialog-box equivalents; that is, each of the statement arguments is equivalent to an option in the dialog box for a corresponding command on the command menu. The following conventions are used:

- Check-box equivalents take the following values: 1 checks the box; 0 (zero) unchecks the box; –1 indicates that the status of the box is unknown.
- Only one option can be selected in an option-button group. Option-button equivalents take the following values: 0 (zero) selects the first option in the group, 1 selects the second option in the group, and so on; –1 indicates that the status is unknown or ambiguous.
- List-box equivalents follow the conventions used for option buttons.
- Combination (combo) boxes are similar to list boxes, but you can select from the list or you can type the desired response. Combo box equivalents take string values.

You can set up the arguments to dialog-box–equivalent statements in two ways: by using the positional form or by using the keyword form. You can use the positional form by listing the argument values after the statement keyword, separated by commas. You can use the keyword form by following the statement keyword with the argument name, preceded by a period (.) and followed by an equal sign (=), which is in turn followed by the argument value. An example of each method follows:

Positional form.

```
EditSearch "Cost of Goods", 1
```

Keyword form.

```
EditSearch .Search = "Cost of Goods", .WholeWord = 1
```

The order in which argument values are specified is important when using the positional form, so this form is most useful for statements with relatively few arguments. When using the keyword form, include only those arguments that you want to change from the default; this form is best if you want to avoid looking up or memorizing the syntax for statements with numerous arguments. You can use both forms for one statement, but arguments specified in the keyword form must follow arguments specified in the positional form.

Recorded macros always use the keyword form. This helps make the programs self-documenting, and allows easy editing of the arguments or replacement of the constant values with variables.

> **NOTE:** *Special mention should be made of the way the macro recorder handles the quotation-mark character (") in string arguments. Quotation marks can be part of arguments when the Unit of Measure for Word is set to inches. For example, the contents of a text box in a recorded dialog might be:*
>
> ```
> 8.5"
> ```
>
> *Normally, the entire argument would be contained in quotation marks as a string literal, but it is not possible to include the quotation-mark character in a string literal. The macro recorder deals with this by using the* **Chr$( )** *function of WordBASIC. The character code for the quotation mark is 34, so the recorded argument would appear as:*
>
> ```
> "8.5" + Chr$(34)
> ```
>
> *For more information, consult the individual entry for the* **Chr$( )** *function in "WordBASIC Cross Reference."*

Command buttons carry out actions. Command-button equivalents are not arguments in the traditional sense and are not included in statement syntax. They are discussed in the text following the syntax line. Command-button equivalents can be specified only using the keyword form and must be appended to the argument list. You can specify only one command button per statement.

WORDBASIC CROSS REFERENCE

This cross reference provides a listing of WordBASIC keywords by function. Keywords are listed alphabetically under each heading or subheading. Some keywords appear under more than one heading. For specific information, see individual entries in this chapter.

BASIC Statements and Functions

The following WordBASIC commands are derived from Microsoft QuickBASIC functions. Syntax and usage is often similar to QuickBASIC.

Definition and Declaration Statements

Declare	**Let**
Dim	**Sub...End Sub**
Function...End Function	**Redim**

Program Branching and Control

Call	**On Error**
For...Next	**Select Case...Case...Case Else...End Select**
Function...End Function	**Stop**
Goto	**Sub...End Sub**
If...ElseIf...Else...End If	**While...Wend**

Screen and Keyboard Input/Output

Input	**Line Input**	**MsgBox**
InputBox$( )	**Print**	**MsgBox( )**

String Functions

Asc( )	**Left$( )**	**Str$( )**
Chr$( )	**Len( )**	**String$( )**
InStr( )	**Mid$( )**	**UCase$( )**
LCase$( )	**Right$( )**	

Numeric Functions

Abs( )	**Sgn( )**	**Val( )**
Int( )	**Rnd( )**	

Error Handling

Err	**Error**	**On Error**

Sequential Files and Disk File Manipulation

ChDir	**Line Input**	**Read**
Close	**Lof( )**	**RmDir**
Eof( )	**MkDir**	**Seek**
Files$( )	**Name**	**Seek( )**
Input	**Open**	**Shell**
Input$( )	**Print**	**Write**
Kill		

BASIC Utility Functions

Beep	**Rem**	**Time$( )**
Date$( )	**Shell**	

Bookmark Statements and Functions

These statements and functions allow the creation, use, and comparison of bookmarks. For more information on bookmarks, see the *Word User's Reference.*

BookmarkName$( )	**ExistingBookmark( )**
CmpBookmarks( )	**GetBookmark$( )**
CopyBookmark	**InsertBookmark**
CountBookmarks( )	**SetEndOfBookmark**
EditGoto	**SetStartOfBookmark**
EmptyBookmark( )	

Environment Statements and Functions

These statements and functions set conditions in or test the status of the overall Word environment:

AppInfo$( )	**GetProfileString$( )**
Cancel	**IsDirty( )**
ChangeRulerMode	**OK**
ColumnSelect	**Overtype**
CountFiles( )	**Overtype( )**
CountWindows( )	**SetDirty**
Date$( )	**SetProfileString**
DisableInput	**Time$( )**
EditSummaryInfo	**Window**
Extend Selection	**WindowName$( )**
FileName$( )	

DDE (Dynamic Data Exchange) Statements and Functions

These statements and functions are used to establish DDE links for exchange of information between Word and other Windows or OS/2 applications:

DDEExecute	**DDETerminate**
DDEInitiate( )	**DDETerminateAll**
DDEPoke	**EditPasteLink**
DDERequest$( )	

Dialog Definition and Control Statements and Functions

These statements and functions allow interaction with the users of your macro using the graphical dialog box interface. Custom dialog boxes can be created, or you can use Word's built-in dialog boxes in your programs.

Begin Dialog	**GetCurValues**
CheckBox	**GroupBox**
ComboBox	**InputBox$( )**
Dialog	**ListBox**
Dim	**MsgBox**
End Dialog	**MsgBox( )**

OKButton and CancelButton	**Text**
OptionGroup and OptionButton	**TextBox**
Redim	

Editing Commands and Functions

These commands and functions are used to edit document text and the various other components that make up a Word document. Commands and functions are also provided for searching a document for matching text or formatting, and for changing that text or formatting if desired.

CopyFormat	**EditSearchChar**
CopyText	**EditSearchFound( )**
DeleteBackWord	**EditSearchPara**
DeleteWord	**EditSelectAll**
EditClear	**EditTable**
EditCopy	**EditUndo**
EditCut	**Insert**
EditGlossary	**InsertFile**
EditGoto	**MoveText**
EditHeaderFooter	**OK**
EditHeaderFooterLink	**Repeat**
EditPaste	**Search**
EditPasteLink	**Selection$( )**
EditReplace	**SelectTable**
EditReplaceChar	**Spike**
EditReplacePara	**UnSpike**
EditSearch	

Field Statements and Functions

These statements and functions allow the insertion, use, and editing of fields. For more information on fields, see Chapter 9, "Fields."

DoFieldClick	**NextField**
InsertDateField	**NextField( )**
InsertField	**PrevField**
InsertFieldChars	**PrevField( )**
InsertFile	**ToggleFieldDisplay**
InsertIndex	**UnLinkFields**
InsertIndexEntry	**UnLockFields**
InsertPageField	**UpdateFields**
InsertPicture	**UpdateSource**
InsertTableOfContents	**ViewFieldCodes**
InsertTimeField	**ViewFieldCodes( )**
LockFields	

File Statements and Functions

These statements and functions deal with document and operating system files as well as document printing functions:

Activate	**FileFind**	**FileSaveAll**
AppActivate	**FileName$( )**	**FileSaveAs**
ChDir	**FileNew**	**Files$( )**
CountFiles( )	**FileOpen**	**InsertFile**
DocClose	**FilePrint**	**Kill**
File1	**FilePrinterSetup**	**MkDir**
File2	**FilePrintMerge**	**Name**
File3	**FilePrintPreview**	**RmDir**
File4	**FilePrintPreviewBoundaries**	**Save**
FileClose	**FilePrintPreviewPages**	**Template**
FileExit	**FileSave**	**UpdateSource**

Formatting Statements and Functions

These statements and functions deal with formatting of characters, paragraphs, tables, headers, footers, and other elements of a Word document:

Bold
Bold( )
CenterPara
CenterPara( )
CountFonts( )
ChangeCase
CharColor
CharColor( )
CloseUpPara
CopyFormat
CountStyles( )
DoubleUnderline
DoubleUnderline( )
EditHeaderFooter
EditHeaderFooterLink
EditReplaceChar
EditReplacePara
EditSearchChar
EditSearchPara
Font
Font$( )
FontSize
FontSize( )
FormatCharacter
FormatDefineStyles
FormatDefineStylesChar
FormatDefineStylesPara
FortmatDefineStylesPosition
FormatDefineStylesTabs
FormatDocument
FormatParagraph
FormatPicture
FormatPosition
FormatSection
FormatStyles
FormatTable
FormatTabsGrow
Font
HangingIndent
Hidden
Hidden( )
Indent
InsertBreak
InsertColumnBreak
InsertFootnote
InsertPageBreak
InsertPageNumbers
InsertPara
InsertPicture
InsertTable
InsertTableToText
Italic
Italic( )
JustifyPara
JustifyPara( )
LeftPara
LeftPara( )
NormalStyle
NormalStyle( )
OpenUpPara
ResetChar
ResetChar( )

ResetFootnoteContNotice
ResetFootnoteContSep
ResetFootnoteSep
ResetPara
ResetPara( )
RightPara
RightPara( )
SelType
SelType( )
ShrinkFont
SmallCaps
SmallCaps( )
SpacePara1
SpacePara1( )
SpacePara2
SpacePara2( )
SpacePara15
SpacePara15( )
StyleName$( )
SubScript
Subscript( )
SuperScript
SuperScript( )
TabLeader$( )
TabType( )
Underline
Underline( )
UnHang
UnIndent
WordUnderline
WordUnderline( )

Glossary Statements and Functions

These statements and functions deal with the use of glossaries. For more information on glossaries, see the *Word User's Reference*.

CountGlossaries( )
EditGlossary
ExpandGlossary
GetGlossary$( )
GlossaryName$( )
SetGlossary
Spike
UnSpike

Help Statements

These statements control Word's on-line help features:

Help
HelpAbout
HelpActiveWindow
HelpContext
HelpIndex
HelpKeyboard
HelpTutorial
HelpUsingHelp

Macro Control, Creation, and Editing Statements and Functions

These statements and functions relate to the creation, editing, and use of macro programs:

CountMacros( )	**MacroRecord**
DisableInput	**MacroRun**
MacroAssignToKey	**OnTime**
MacroAssignToMenu	**PauseRecorder**
MacroEdit	**RecordNextCommand**
MacroName$( )	**ShowVars**

Mode Statements and Functions

These statements and functions control the state of Word's various modes. These modes often affect how many other statements operate.

AppInfo$( )	**IconBarMode**
Cancel	**MenuMode**
ChangeRulerMode	**MoveText**
ColumnSelect	**OverType**
CopyFormat	**OverType( )**
CopyText	**RulerMode**

Outlining Statements and Functions

These statements and functions control Word's built-in outlining capabilities. For more information on outlining, see the *Word User's Reference.*

OutlineCollapse	**ShowHeading2**
OutlineDemote	**ShowHeading3**
OutlineExpand	**ShowHeading4**
OutlineLevel( )	**ShowHeading5**
OutlineMoveDown	**ShowHeading6**
OutlineMoveUp	**ShowHeading7**
OutlinePromote	**ShowHeading8**
OutlineShowFirstLineView	**ShowHeading9**
ShowAllHeadings	**ViewOutline**
ShowHeading1	**ViewOutline( )**

Selection and Insertion Point Definition and Control Statements and Functions

These statements and functions deal with the location and movement of the selection or insertion point:

CharLeft
CharLeft( )
CharRight
CharRight( )
EditGoto
EditSelectAll
EndOfColumn
EndOfDocument
EndOfLine
EndOfRow
EndOfWindow
ExtendSelection
GoBack
Insert
LineDown
LineDown( )
LineUp
LineUp( )
NextCell
NextCell( )
NextField
NextField( )
NextObject
NextObject( )
NextPage
NextPage( )
NextTab( )
PageDown
PageDown( )
PageUp
PageUp( )
ParaDown
ParaDown( )
ParaUp
ParaUp( )
PrevCell
PrevCell( )
PrevField
PrevField( )
PrevObject
PrevObject( )
PrevPage
PrevPage( )
PrevTab( )
Selection$( )
SelectTable
SentLeft
SentLeft( )
SentRight
SentRight( )
StartOfColumn
StartOfDocument
StartOfLine
StartOfRow
StartOfWindow
WordLeft
WordLeft( )
WordRight
WordRight( )

Table Creation and Editing Statements and Functions

These Statements and functions control the creation and editing of tables and cells:

EditTable	**NextCell( )**
EndOfColumn	**PrevCell**
EndOfRow	**PrevCell( )**
FormatTable	**SelectTable**
InsertTable	**StartOfColumn**
InsertTableToText	**StartOfRow**
NextCell	

Utility Statements and Functions

This category of statements and functions includes all the commands from Word's Utility menu, as well as other commands and statements of general use:

Activate	**UtilRenumber**
AppActivate	**UtilRepaginateNow**
ControlRun	**UtilRevisionMarks**
Declare	**UtilSort**
GetProfileString$( )	**UtilSpelling**
RenameMenu	**UtilSpellSelection**
Repeat	**UtilThesaurus**
SendKeys	**ViewFullMenus**
SetProfileString	**ViewMenus( )**
UtilCalculate( )	**ViewRibbon**
UtilCompareVersions	**ViewRibbon( )**
UtilCustomize	**ViewRuler**
UtilGetSpelling	**ViewRuler( )**
UtilGetSpelling( )	**ViewShortMenus**
UtilGetSynonyms	**ViewStatusBar**
UtilGetSynonyms( )	**ViewStatusBar( )**
UtilHyphenate	

View Control Statements and Functions

These statements and functions deal with the various visual elements of the Word program and its editing environment:

FilePrintPreview	**ViewFieldCodes**
FilePrintPreview( )	**ViewFieldCodes( )**
ShowAll	**ViewFootnotes**
ShowAllHeadings	**ViewFootnotes( )**
ShowHeading1	**ViewFullMenus**
ShowHeading2	**ViewMenus( )**
ShowHeading3	**ViewOutline**
ShowHeading4	**ViewOutline( )**
ShowHeading5	**ViewPage**
ShowHeading6	**ViewPage( )**
ShowHeading7	**ViewPreferences**
ShowHeading8	**ViewRibbon**
ShowHeading9	**ViewRibbon( )**
ToggleFieldDisplay	**ViewRuler**
ViewAnnotations	**ViewRuler( )**
ViewAnnotations( )	**ViewShortMenus**
ViewDraft	**ViewStatusBar**
ViewDraft( )	**ViewStatusBar( )**

Window Control Statements and Functions

These statements and functions control windows, such as the Word window itself or various document windows and panes. Windows can be opened, closed, split, resized, scrolled, or moved.

Activate	**HScroll**
AppActivate	**HScroll( )**
AppInfo( )	**NextWindow**
AppMaximize	**OtherPane**
AppMaximize( )	**PrevWindow**
AppMinimize	**StartOfWindow**
AppMinimize( )	**VLine**
AppMove	**VPage**
AppRestore	**VScroll**
AppSize	**VScroll( )**
ClosePane	**Window( )**
CountWindows( )	**Window1**
DocClose	**Window2**
DocMaximize	**Window3**
DocMaximize( )	**Window4**
DocMove	**Window5**
DocRestore	**Window6**
DocSize	**Window7**
DocSplit	**Window8**
DocSplit( )	**Window9**
EndOfWindow	**WindowArrangeAll**
FileClose	**WindowName$( )**
HLine	**WindowNewWindow**
HPage	**WindowPane( )**

ALPHABETIC LISTING OF WORDBASIC STATEMENTS AND FUNCTIONS

Abs( )

Num = **Abs(***n***)**

Returns the absolute unsigned value of *n*.

Function	Return value
`Print Abs(5)`	5
`Print Abs(-5)`	5

For related commands, see "BASIC Statements and Functions" in the section "WordBASIC Cross Reference," earlier in this chapter.

Activate

Activate *WindowText$, [PaneNum]*

Activates the window whose title bar is specified by the *WindowText$* argument. If the *PaneNum* argument is 1 or 2, the top pane is activated; if *PaneNum* is 3 or 4, the bottom pane is activated.

Syntax examples.

```
Activate "DOC5.DOC",1
```

```
Document$ - "DOC5.DOC"
Pane - 1
Activate Document$,Pane
```

The statements in these examples activate the upper pane of the window titled DOC5.DOC.

For related commands, see "Window Control Statements and Functions" in the section "WordBASIC Cross Reference," earlier in this chapter.

AppActivate

AppActivate *WindowText$, [Immediate]*

Activates the window whose title bar is specified by *WindowText$*. Use this statement for activating windows in other applications. For Word windows, use **Activate**. If the *Immediate* argument is 1, Word immediately switches the focus to the other application, even if Word does not have the focus. If *Immediate* is 0 (zero) and Word does not have the focus, Word flashes its title bar, waits for the user to give the focus to Word, and then activates the application.

Syntax examples.

```
AppActivate "Microsoft Excel",1
```

```
Program2$ = "Microsoft Excel"
AppActivate Program2$,1
```

The statements in the examples activate the window named `"Microsoft Excel"`.

You should be careful when using this command because window names can change. Many applications will append the name of the working file to the application name used in the window title bar. For example, the Windows Cardfile application might have window names like:

```
Cardfile - (untitled)
```

```
Cardfile - PHONE.CRD
```

For related commands, see "File Statements and Functions," "Utility Statements and Functions," and "Window Control Statements and Functions" in the section "WordBASIC Cross Reference," earlier in this chapter.

AppInfo$( )

*A$* = **AppInfo$(***TypeOfInfo***)**

Returns information about the state of Word.

If *TypeOfInfo* is	Result is
1	The environment string; for example, `"Windows 2.11"`.
2	The version number of Word; for example, `"1.00"`.
3	Word is in a special mode; for example, CopyText or MoveText mode.

(continued)

Continued

If *TypeOfInfo* is	Result is
4	X position of the Word window, measured in points from the left of the screen.
5	Y position of the Word window, measured in points from the top of the screen.
6	Width of the current document workspace, in points.
7	Height of the current document workspace, in points.
8	Returns –1 if the application is maximized.
9	Total conventional memory (do not use in Word for OS/2).
10	Amount of conventional memory available (do not use in Word for OS/2).
11	Total expanded memory (do not use in Word for OS/2).
12	Amount of expanded memory available (do not use in Word for OS/2).
13	Returns –1 if a math coprocessor is installed.
14	Returns –1 if a mouse is present.
15	Amount of disk space available.

Syntax example.

```
Ver$ = AppInfo$(2)
MsgBox Ver$, "Microsoft Word Version", 64
```

Displays a message box with the version number of Word. Values are returned as strings. Use **Val(AppInfo$(*n*))** to convert the string to a number, if appropriate.

Syntax example.

```
DiskFree = Val(AppInfo$(15))
Print DiskFree
```

This example displays the available disk space as a numeric value instead of as string data.

Several **AppInfo$( )** arguments deal with memory. These values have limited use under Windows, because the available memory can change from moment to moment. They are meaningless under OS/2 due to the memory management techniques involved, and they should not be used.

For related commands, see "Environment Statements and Functions" in the section "WordBASIC Cross Reference," earlier in this chapter.

AppMaximize

AppMaximize

If the Word window is less than full screen, zooms the window to full screen size. If the window is already full screen, performs the same action as **AppRestore**.

For related commands, see "Window Control Statements and Functions" in the section "WordBASIC Cross Reference," earlier in this chapter.

AppMaximize( )

Log = **AppMaximize( )**

Returns a nonzero value if the window is maximized.

Syntax example.

```
If AppMaximize() = 0 Then AppMaximize
```

For related commands, see "Window Control Statements and Functions" in the section "WordBASIC Cross Reference," earlier in this chapter.

AppMinimize

AppMinimize

If Word is not minimized, minimizes the Word window to an icon. If Word is already minimized, performs the same action as **AppRestore**.

NOTE: *If an untrapped error occurs in a macro while Word is minimized, the macro halts, Word remains minimized, and the Word icon flashes. When Word is maximized, an error message box that indicates the nature of the error is displayed.*

For related commands, see "Window Control Statements and Functions" in the section "WordBASIC Cross Reference," earlier in this chapter.

AppMinimize( )

Log = **AppMinimize( )**

Returns a nonzero value if the window is minimized.

For related commands, see "Window Control Statements and Functions" in the section "WordBASIC Cross Reference," earlier in this chapter.

AppMove

AppMove *XPos, YPos*

Moves the Word window to *XPos, YPos* relative to the upper-left corner of the screen. Values are given in points.

Statement	Result
`AppMove 20, 40`	Moves the Word window 20 points right and 40 points down from the upper left corner of the screen.

For related commands, see "Window Control Statements and Functions" in the section "WordBASIC Cross Reference," earlier in this chapter.

AppRestore

AppRestore

Restores the Word window from a maximized/minimized state.

For related commands, see "Window Control Statements and Functions" in the section "WordBASIC Cross Reference," earlier in this chapter.

AppSize

AppSize *Width, Height*

Resizes the Word window. Values are given in points.

Syntax example.

```
AppMove 0, 0
AppSize 480, 350
```

Places the Word window at the upper left corner of the screen and extends it to the lower right corner of a standard EGA screen. The location of the lower right corner varies depending on the type of video display used. Use **AppMaximize** to make the window full screen on any type of display.

Syntax example.

```
AppSize 240, 175
AppMove 120, 87
```

This example sizes the Word window to half-screen size and places it in the center of a standard EGA screen.

For related commands, see "Window Control Statements and Functions" in the section "WordBASIC Cross Reference," earlier in this chapter.

Asc( )

Num = **Asc(***A$***)**

Returns the character code of the first character in ***A$***. **Asc** is short for the ASCII character set used with earlier versions of BASIC and is so named for compatibility purposes. The actual codes returned are those used by Word's operating environment—ANSI.

Function	Return value
`Print Asc("Signature authority")`	83

For related commands, see "BASIC Statements and Functions" in the section "WordBASIC Cross Reference," earlier in this chapter.

Beep

Beep *[BeepType]*

Causes the computer's speaker to beep. A typical use of **Beep** is for signaling the end of a macro. *BeepType* is 1, 2, 3, or 4. If *BeepType* is omitted, it is assumed to be 1. The value of *BeepType* is passed to the operating environment. Current operating environments do not make use of this value. *BeepType* is provided for compatibility with future versions of Microsoft Windows or OS/2.

For related commands, see "BASIC Statements and Functions" in the section "WordBASIC Cross Reference," earlier in this chapter.

Begin Dialog

Begin Dialog UserDialog *[x], [y], dx, dy*

Starts the dialog-box declaration. The *dx* and *dy* arguments are the width and height of the dialog box (relative to the given *x* and *y* coordinates). If *x* and *y* are not supplied,Word automatically positions the dialog box at the point where dialog boxes usually appear on the screen.

For related commands, see "Dialog Definition and Control Statements and Functions" in the section "WordBASIC Cross Reference," earlier in this chapter.

Bold

Bold *[On]*

If *On* is omitted, toggles bold for the entire selection. If *On* is nonzero, makes the entire selection bold. If *On* is 0 (zero), removes bold from the entire selection.

Statement	If text is	New text is
Bold	Trey Research Company	**Trey Research Company**
Bold	Trey **Research** Company	**Trey Research Company**
Bold	**Trey Research Company**	Trey Research Company
Bold 1	Trey Research Company	**Trey Research Company**
Bold 0	Trey **Research** Company	Trey Research Company

For related commands, see "Formatting Statements and Functions" in the section "WordBASIC Cross Reference," earlier in this chapter.

Bold( )

Num = **Bold( )**

Returns 0 (zero) if none of the selection is bold, 1 if all of the selection is bold, or –1 if part of the selection is bold.

For related commands, see "Formatting Statements and Functions" in the section "WordBASIC Cross Reference," earlier in this chapter.

BookmarkName$( )

*A$* = **BookmarkName$(***Count***)**

Returns the name of the bookmark defined by *Count*. *Count* must be in the range 1 to *CountBookmarks( )*.

Example.

```
.
.
.
Dim Mark$(CountBookmarks()-1)              'Define array Mark$ to
                                           'hold bookmark names
```

```
For Count = 1 To CountBookmarks()         'Loop from 1 (first
                                          'bookmark) to CountBookmarks()
                                          '(last bookmark)
   Mark$(Count-1) = BookmarkName$(Count) 'Load bookmark into array
Next                                      'Next Count
.
.
.
```

For related commands, see "Bookmark Statements and Functions" in the section "WordBASIC Cross Reference," earlier in this chapter.

Call

[**Call**] *SubName [ParameterList]*

Transfers control to a subroutine. The use of **Call** is optional. New users of WordBASIC may use it to prevent confusing a WordBASIC keyword with a subroutine name while reading programs.

Statement	Result
`Call FindName`	Calls the subroutine `FindName`.
`FindName`	Calls the subroutine `FindName`.

Example.

```
Sub MAIN
   If IsDirty() = -1 Then
      Call BeepThreeTimes      'Call subroutine BeepThreeTimes
      AlertMsg                 'Call subroutine AlertMsg
   End If
End Sub
Sub BeepThreeTimes             'Start subroutine
   For Count = 1 To 3
      Beep
      For Timer = 1 To 100     'Delay loop between beeps
      Next Timer
   Next Count
End Sub                        'End subroutine BeepThreeTimes
Sub AlertMsg                   'Start subroutine
   MsgBox"Document Has Been Changed Since Last Save",,48
End Sub                        'End subroutine AlertMsg
```

For related commands, see "BASIC Statements and Functions" in the section "WordBASIC Cross Reference," earlier in this chapter.

Cancel

Cancel

Terminates a mode (for example, **ColumnSelect**) and does not perform the action. For more information, see the entry for **OK**, later in this chapter.

For related commands, see "Mode Statements and Functions" in the section "WordBASIC Cross Reference," earlier in this chapter.

CenterPara

CenterPara

Centers the currently selected paragraph(s).

For related commands, see "Formatting Statements and Functions" in the section "WordBASIC Cross Reference," earlier in this chapter.

CenterPara( )

Num = **CenterPara( )**

Returns 0 (zero) if none of the selected paragraphs is centered, 1 if all of the selected paragraphs are centered, or –1 if more than one kind of paragraph alignment is used.

For related commands, see "Formatting Statements and Functions" in the section "WordBASIC Cross Reference," earlier in this chapter.

ChangeCase

ChangeCase *[Type]*

If *Type* is omitted, alternates the case of the current selection between all lowercase, all uppercase, and initial capitals based on the first two characters of the selection. If *Type* is 0 (zero), sets the text to all lowercase. If *Type* is 1, sets the text to all uppercase. If *Type* is 2, sets the text to initial capitals. If the selection is an insertion point, Word does not perform an action.

Statement	If selected text is	New text is
`ChangeCase 0`	`How many shares?`	`how many shares?`
`ChangeCase 1`	`How many shares?`	`HOW MANY SHARES?`
`ChangeCase 2`	`How many shares?`	`How Many Shares?`
`ChangeCase`	`How many shares?`	`how many shares?`
	`how many SHARES?`	`HOW MANY SHARES?`

For related commands, see "Formatting Statements and Functions" in the section "WordBASIC Cross Reference," earlier in this chapter.

ChangeRulerMode

ChangeRulerMode

Cycles the ruler between paragraph view and margin view. If the insertion point or selection is in a table, cycles between paragraph view, margin view, and column view.

For related commands, see "Mode Statements and Functions" in the section "WordBASIC Cross Reference," earlier in this chapter.

CharColor

CharColor *Color*

Sets the character color of the selection to *Color*, which can be one of the following:

Color argument	Description
0	Auto (color specified by the Control Panel setting)
1	Black
2	Blue
3	Cyan
4	Green
5	Magenta
6	Red
7	Yellow
8	White

For related commands, see "Formatting Statements and Functions" in the section "WordBASIC Cross Reference," earlier in this chapter.

CharColor( )

Num = **CharColor( )**

Returns the numbers set by the **CharColor** statement, or –1 if all the selected text is not the same color.

For related commands, see "Formatting Statements and Functions" in the section "WordBASIC Cross Reference," earlier in this chapter.

CharLeft

CharLeft *[Repeat], [Select]*

Moves the insertion point left by *Repeat* characters. If *Repeat* is omitted, 1 is assumed. If *Select* is nonzero, the selection is extended to the left by *Repeat* characters. If there is a selection, `CharLeft 1` changes the selection to an insertion point positioned at the left edge of the original selection.

Statement	Result
`CharLeft 5, 1`	Extends the selection five characters to the left of the insertion point.

For related commands, see "Selection and Insertion Point Definition and Control Statements and Functions" in the section "WordBASIC Cross Reference," earlier in this chapter.

CharLeft( )

Log = **CharLeft(***[Repeat], [Select]***)**

Moves the selection left by *Repeat* characters. If *Repeat* is omitted, 1 is assumed. Returns 0 (zero) if the action cannot be performed. If there is a selection, `CharLeft (1)` changes the selection to an insertion point positioned at the left edge of the original selection.

For related commands, see "Selection and Insertion Point Definition and Control Statements and Functions" in the section "WordBASIC Cross Reference," earlier in this chapter.

CharRight

CharRight *[Repeat], [Select]*

Moves the selection right by *Repeat* characters. If *Repeat* is omitted, 1 is assumed. If *Select* is nonzero, the selection is extended to the right by *Repeat* characters. If there is a selection, `CharRight 1` changes the selection to an insertion point positioned at the right edge of the original selection. If *Select* is 0 (zero) or omitted, the selection is not extended.

Statement	Result
`CharRight 10`	If there is no selection, moves the insertion point 10 characters to the right of the original insertion point, but does not extend the selection. If there is a selection, moves the insertion point 9 characters to the right.

For related commands, see "Selection and Insertion Point Definition and Control Statements and Functions" in the section "WordBASIC Cross Reference," earlier in this chapter.

CharRight( )

Log = **CharRight(***[Repeat], [Select]***)**

Moves the selection right by *Repeat* characters, extending the selection if *Select* is nonzero. Returns 0 (zero) if the action cannot be performed. If there is a selection, `CharRight (1)` changes the selection to an insertion point positioned at the right edge of the original selection.

For related commands, see "Selection and Insertion Point Definition and Control Statements and Functions" in the section "WordBASIC Cross Reference," earlier in this chapter.

ChDir

ChDir *Name$*

Changes to the directory specified by *Name$*.

Syntax example.

```
ChDir "\Windows\Excel\JulyRpt"
```

For related commands, see "BASIC Statements and Functions" in the section "WordBASIC Cross Reference," earlier in this chapter.

CheckBox

CheckBox *x, y, dx, dy, Text$, .Field*

Creates a check box with label *Text$*. An amersand (&) preceding a character in *Text$* makes it the keyboard equivalent of selecting in the dialog box. When the dialog box that contains the check box is used, *.Field* contains the current setting: if this value is 0 (zero), the box is not checked; any other value means the box is checked. The result is a numeric field with the value 0 (not checked), 1 (checked), or –1 (grayed) in the dialog record returned from **Dialog**.

Example.

```
CheckBox 97,54,36,12 "&Bold", .bold
```

For related commands, see "Dialog Definition and Control Statements and Functions" in the section "WordBASIC Cross Reference," earlier in this chapter.

Chr$( )

*A$* = **Chr$(***CharCode***)**

Returns the character whose ANSI character code is *CharCode*. The following table shows some of the special characters that can be returned using **Chr$( )**.

Value	Character inserted
Chr$(9)	Tab
Chr$(11)	New line character
Chr$(30)	Nonbreaking hyphen
Chr$(31)	Optional hyphen
Chr$(34)	Quotation mark
Chr$(160)	Nonbreaking space (Windows only)
Chr$(22)	Nonbreaking space (OS/2 only)

Example.

```
Print "Title:" + Chr$(9) + Chr$(34) + "Executive Director" + Chr$(34)
```

Result.

```
Title:   "Executive Director"
```

For related commands, see "BASIC Statements and Functions" in the section "WordBASIC Cross Reference," earlier in this chapter.

Close

Close *[[#]StreamNumber]*

Closes the file attached to *StreamNumber*. If *StreamNumber* is omitted, all open files are closed.

Statement	Result
`Close`	Closes all open files.
`Close #2`	Closes file attached to stream number 2.
`Close #Handle`	Closes the file attached to the stream indicated by the value of Handle.

For related commands, see "BASIC Statements and Functions" in the section "WordBASIC Cross Reference," earlier in this chapter.

ClosePane

ClosePane

Closes the lower window pane. Use this statement to close a pane in a split document, a header/footer pane, a footnote pane, and so on. This statement does not close a document window, only a pane in a window.

For related commands, see "Window Control Statements and Functions" in the section "WordBASIC Cross Reference," earlier in this chapter.

CloseUpPara

CloseUpPara

Makes the Space Before option (in the Format Paragraph dialog box) for the selected paragraph 0 (zero).

For related commands, see "Formatting Statements and Functions" in the section "WordBASIC Cross Reference," earlier in this chapter.

CmpBookmarks( )

Num = **CmpBookmarks(***Bookmark1$, Bookmark2$***)**

Compares two named bookmarks and returns one of the following values:

Return value	Meaning
0	*Bookmark1$* and *Bookmark2$* are equivalent.
1	*Bookmark1$* is entirely below *Bookmark2$*.
2	*Bookmark1$* is entirely above *Bookmark2$*.
3	*Bookmark1$* is below and inside *Bookmark2$*.
4	*Bookmark1$* is inside and above *Bookmark2$*.
5	*Bookmark1$* encloses *Bookmark2$*.
6	*Bookmark2$* encloses *Bookmark1$*.
7	*Bookmark1$* and *Bookmark2$* begin at the same point, but *Bookmark1$* is longer.
8	*Bookmark1$* and *Bookmark2$* begin at the same point, but *Bookmark2$* is longer.
9	*Bookmark1$* and *Bookmark2$* end at the same place, but *Bookmark1$* is longer.
10	*Bookmark1$* and *Bookmark2$* end at the same place, but *Bookmark2$* is longer.
11	*Bookmark1$* is below and adjacent to *Bookmark2$*.
12	*Bookmark1$* is above and adjacent to *Bookmark2$*.
13	One or more of the bookmarks do not exist.

For more information about bookmarks, see the section entitled "Instructions" in Chapter 9, "Fields."

For related commands, see "Bookmark Statements and Functions" in the section "WordBASIC Cross Reference," earlier in this chapter.

ColumnSelect

ColumnSelect

Starts the column selection mode. **Cancel**, **OK**, and any command acting on the column selection ends this mode.

For related commands, see "Mode Statements and Functions" in the section "WordBASIC Cross Reference," earlier in this chapter.

ComboBox

ComboBox *x*, *y*, *dx*, *dy*, *ArrayVariable$*, *.Field*

Creates an expanded combo box with the list box filled from the *ArrayVariable$*. When the dialog box is used, *.Field* contains the current setting (the selected choice, returned as a string from **Dialog**).

Syntax example.

```
ComboBox 6, 31, 49, 33, Arr$(), .LB
```

For related commands, see "Dialog Definition and Control Statements and Functions" in the section "WordBASIC Cross Reference," earlier in this chapter.

ControlRun

ControlRun *Application*

Equivalent to the Control Run dialog box. Runs an application listed in the Word Control Run dialog box.

Statement	Result
`ControlRun 0`	Runs Clipboard.
`ControlRun 1`	Runs Control Panel.

CopyBookmark

CopyBookmark *Bookmark1$*, *Bookmark2$*

Sets *Bookmark2$* equal to *Bookmark1$*.

Statement	Result
`CopyBookmark "sales_receipts", "month_sales"`	Causes the bookmark `"month_sales"` to be associated with the same text as the bookmark `"sales_receipts"`.

For related commands, see "Bookmark Statements and Functions" in the section "WordBASIC Cross Reference," earlier in this chapter.

CopyFormat

CopyFormat

Copies the formatting of the selected text. To use this statement, include in the macro statements for the following steps:

1. Make a selection.
2. Run **CopyFormat**.
3. Select where you want to paste the formatting.
4. Run **OK** (press Enter).

Syntax example.

```
StartOfLine      'Move insertion to start of current line
EndOfLine 1      'Move insertion to end of line while selecting
CopyFormat       'Copy formatting
EndOfColumn      'Move insertion to end of column
StartOfLine 1    'Move insertion to start of line while selecting
OK               'Apply copied format to selected text
```

For related commands, see "Formatting Statements and Functions" in the section "WordBASIC Cross Reference," earlier in this chapter.

CopyText

CopyText

Copies selected text without putting it in the Clipboard. Equivalent to the COPY TO key (Shift+F2). To use this statement, include in the macro statements for the following steps:

1. Make a selection.
2. Run **CopyText**.
3. Select where you want to paste the text.
4. Run **OK** (press Enter).

For related commands, see "Editing Commands and Functions" in the section "WordBASIC Cross Reference," earlier in this chapter.

CountBookmarks( )

Num = **CountBookmarks( )**

Returns the number of bookmarks defined in the current document.

For related commands, see "Bookmark Statements and Functions" in the section "WordBASIC Cross Reference," earlier in this chapter.

CountFiles( )

Num = **CountFiles( )**

Returns the number of names in the file list on the File menu.

Syntax example.

```
For Count = 1 To CountFiles()            'Load names of all files
                                         'in File menu into
   FileArray$(Count) = FileName$(Count) 'string array called FileArray$
Next Count
```

For related commands, see "File Statements and Functions" in the section "WordBASIC Cross Reference," earlier in this chapter.

CountFonts( )

Num = **CountFonts( )**

Returns the number of fonts available with the selected printer. This is the number of the fonts that appear both in the Format Character dialog box and on the ribbon's font list.

Syntax example.

```
For Count = 1 To CountFonts()           'Load names of all current
                                        'printer fonts into
   FontName$(Count) = Font$(Count)      'string array called FontName$
Next Count
Font FontName$(Count)                   'Apply last font in list
                                        'to selected text
```

For related commands, see "Formatting Statements and Functions" in the section "WordBASIC Cross Reference," earlier in this chapter.

CountGlossaries( )

Num = **CountGlossaries(***[Context]***)**

Returns the number of glossaries defined in the context specified by *Context*. *Context* can be 0 (zero) for global or nonzero for document template. The default is global.

For related commands, see "Glossary Statements and Functions" in the section "WordBASIC Cross Reference," earlier in this chapter.

CountMacros( )

Num = **CountMacros(***[Context], [All]***)**

Returns the number of macro programs defined in the context specified by *Context*. *Context* can be 0 (zero) for global or nonzero for document template. The default is global.

If *All* is nonzero, built-in commands are included in the count. Word contains over 230 built-in commands.

For related commands, see "Macro Control, Creation, and Editing Statements and Functions" in the section "WordBASIC Cross Reference," earlier in this chapter.

CountStyles( )

Num = **CountStyles(***[Context], [All]***)**

Returns the number of styles defined in the context specified by *Context*. *Context* can be 0 (zero) for the document, or nonzero for the document template. The default is document.

If *All* is nonzero, unused built-in styles are included. Word contains 34 built-in styles.

CountStyles(0,0) returns any built-in styles that have been used and heading 1 through heading 3 (the styles shown in the dialog). CountStyles(0,1) returns the number of all built-in styles and the number of user-created styles. Press Ctrl+A in the dialog to see a list of the styles.

For related commands, see "Formatting Statements and Functions" in the section "WordBASIC Cross Reference," earlier in this chapter.

CountWindows( )

Num = **CountWindows( )**

Returns the number of windows listed on the Window menu.

For related commands, see "Window Control Statements and Functions" in the section "WordBASIC Cross Reference," earlier in this chapter.

Date$( )

*A$* = **Date$( )**

Returns today's date. The date format is determined by the date setting in the operating environment's control panel.

For related commands, see "BASIC Statements and Functions" in the section "WordBASIC Cross Reference," earlier in this chapter.

DDEExecute

DDEExecute *ChanNum, ExecuteString$*

Sends an execute message over the channel *ChanNum* with an *ExecuteString$* that is defined by the receiving application. Use the format described under **SendKeys** to send specific key sequences.

The channel number must have been opened by the **DDEInitiate( )** function. If the channel is not valid or if the receiving application refuses to execute the instructions, an error is generated.

For related commands, see "DDE (Dynamic Data Exchange) Statements and Functions" in the section "WordBASIC Cross Reference," earlier in this chapter.

DDEInitiate( )

ChanNum = **DDEInitiate(***App$, Topic$***)**

Opens a DDE channel to an application. *App$* is the application name defined by the other application. *Topic$* describes something in the application you are accessing, usually the document that contains the data you want to use.

If **DDEInitiate( )** is successful, it returns the number of the open channel. All subsequent **DDE** macro functions use this number to specify the channel. This function returns 0 (zero) if it fails to open a channel.

Function	Result
`ChanNum = DDEInitiate("EXCEL", "LOAN.XLS")`	Initiates a channel to Microsoft Excel and the file LOAN.XLS; the *ChanNum* variable holds the channel number returned.

For related commands, see "DDE (Dynamic Data Exchange) Statements and Functions" in the section "WordBASIC Cross Reference," earlier in this chapter.

DDEPoke

DDEPoke *ChanNum, Item$, Data$*

Sends the data to the item specified by *Item$* in the application connected to channel *ChanNum*. The channel must have been opened by the **DDEInitiate( )** function. If **DDEPoke** is unsuccessful, an error is generated.

For related commands, see "DDE (Dynamic Data Exchange) Statements and Functions" in the section "WordBASIC Cross Reference," earlier in this chapter.

DDERequest$( )

*A$* = **DDERequest$(***ChanNum, Item$***)**

Requests the information specified by *Item$* over the DDE channel specified by *ChanNum*. The channel must have been opened by the **DDEInitiate( )** function. If **DDERequest$( )** is unsuccessful, a null string ("") is returned.

DDERequest$( ) returns the data in CF_TEXT format. Pictures or text in Rich Text Format cannot be transferred.

For related commands, see "DDE (Dynamic Data Exchange) Statements and Functions" in the section "WordBASIC Cross Reference," earlier in this chapter.

DDETerminate

DDETerminate *ChanNum*

Closes the channel *ChanNum*. The channel must have been opened with the **DDEInitiate( )** function.

For related commands, see "DDE (Dynamic Data Exchange) Statements and Functions" in the section "WordBASIC Cross Reference," earlier in this chapter.

DDETerminateAll

DDETerminateAll

Similar to **DDETerminate**, but closes all open channels.

For related commands, see "DDE (Dynamic Data Exchange) Statements and Functions" in the section "WordBASIC Cross Reference," earlier in this chapter.

Declare

Declare Sub *SubName* **Lib** *LibName [ParameterList]* [**Alias** *ModuleName]*

Declare Function *FunctionName* **Lib** *LibName [ParameterList]* [**Alias** *ModuleName]*

In Word for Windows only, declares an external library function as a subroutine or function inside a macro. This command and the use of Dynamic Link Libraries in WordBASIC is not currently supported under OS/2. Use of this feature requires knowledge of Windows programming. For more information on the **Declare** statement, see Appendix C, "Dynamic Link Libraries."

Example.

```
Declare Function, 'IsAppLoaded Lib "kernel" (name$) As Integer Alias "GetModuleHandle"
Sub MAIN
   If IsAppLoaded("EXCEL") = 0 Then
      MsgBox "Excel is not running"
   Else
      MsgBox "Excel is loaded"
   End If
End Sub
```

For related commands, see "Utility Statements and Functions" in the section "WordBASIC Cross Reference," earlier in this chapter.

DeleteBackWord

DeleteBackWord

Deletes the word immediately preceding the selection but does not place it on the Clipboard. This is the equivalent of pressing Ctrl+Backspace.

For related commands, see "Editing Commands and Functions" in the section "WordBASIC Cross Reference," earlier in this chapter.

DeleteWord

DeleteWord

Deletes the word immediately following the insertion point or the first word included in the selection but does not place it on the Clipboard. The current contents of the clipboard are not disturbed. This is the equivalent of pressing Ctrl+Del.

For related commands, see "Editing Commands and Functions" in the section "WordBASIC Cross Reference," earlier in this chapter.

Dialog

Dialog *DialogRecord*

Displays for editing the dialog box specified by *DialogRecord.* After editing, you can store edits in *DialogRecord* by choosing OK, or you can lose edits by choosing Cancel. Choosing Cancel produces a run-time error that you can trap with **On Error.**

For related commands, see "Dialog Definition and Control Statements and Functions" in the section "WordBASIC Cross Reference," earlier in this chapter.

Dim

Dim [**Shared**] *Var [(Size)] [, Var [(Size)]...]*

Declares a variable array's type and allocates storage space for the array. Also used in defining dialog records. For more information on using the **Dim** statement with arrays, see Chapter 4, "Interlude—WordBASIC for Beginners." For information on using **Dim** to define dialog records, see Chapter 6, "More WordBASIC Programming Concepts."

For related commands, see "BASIC Statements and Functions" and "Dialog Definition and Control Statements and Functions" in the section "WordBASIC Cross Reference," earlier in this chapter.

DisableInput

DisableInput *[Disable]*

Prevents the Esc key from interrupting a macro. The Esc key is enabled by setting *Disable* to 0 (zero). Setting *Disable* to 1 disables the Esc key; 1 is the default.

Statement	Result
`DisableInput 0`	Disable inactive
`DisableInput 1`	Disable active

For related commands, see "Macrol Control, Creation, and Editing Statements and Functions" in the section "WordBASIC Cross Reference," earlier in this chapter.

DocClose

DocClose *[Save]*

Closes the current window or pane. If *Save* is 1, Word saves the document; if *Save* is 2, Word closes the window or pane but does not save the document. If *Save* is 0 (zero) or omitted, prompts the user to save if the document is "dirty" (that is, changes have been made since the last time the document was saved).

For related commands, see "File Statements and Functions" in the section "WordBASIC Cross Reference," earlier in this chapter.

DocMaximize

DocMaximize

Zooms the document window to application window size. If it is already maximized, the screen is displayed in the restored state.

For related commands, see "Window Control Statements and Functions" in the section "WordBASIC Cross Reference," earlier in this chapter.

DocMaximize( )

Log = **DocMaximize( )**

Returns –1 if the window is maximized.

Function	Result
`If Not DocMaximize() Then DocMaximize`	Tests the document window to see if it is maximized. If the window is maximized, no action is performed; if the window is not maximized, maximizes the window.

For related commands, see "Window Control Statements and Functions" in the section "WordBASIC Cross Reference," earlier in this chapter.

DocMove

DocMove *XPos, YPos*

Moves the document window to *XPos, YPos* relative to the upper left corner of the document area. Values are given in points.

Statement	Result
`DocMove 20, 40`	Moves the window to the position 20 points to the right and 40 points down from the upper left corner of the document area.

For related commands, see "Window Control Statements and Functions" in the section "WordBASIC Cross Reference," earlier in this chapter.

DocRestore

DocRestore

Restores the document window from a maximized state.

For related commands, see "Window Control Statements and Functions" in the section "WordBASIC Cross Reference," earlier in this chapter.

DocSize

DocSize *Width, Height*

Sizes the document window to the width and height specified by *Width, Height*. Values are given in points.

For related commands, see "Window Control Statements and Functions" in the section "WordBASIC Cross Reference," earlier in this chapter.

DocSplit

DocSplit *Percentage*

Splits the current window at the given *Percentage* height.

Statement	Result
`DocSplit 50`	Splits the current window in the middle.

For related commands, see "Window Control Statements and Functions" in the section "WordBASIC Cross Reference," earlier in this chapter.

DocSplit( )

Num = **DocSplit( )**

Returns the current window split position as a percentage of the window height, or returns 0 (zero) if the window is not split.

Function	Result
`If DocSplit() > 50 Then DocSplit 50`	If the current window is split more than 50% of the way down its height, then the window is split in the middle.

For related commands, see "Window Control Statements and Functions" in the section "WordBASIC Cross Reference," earlier in this chapter.

DoFieldClick

DoFieldClick

Simulates the double-clicking of a mouse button or pressing the DO FIELD CLICK key combination (Alt+Shift+F9) within the GOTOBUTTON and

MACROBUTTON fields' prompts. For information on these fields, see Chapter 9, "Fields."

For related commands, see "Field Statements and Functions" in the section "WordBASIC Cross Reference," earlier in this chapter.

DoubleUnderline

DoubleUnderline *[On]*

If *On* is omitted, toggles double underlining for the entire selection. If part of the selection has double underlining, toggles on for entire selection. If *On* is 1, Word double underlines the entire selection. If *On* is 0 (zero), Word removes double underlining from the entire selection.

Statement	If text is	New text is
`DoubleUnderline`	Trey Research Company	Trey Research Company
`DoubleUnderline`	Trey Research Company	Trey Research Company
`DoubleUnderline`	Trey Research Company	Trey Research Company
`DoubleUnderline 1`	Trey Research Company	Trey Research Company
`DoubleUnderline 0`	Trey Research Company	Trey Research Company

For related commands, see "Formatting Statements and Functions" in the section "WordBASIC Cross Reference," earlier in this chapter.

DoubleUnderline( )

Num = **DoubleUnderline( )**

Returns 0 (zero) if none of the selection is double underlined, 1 if all of the selection is double underlined, or –1 if part of the selection is double underlined or more than one kind of underlining is used.

If selected text is	Function returns
Trey Research Journal	0; the selection is not double underlined.
Trey Research Journal	1; the entire selection is double underlined.
Trey Research Journal	–1; only part of the selection is double underlined.

For related commands, see "Formatting Statements and Functions" in the section "WordBASIC Cross Reference," earlier in this chapter.

EditClear

EditClear *[Count]*

Deletes the selection without changing the contents of the Clipboard. If the selection is an insertion point, deletes the character to the right of the insertion point. If *Count* is a positive number, deletes the specified number of characters from the right of the insertion point. If *Count* is a negative number, deletes the specified number of characters from the left of the insertion point.

For related commands, see "Editing Commands and Functions" in the section "WordBASIC Cross Reference," earlier in this chapter.

EditCopy

EditCopy

Equivalent to the Copy command on the Edit menu. Copies the selection to the Clipboard.

For related commands, see "Editing Commands and Functions" in the section "WordBASIC Cross Reference," earlier in this chapter.

EditCut

EditCut

Equivalent to the Cut command on the Edit menu. Places the selection on the Clipboard and then deletes it from the document.

For related commands, see "Editing Commands and Functions" in the section "WordBASIC Cross Reference," earlier in this chapter.

EditGlossary

EditGlossary *Name$* [**.Insert**]

EditGlossary *Name$, [Context,]* **.Define**

EditGlossary *Name$*, **.Delete**

Equivalent to the Edit Glossary dialog box. Used to define, delete, and insert glossary entries. *Context* can be 0 (zero) for global, or 1 for document template. The default is global. *Context* is used only for **.Define**.

The default action is insert. You can perform other actions by appending the command button name from the dialog box (**Define** or **Delete**) to the statement.

Statement	Result
`EditGlossary "CPR"`	Inserts the glossary entry named `"CPR"` at the insertion point.
`EditGlossary "CPR", .Define`	Defines the glossary entry named `"CPR"`.
`EditGlossary "CPR", .Delete`	Deletes the glossary entry named `"CPR"`.

For related commands, see "Editing Commands and Functions" and "Glossary Statements and Functions" in the section "WordBASIC Cross Reference," earlier in this chapter.

EditGoTo

EditGoTo *Destination$*

Equivalent to the Edit Go To dialog box and GOTO key (F5). *Destination$* is a bookmark name or goto string. For more information on bookmarks, see the special bookmarks in the preceding section and "Moving the Insertion Point" in the *Word User's Reference.*

Statement	Result
`EditGoTo "l+10"`	Moves the insertion point 10 lines down.
`EditGoTo "s1l50"`	Moves the insertion point to line 50 of section 1.
`EditGoTo "Disclaim"`	Moves the insertion point to the bookmark `"Disclaim"`.
`EditGoTo "f1"`	Moves the insertion point to footnote 1.

(continued)

Continued

Statement	Result
`EditGoTo "\StartOfDoc"`	Uses a special bookmark to move the insertion point to the beginning of the document.
`EditGoTo "a"`	Moves the insertion point to the next annotation.
`EditGoTo "%50"`	Moves the insertion point to the middle of the document.
`EditGoTo "5"`	Goes to page 5.
`EditGoTo "s1"`	Goes to section 1.

For related commands, see "Editing Commands and Functions" and "Bookmark Statements and Functions" in the section "WordBASIC Cross Reference," earlier in this chapter.

EditHeaderFooter

EditHeaderFooter *[Type], [StartingNum[$]], [NumFormat], [HeaderDistance[$]], [FooterDistance[$]], [FirstPage], [OddAndEvenPages]*

Equivalent to the Edit Header/Footer dialog box. Opens the header or footer pane for editing.

The following table summarizes the arguments. Some arguments correspond to check boxes. If the argument is 1, the check box is on. If the argument is 0 (zero), it is off.

Argument	Description
Type	Specifies header type, as described in the following table.
StartingNum[$]	Value at which to start page numbers, or 0 for Auto.
NumFormat	Format for page numbers, as described in the following table.
HeaderDistance[$]	Distance from the top of the page, in points.
FooterDistance[$]	Distance from the bottom of the page, in points.
FirstPage	Corresponds to Different First Page check box.
OddAndEvenPages	Corresponds to Different Odd And Even Pages check box.

If *FirstPage* is	and *OddAndEvenPages* is	*Type* values
0	0	0 = Header 1 = Footer
1	0	0 = Header 1 = Footer 2 = First Header 3 = First Footer
0	1	0 = Even Header 1 = Even Footer 2 = Odd Header 3 = Odd Footer
1	1	0 = First Header 1 = First Footer 2 = Even Header 3 = Even Footer 4 = Odd Header 5 = Odd Footer

If *NumFormat* is	Numbers are printed as
0	1 2 3...
1	a b c...
2	A B C...
3	i ii iii...
4	I II III...

For related commands, see "Editing Commands and Functions" and "Formatting Statements and Functions" in the section "WordBASIC Cross Reference," earlier in this chapter.

EditHeaderFooterLink

EditHeaderFooterLink

Links the header/footer with a previous section. This is not possible in the first section of a document.

For related commands, see "Editing Commands and Functions" and "Formatting Statements and Functions" in the section "WordBASIC Cross Reference," earlier in this chapter.

EditPaste

EditPaste

Equivalent to the Paste command on the Edit menu. Copies the contents of the Clipboard to the insertion point.

For related commands, see "Editing Commands and Functions" in the section "WordBASIC Cross Reference," earlier in this chapter.

EditPasteLink

EditPasteLink *[AutoUpdate]*

Equivalent to the Edit Paste Link dialog box. Pastes a Dynamic Data Exchange (DDE) field. If *AutoUpdate* is 1, pastes a DDEAUTO field. This statement requires that the Clipboard contain linkable contents. If it does not, an error message appears.

For information on DDE, see Chapter 8, "Dynamic Data Exchange," and Chapter 9, "Fields."

For related commands, see "Editing Commands and Functions" and "DDE (Dynamic Data Exchange) Statements and Functions" in the section "WordBASIC Cross Reference," earlier in this chapter.

EditReplace

EditReplace *[Search$], [Replace$], [WholeWord], [MatchCase], [Confirm], [Format]*

Equivalent to the Edit Replace dialog box. Replaces the *Search$* string with the *Replace$* string. If *Search$* and *Replace$* are omitted, the strings used in the previous search and/or replace are used.

The following table summarizes the arguments:

Argument	Description
WholeWord	Corresponds to the Whole Word check box.
MatchCase	Corresponds to the Match Upper/Lowercase check box.
Confirm	Corresponds to the Confirm Changes check box.
Format	Replaces formatting in addition to, or instead of, text.

To replace formatting in addition to, or instead of, text, first use the **EditReplaceChar**, **EditReplacePara**, **EditSearchChar**, or **EditSearchPara** statement to set up the formatting, and then use **EditReplace** or **EditSearch** with *Format* set to 1.

For related commands, see "Editing Commands and Functions" in the section "WordBASIC Cross Reference," earlier in this chapter.

EditReplaceChar

EditReplaceChar *[Font$], [Points[$]], [Color], [Bold], [Italic], [SmallCaps], [Hidden], [Underline], [WordUnderline], [DoubleUnderline], [Position[$]], [Spacing[$]]*

Dialog-box equivalent; defines the character formatting **EditReplace** uses to format replacement text. The arguments specify options available in the Format Character dialog box. For a description of the arguments, see **FormatCharacter**, later in this section.

For related commands, see "Editing Commands and Functions" and "Formatting Statements and Functions" in the section "WordBASIC Cross Reference," earlier in this chapter.

EditReplacePara

EditReplacePara *[Alignment], [LeftIndent[$]], [RightIndent[$]], [FirstIndent[$]], [Before[$]], [After[$]], [LineSpacing[$]], [Style$], [KeepTogether], [KeepWithNext], [Border], [Pattern], [PageBreak], [NoLineNum]*

Dialog box equivalent; defines the paragraph formatting **EditReplace** uses to format replacement text. The arguments specify options available in the Format

Paragraph dialog box. For a description of the arguments, see **FormatParagraph**, later in this section.

For related commands, see "Editing Commands and Functions" and "Formatting Statements and Functions" in the section "WordBASIC Cross Reference," earlier in this chapter.

EditSearch

EditSearch *[Search$], [WholeWord], [MatchCase], [Direction], [Format]*

Equivalent to the Edit Search dialog box. Searches for the string specified by the *Search$* argument.

The following table summarizes the arguments. Some arguments correspond to check boxes. If the argument is 1, the check box is on. If the argument is 0 (zero), it is off.

Argument	Description
WholeWord	Corresponds to the Whole Word check box.
MatchCase	Corresponds to the Match Upper/Lowercase check box.
Direction	0 (zero) searches toward beginning of document, without prompt; 1 searches toward end of document, with prompt; 2 searches toward end of document, without prompt. The default is the last direction argument used, or 1 the first time **EditSearch** is executed.
Format	Searches for formatting in addition to, or instead of, text; 0 (zero) ignores formatting (default), 1 uses formatting.

For related commands, see "Editing Commands and Functions" in the section "WordBASIC Cross Reference," earlier in this chapter.

EditSearchChar

EditSearchChar *[Font$], [Points[$]], [Color], [Bold], [Italic], [SmallCaps], [Hidden], [Underline], [WordUnderline], [DoubleUnderline], [Position[$]], [Spacing[$]]*

Dialog-box equivalent; defines the character formatting **EditSearch** and **EditReplace** use to find formatted text. The arguments specify options available in the Format Character dialog box. For a description of the arguments, see **FormatCharacter**, later in this section.

For related commands, see "Editing Commands and Functions" and "Formatting Statements and Functions" in the section "WordBASIC Cross Reference," earlier in this chapter.

EditSearchFound( )

Log = **EditSearchFound( )**

Returns –1 if the last **EditSearch** was successful. Returns 0 (zero) if the last **EditSearch** was not successful.

Example.

```
Sub MAIN
   Count = 0
   StartOfDocument
   EditSearch "macro", .Direction = 2
   While EditSearchFound()
      Count = Count + 1
      EditSearch "macro"
   Wend
   Print "macro was found ";Count; " times"
End Sub
```

For related commands, see "Editing Commands and Functions" in the section "WordBASIC Cross Reference," earlier in this chapter.

EditSearchPara

EditSearchPara *[Alignment], [LeftIndent[$]], [RightIndent[$]], [FirstIndent[$]], [Before[$]], [After[$]], [LineSpacing[$]], [Style$], [KeepTogether], [KeepWithNext], [Border], [Pattern], [PageBreak], [NoLineNum]*

Dialog-box equivalent; defines the paragraph formatting **EditSearch** and **EditReplace** use to find formatted text. The arguments specify options available in the Format Paragraph dialog box. For a description of the arguments, see **FormatParagraph**, later in this section.

For related commands, see "Editing Commands and Functions" and "Formatting Statements and Functions" in the section "WordBASIC Cross Reference," earlier in this chapter.

EditSelectAll

EditSelectAll

Selects the entire document.

For related commands, see "Editing Commands and Functions" and "Selection and Insertion Point Definition and Control Statements and Functions" in the section "WordBASIC Cross Reference," earlier in this chapter.

EditSummaryInfo

EditSummaryInfo *[Title$], [Subject$], [Author$], [Keywords$], [Comments$], [Directory$], [Template$], [CreateDate$], [LastSavedDate$], [LastSavedBy$], [RevisionNumber], [EditTime$], [LastPrintedDate$], [NumPages], [NumWords], [NumChars], [FileName$]*

Equivalent to the Edit Summary Info dialog box. Sets the summary information and allows access to the Statistics dialog box. All the options in the Statistics dialog box are read-only.

You can append the Update command button name (**.Update**) to update the summary information.

Argument	Description
Title$	Title.
Subject$	Subject.
Author$	Author.
Keywords$	Key words used to identify the document.
Comments$	Comments on the document.
Directory$	The document's directory location; read-only.
Template$	Document template; read-only.
CreateDate$	Creation date; read-only.
LastSavedDate$	Date the document was last saved; read-only.
LastSavedBy$	Name of the person last saving the document; read-only.
RevisionNumber	Number of times the document has been saved; read-only.
EditTime$	Total time the document has been open, in minutes.
LastPrintedDate$	Date document was last printed; read-only.
NumPages	Number of pages; read-only.

(continued)

Continued

Argument	Description
NumWords	Number of words; read-only.
NumChars	Number of characters; read-only.
FileName$	Makes changes to summary information for the specified file name.

For related commands, see "Editing Commands and Functions"and "Environment Statements and Functions" in the section "WordBASIC Cross Reference," earlier in this chapter.

EditTable

EditTable *[Modify], [ShiftCells]*

Equivalent to the Edit Table dialog box. *Modify* is 0 (zero) for Row, 1 for Column, or 2 for Selection. *ShiftCells* is 0 (zero) to shift Horizontally, or 1 to shift Vertically. You can insert, delete, merge, or split cells by appending the Insert (**.Insert**), Delete (**.Delete**), MergeCells (**.MergeCells**), or SplitCells (**.SplitCells**) command button name.

For related commands, see "Editing Commands and Functions" and "Table Creation and Editing Statements and Functions" in the section "WordBASIC Cross Reference," earlier in this chapter.

EditUndo

EditUndo

Equivalent to the Undo command on the Edit menu. Undoes the last action, if possible. You can undo certain Word actions (for example, Cut and Paste). Some actions cannot be undone.

For related commands, see "Editing Commands and Functions" in the section "WordBASIC Cross Reference," earlier in this chapter.

EmptyBookmark( )

Log = **EmptyBookmark(***Name$***)**

Returns –1 if the bookmark *Name$* is empty (an insertion point), or 0 (zero) if *Name$* is not empty.

For related commands, see "Bookmark Statements and Functions" in the section "WordBASIC Cross Reference," earlier in this chapter.

End Dialog

End Dialog

Ends the definition of the dialog box.

For related commands, see "Dialog Definition and Control Statements and Functions" in the section "WordBASIC Cross Reference," earlier in this chapter.

EndOfColumn

EndOfColumn *[Select]*

Moves the insertion point to the bottom cell in the table column. If *Select* is nonzero, the selection is extended or shrunk.

For related commands, see "Selection and Insertion Point Definition and Control Statements and Functions" in the section "WordBASIC Cross Reference," earlier in this chapter.

EndOfDocument

EndOfDocument *[Select]*

Moves the insertion point to the end of the document. If *Select* is nonzero, the selection is extended or shrunk.

For related commands, see "Selection and Insertion Point Definition and Control Statements and Functions" in the section "WordBASIC Cross Reference," earlier in this chapter.

EndOfLine

EndOfLine *[Select]*

Moves the insertion point to the end of the line. If *Select* is nonzero, the selection is extended or shrunk.

For related commands, see "Selection and Insertion Point Definition and Control Statements and Functions" in the section "WordBASIC Cross Reference," earlier in this chapter.

EndOfRow

EndOfRow *[Select]*

Moves the selection to the end of the last cell in the table row. If *Select* is nonzero, the selection is extended or shrunk.

For related commands, see "Selection and Insertion Point Definition and Control Statements and Functions" in the section "WordBASIC Cross Reference," earlier in this chapter.

EndOfWindow

EndOfWindow *[Select]*

Moves the selection to the end of the window. If *Select* is nonzero, the selection is extended or shrunk.

For related commands, see "Selection and Insertion Point Definition and Control Statements and Functions" in the section "WordBASIC Cross Reference," earlier in this chapter.

Eof( )

Log = **Eof(***StreamNumber***)**

Returns –1 when the end of the file attached to the *StreamNumber* has been reached.

For information on sequential files, see Chapter 6, "More WordBASIC Programming Concepts."

For related commands, see "BASIC Statements and Functions" in the section "WordBASIC Cross Reference," earlier in this chapter.

Err

Num = **Err**

Err = 0

This is a special variable that contains the error code for the most recent error condition. (For more information, see the list of error codes at the end of this chapter.)

The form **Err = 0** is used to reset error trapping after an error has occurred. This form is normally used at the end of an error trapping routine. If **Err = 0** is not included, only the first error that occurs is trapped. Future errors generate an error message and cause the macro to halt.

Example.

```
Sub MAIN
   On Error Goto Trouble
   Port = 1
Start:
   Print WindowName$(Port)
   Port = Port + 1
Goto Start
Trouble:
   Error Err
End Sub
```

This example first sets up an error trap using the **On Error Goto** statement. The value of the variable **Port** is set to 1. The name of window with the number of **Port** (1) is printed. The value of **Port** is increased by one and the process is repeated until the value of **Port** exceeds the number of open windows. At this point, an error occurs and the error trap directs the program to the label **Trouble**. The statement **Error** prints an error message for the designated error number and causes the macro to halt. The number of the last occurring error is stored in **Err**.

As shown here, with a slightly altered error routine, the preceding program could deal with the error and allow the program to continue:

```
.
.
.
Trouble:
   If Err = 5 Then          'Check for error 5, Illegal Function Call
      Port = 1              'If found, set value of Port to 1
      Err = 0               'Reset error trap
      Goto Start            'Return to main program
   Else                     'If a different error occurs
      Error Err             'Print error message and halt
End Sub                     'End of program
```

Errors with numbers 1000 or greater are generated by Word and not by the programming language itself. If such an error occurs, an error message box is displayed, and the user must respond before the macro can continue. If OK is selected, control of the program then passes to the error-handling routine.

For related commands, see "BASIC Statements and Functions" in the section "WordBASIC Cross Reference," earlier in this chapter.

Error

Error *ErrorNumber*

Generates an error condition specified by *ErrorNumber*. *ErrorNumber* is an error code. (For more information, see "Macro Error Messages" and "Other Error Messages," later in this chapter.)

Error serves two functions. It can be used to generate a specified error condition in order to test an error handling routine, or it can be used to display an error message and terminate operation of the macro program.

Errors with numbers 1000 or greater are generated by Word and not by the programming language itself. If such an error occurs, an error message box is displayed, and the user must respond before the macro can continue. If OK is selected, control of the program then passes to the current **On Error** statement. If an argument of 1000 or greater is used with **Error**, no message box is displayed, but the error trap (if any) is triggered.

In the following example, **Error** is used for both purposes: first, to generate a simulated error that triggers the error handling routine, and second, to display a message and end the macro if the error is not specifically handled.

Example.

```
Sub MAIN
   On Error Goto ErrorHandler
   Error 530          'Generate error 530 "Dialog box too complex"
ErrorHandler:
   Select Case Err    'Branch based on error number in Err
   Case 5             'Statements to deal with error 5 follow
      .
      .
      .
   Case 11            'Statements to deal with error 11 follow
      .
      .
      .
   Case 71            'Statements to deal with error 71 follow
      .
      .
      .
   Case Else          'Error (such as 530) not handled above
      Error Err       'Generate error message and end macro
   End Select
End Sub               'End MAIN
```

For related commands, see "BASIC Statements and Functions" in the section "WordBASIC Cross Reference," earlier in this chapter.

ExistingBookmark( )

ExistingBookmark(*Bookmark$***)**

Used to test for the presence of a particular bookmark. Returns –1 if *Bookmark$* exists, or 0 (zero) if it does not exist.

For related commands, see "Bookmark Statements and Functions" in the section "WordBASIC Cross Reference," earlier in this chapter.

ExpandGlossary

ExpandGlossary

Expands the word closest to the insertion point into the corresponding glossary text.

For related commands, see "Glossary Statements and Functions" in the section "WordBASIC Cross Reference," earlier in this chapter.

ExtendSelection

ExtendSelection *[Character$]*

Turns on extend mode, if it is not already turned on. If extend mode is already turned on, the selection is extended to the next unit; for example, if extend mode is already on and a character is selected, **ExtendSelection** extends the selection to the whole word. If *Character$* is specified, the selection is extended to that character. Use the **Cancel** command to exit this mode.

For related commands, see "Glossary Statements and Functions" and "Mode Statements and Functions" in the section "WordBASIC Cross Reference," earlier in this chapter.

File1

File1

Equivalent to selecting the first file listed on the File menu. Opens the first file. An error is generated if you attempt to open a nonexistent file slot; that is, you cannot use **File1** if the File menu lists no files.

For related commands, see "File Statements and Functions" in the section "WordBASIC Cross Reference," earlier in this chapter.

File2

File2

Equivalent to selecting the second file listed on the File menu. Opens the second file. An error is generated if you attempt to open a nonexistent file slot; that is, you cannot use **File2** if the File menu lists only one file or no file.

For related commands, see "File Statements and Functions" in the section "WordBASIC Cross Reference," earlier in this chapter.

File3

File3

Equivalent to selecting the third file listed on the File menu. Opens the third file. An error is generated if you attempt to open a nonexistent file slot; that is, you cannot use **File3** if the File menu lists two or fewer files.

For related commands, see "File Statements and Functions" in the section "WordBASIC Cross Reference," earlier in this chapter.

File4

File4

Equivalent to selecting the fourth file listed on the File menu. Opens the fourth file. An error is generated if you attempt to open a nonexistent file slot; that is, you cannot use **File4** if the File menu lists three or fewer files.

For related commands, see "File Statements and Functions" in the section "WordBASIC Cross Reference," earlier in this chapter.

FileClose

FileClose *[Save]*

Equivalent to the Close command on the File menu. Closes the current file and associated windows. (Use **DocClose** to close only the active window of a document.) The *Save* argument determines whether a save is forced: 1 forces a save, 2 forces no save. If *Save* is 0 (zero) or omitted, the user will be prompted to save if the file is "dirty" (that is, changes have been made since the last time the file was saved).

For related commands, see "File Statements and Functions" in the section "WordBASIC Cross Reference," earlier in this chapter.

FileExit

FileExit *[Save]*

Equivalent to the Exit command on the File menu. Quits Word. If any open documents have been edited and if *Save* is omitted or is 0 (zero), the user is prompted to save each changed document. If *Save* is 1, all edited documents are automatically saved before exiting. If *Save* is 2, the documents are not saved.

For related commands, see "File Statements and Functions" and "Environment Statements and Functions" in the section "WordBASIC Cross Reference," earlier in this chapter.

FileFind

FileFind *[SortBy], [SearchList$], [Title$], [Subject$], [Author$], [Keywords$], [SavedBy$], [Text$], [DateCreatedFrom$], [DateCreatedTo$], [DateSavedFrom$], [DateSavedTo$], [MatchCase], [SearchAgain]*

Equivalent to the File Find dialog box. Can be used to change the search criteria in subsequent **FileFind** statements. If you record a macro with **FileFind**, any other actions you perform in the File Find dialog box at that time (for example, opening or deleting a document, editing summary information, or printing) are recorded as separate statements.

Argument	Description
SortBy	Specifies what information the documents are sorted by; see the following table.
SearchList$	List of existing directories.
Title$	Title.
Subject$	Subject.
Author$	Author.
Keywords$	Key words used to identify the document.

(continued)

Continued

Argument	Description
SavedBy$	Name of the person who last saved the document.
Text$	Text in the document.
DateCreatedFrom$	Document creation date you want to search from.
DateCreatedTo$	Document creation date you want to search to.
DateSavedFrom$	Document save date you want to search from.
DateSavedTo$	Document save date you want to search to.
MatchCase	Specifies whether to match the case of the search text exactly: 0 (zero) is no (default), 1 is yes.
SearchAgain	Specifies whether to begin the search again: 0 (zero) is no (default), search the current list of files; 1 is yes, search all directories in the search list and generate a new list of files.

If *SortBy* is	Word sorts files
0	Alphabetically by name.
1	Alphabetically by author.
2	Chronologically by creation date.
3	Chronologically by date last saved.
4	Alphabetically by the name of the person who last saved the document.
5	By size, with smallest document listed first.

For related commands, see "File Statements and Functions" in the section "WordBASIC Cross Reference," earlier in this chapter.

FileName$( )

*A$* = **FileName$(***n***)**

Returns the name of the *n*th file in the file list. If *n* is 0 (zero), the name of the current file is returned. If there is no current document, **FileName$(0)** returns an empty string. If *n* is greater than the number of files listed on the File menu, an error is generated.

For related commands, see "File Statements and Functions" in the section "WordBASIC Cross Reference," earlier in this chapter.

FileNew

FileNew *[NewTemplate], [Template$]*

Equivalent to the File New dialog box. The following table summarizes the arguments:

Argument	Description
NewTemplate	If 1, file is a document template; if 0 (zero), file is a document (default).
Template$	Name of the document template or document on which to base the document.

For related commands, see "File Statements and Functions" in the section "WordBASIC Cross Reference," earlier in this chapter.

FileOpen

FileOpen *Name$, [ReadOnly]*

Equivalent to the File Open dialog box. Opens the document specified by *Name$*. An error is generated if the document does not exist. If *ReadOnly* is 1, the document is opened as read-only.

For related commands, see "File Statements and Functions" in the section "WordBASIC Cross Reference," earlier in this chapter.

FilePrint

FilePrint *[Type], [NumCopies], [Range], [From$], [To$], [Reverse], [Draft], [UpdateFields], [PaperFeed], [Summary], [Annotations], [ShowHidden], [ShowCodes], [FileName$]*

Equivalent to the File Print dialog box. Prints a document. The following table summarizes the arguments:

Argument	Description
Type	Type of document to print; can be 0 (zero) for document, 1 for summary information, 2 for annotations, 3 for style sheet, 4 for glossary, or 5 for key assignments.
NumCopies	Number of copies.

(continued)

Continued

Argument	Description
Range	Page range; 0 (zero) prints all of the document, 1 prints the selection, 2 prints the specified range of pages.
From$	Beginning of the range; can be page and/or section; ignored if *Range* equals 0 (zero) or 1.
To$	End of the range; can be page and/or section; ignored if *Range* equals 0 (zero) or 1.
Reverse	If 0 (zero), prints the document from the first page to the last; if 1, prints the document in reverse order.
Draft	Prints in draft mode.
UpdateFields	Updates fields before printing (some fields are automatically updated at printing; this argument updates fields not normally updated).
PaperFeed	0 (zero) is Manual, 1 is Envelope, 2 is Tractor, 3 is Auto, 4 selects Bin1, 5 selects Bin2, 6 selects Bin3, 7 selects Mixed.
Summary	Instructs Word to include summary information when printing.
Annotations	Instructs Word to include annotations when printing.
ShowHidden	Instructs Word to include hidden text when printing.
ShowCodes	Instructs Word to show field codes when printing.
FileName$	If supplied, the specified file is printed. Recording **Print** from **FileFind** records **FilePrint** with this field.

For related commands, see "File Statements and Functions" in the section "WordBASIC Cross Reference," earlier in this chapter.

FilePrinterSetup

FilePrinterSetup *[Printer$]*

Equivalent to the File Printer Setup dialog box. *Printer$* is the name of the new printer to be activated. Enter this argument exactly as it appears in the File Printer Setup dialog box.

The Setup command button name (.**Setup**) can be appended to display the dialog box showing the printer options.

Printer setting	Result
`FilePrinterSetup "PostScript printer on COM2:"`	Changes the printer to the PostScript printer attached to the COM2: port.

For related commands, see "File Statements and Functions" in the section "WordBASIC Cross Reference," earlier in this chapter.

FilePrintMerge

FilePrintMerge *[MergeRecords], [From], [To]*

Equivalent to the File Print Merge dialog box. If *MergeRecords* is nonzero, Word merges only the records specified between *From* and *To*, one of which must be nonzero. If *MergeRecords* is zero or omitted, *From* and *To* are ignored.

The NewDocument command button name (**.NewDocument**) can be appended to direct the output to a new document.

For related commands, see "File Statements and Functions" in the section "WordBASIC Cross Reference," earlier in this chapter.

FilePrintPreview

FilePrintPreview *[On]*

Equivalent to the Print Preview command on the File menu. If *On* is omitted, toggles print preview mode. If *On* is nonzero, turns on print preview mode. If *On* is 0 (zero), turns off print preview mode.

For related commands, see "File Statements and Functions" and "View Control Statements and Functions" in the section "WordBASIC Cross Reference," earlier in this chapter.

FilePrintPreview( )

A$ = **FilePrintPreview( )**

Returns –1 if print preview mode is on, or 0 (zero) if it is off.

For related commands, see "File Statements and Functions" and "View Control Statements and Functions" in the section "WordBASIC Cross Reference," earlier in this chapter.

FilePrintPreviewBoundaries

FilePrintPreviewBoundaries *[On]*

Displays the text boundaries if *On* is nonzero; if *On* is 0 (zero), turns off display. If *On* is omitted, toggles the display of text boundaries.

For related commands, see "File Statements and Functions" and "View Control Statements and Functions" in the section "WordBASIC Cross Reference," earlier in this chapter.

FilePrintPreviewPages

FilePrintPreviewPages *[Pages]*

If *Pages* is omitted, toggles display between one and two pages.

Pages **argument**	**Description**
0	Toggles the display state (default).
1	Displays one page.
2	Displays two pages.

For related commands, see "File Statements and Functions" and "View Control Statements and Functions" in the section "WordBASIC Cross Reference," earlier in this chapter.

FileSave

FileSave

Equivalent to the Save command on the File menu. Saves the current document. If the document is not named, displays the Save As dialog box and prompts the user for the file name.

For related commands, see "File Statements and Functions" in the section "WordBASIC Cross Reference," earlier in this chapter.

FileSaveAll

FileSaveAll *[Save]*

Equivalent to the Save All command on the File menu. Prompts the user to save all changed files, including NORMAL.DOT. If *Save* is 0 (zero), the user is prompted to save all files marked as "dirty" (that is, changes have been made since the last time the file was saved). If *Save* is 1, all edited documents are automatically saved.

For related commands, see "File Statements and Functions" in the section "WordBASIC Cross Reference," earlier in this chapter.

FileSaveAs

FileSaveAs *[Name$], [Format], [FastSave], [CreateBackup], [LockAnnot]*

Equivalent to the File Save As dialog box. Saves the current document with a new name and/or format. *Name$* specifies the new name. *Format* specifies the new format.

Argument	Description
FastSave	Saves changes made since last time the file was saved.
CreateBackup	Creates a backup copy of the document.
LockAnnot	Locks the document for annotations.

Format argument	Document type
0	Normal (Word format).
1	Document Template.
2	Text Only (extended characters saved in ANSI character set).
3	Text+Breaks (plain text with line breaks; extended characters saved in ANSI character set).
4	Text Only (PC-8) (extended characters saved in IBM PC character set).
5	Text+Breaks (PC-8) (text with line breaks; extended characters saved in IBM PC character set).
6	Rich Text Format (RTF).
7	WinWord (OS/2 only).
8	WinWord Template (OS/2 only).

Other file formats can be specified for *Format*. They must be listed in the WIN.INI file under the Microsoft Word entry (Windows) or in the OS2.INI file

(OS/2). The numbers for other formats begin at 100. The number for a format is its CONVNUM number in the INI file plus 100 minus 1.

Example.

```
FileSaveAs "TEST.RTF",6,0,1,0
```

This example saves the current document under the name TEST.RTF, in RTF format, with fastsave off, make backup on, and lock annotations off.

For related commands, see "File Statements and Functions" in the section "WordBASIC Cross Reference," earlier in this chapter.

Files$( )

*A$* = **Files$(***FileSpec$***)**

Returns the first file name that matches *FileSpec$*. If the *FileSpec$* argument is omitted, the next file that matches the last-used *FileSpec$* file name is returned. By specifying the *FileSpec$* file name on the first iteration and omitting it thereafter, this function can also be used to get a list of files that match *FileSpec$*. If no files match, a null string (" ") is returned. `Files$(".")` returns the current directory.

Function	Return value
`A$ = Files$("WIN.*")`	WIN.DOC, WIN.COM, WIN.TXT, or any file with the name `WIN`.
`CurrDir$ = Files$(".")`	The current directory (for example, `"C:\OS2\WORD\"`).

For related commands, see "File Statements and Functions" in the section "WordBASIC Cross Reference," earlier in this chapter.

Font

Font *Name$, [Size]*

Applies the font named by *Name$* to the selection. You can include the *Size* argument instead of following this statement with the **FontSize** statement.

Statement	If selected text is	New text is
`Font "Helv", 8`	Figures are current as of 12 November 1989.	Figures are current as of 12 November 1989.

For related commands, see "Formatting Statements and Functions" in the section "WordBASIC Cross Reference," earlier in this chapter.

Font$( )

*A$* = **Font$( )**

*A$* = **Font$(***Count***)**

Returns the font name of the current selection. If the selection has more than one font, a null string is returned. If a *Count* argument is supplied, **Font$( )** returns the name of the font *Count*. *Count* must be in the range 1 to *CountFonts( )*.

If selected text is	Function returns
Of course, not everyone needs the services of Trey Research	Helv
Of course, not everyone needs the services of Trey Research	Null string

For related commands, see "Formatting Statements and Functions" in the section "WordBASIC Cross Reference," earlier in this chapter.

FontSize

FontSize *Size*

Sets the size of the current selection, in points.

For related commands, see "Formatting Statements and Functions" in the section "WordBASIC Cross Reference," earlier in this chapter.

FontSize( )

Num = **FontSize( )**

Returns the font size of the current selection. If the selection has more than one font size, 0 (zero) is returned.

If selected text is	Function returns
Trey Research...When you need us, we're there.	8
Trey Research...When you need us, we're there.	10

For related commands, see "Formatting Statements and Functions" in the section "WordBASIC Cross Reference," earlier in this chapter.

For...Next

For *CounterVariable* = *Start* **To** *End* [**Step** *Increment*]
    Statement(s)
Next *[CounterVariable]*

Executes the statements between **For** and **Next** as many times as it takes the *CounterVariable* to go from the *Start* value to the *End* value. *Increment* is the value used to increment the counter (default is 1).

The *CounterVariable* with **Next** is optional. If *CounterVariable* is omitted, **Next** causes WordBASIC to loop back to the first incompleted **For...Next** statement. Use of *CounterVariable* does slow program operation somewhat, and this can be important in longer and more complex programs. Using *CounterVariable* aids the readability of the program, but the same result can be obtained by adding a comment after the **Next** statement. (For more information, see the entry for **Rem** and Appendix A, "Programming Style.") Including *CounterVariable* does help check program logic for errors. You may want to use the form **Next** *CounterVariable* when writing and testing your programs and then delete the *CounterVariable* argument when the program has been finished and tested.

Example	Action	Values of Count
`For Count = 1 To 5` `Next Count`	Value of Count is incremented from 1 to 5 in steps of 1.	1, 2, 3, 4, 5

`For Count = 1 To 3`
`Beep`
`Next Count`
	Value of Count is incremented from 1 to 3 in steps of 1. The command Beep is repeated three times.	1, 2, 3

(continued)

Continued

Example	Action	Values of Count
`For Count = 5 To 1 Step -1` `Next Count`	Value of Count is decremented from 5 to 1 in steps of –1.	5, 4, 3, 2, 1
`For Count = 1 To 2 Step .2` `Next Count`	Value of Count is incremented from 1 to 2 in steps of .2.	1, 1.2, 1.4, 1.6, 1.8, 2

For related commands, see "BASIC Statements and Functions" in the section "WordBASIC Cross Reference," earlier in this chapter.

FormatCharacter

FormatCharacter *[Font$], [Points[$]], [Color], [Bold], [Italic], [SmallCaps], [Hidden], [Underline], [WordUnderline], [DoubleUnderline], [Position[$]], [Spacing[$]]*

Equivalent to the Format Character dialog box. Applies character formatting to the selection. The following table summarizes the arguments. Some arguments take measurements in points. Other arguments correspond to check boxes.

Argument	Description
Font$	Name of font.
Points[$]	Size, in points.
Color	Color of the text; for a list of colors, see **CharColor**, earlier in this chapter.
Bold	Corresponds to the Bold check box.
Italic	Corresponds to the Italic check box.
SmallCaps	Corresponds to the Small Kaps check box.
Hidden	Corresponds to the Hidden check box.
Underline	Corresponds to the Underline check box.
WordUnderline	Corresponds to the Word underline check box.
DoubleUnderline	Corresponds to the Double underline check box.
Position[$]	Refers to the character position on the line, as shown in the following table.
Spacing[$]	Specifies the amount of character spacing, in points, as shown in the following table.

Position[$] **argument**	**Position**
0 (zero)	Normal.
A positive number	Superscript by the specified number of points.
A negative number	Subscript by the specified number of points.

Spacing[$] **argument**	**Spacing**
0 (zero)	Normal.
A positive number	Expanded by the specified number of points.
A negative number	Condensed by the specified number of points.

For related commands, see "Formatting Statements and Functions" in the section "WordBASIC Cross Reference," earlier in this chapter.

FormatDefineStyles

FormatDefineStyles *Name$, [BasedOn$], [NextStyle$], [AddToTemplate], [NewName$], [FileName$], [Source]*

Equivalent to the Format Define Styles dialog box. Defines a new style with the specified *Name$*. If a style with that name already exists, that style is made the current style. **FormatDefineStyles** sets up the style; to define the character, paragraph, and tab formats, use the **FormatDefineStylesChar**, **FormatDefineStylesPara**, **FormatDefineStylesPosition**, and **FormatDefineStylesTabs** statements described later in this chapter. To redefine an existing style, include the specific arguments with the **FormatDefineStyles** statement.

Examples are shown in the following table:

Statement	**Result**
`FormatDefineStyles "Title"`	Defines the new style `"Title"`.
`FormatDefineStylesChar .Bold = 1`	Redefines the current style (`"Title"`) to include bold formatting.
`FormatDefineStylesPara .Alignment = 2`	Redefines the current style (`"Title"`) to include centered formatting.
`FormatDefineStyles "Headline", .Delete`	Deletes the style `"Headline"`.

The *BasedOn$* argument specifies a style on which to base the style. The *NextStyle$* argument specifies the style to be applied after the style.

AddToTemplate can be 0 (zero) for the document only, or 1 for the document and its template.

The Delete (**.Delete**), Rename (**.Rename**), and Merge (**.Merge**) command button names can be appended.

The *NewName$* argument specifies a new name for the style; it is used only in conjunction with the Rename command button.

The *FileName$* argument is used only with the Merge command button. It specifies the template or document whose style sheet is to be merged with that of the current document or template.

The *Source* argument is used only in conjunction with the Merge command button, and can be 0 (from the current document or template to a specified document or template), or 1 (from a specified document or template to the current document or template). If no filename and argument is specified, the template of the current document is assumed.

For related commands, see "Formatting Statements and Functions" in the section "WordBASIC Cross Reference," earlier in this chapter.

FormatDefineStylesChar

Dialog-box equivalent; defines the current style with the specified character properties. This statement takes the same arguments as **FormatCharacter**. For more information, see **FormatCharacter**, earlier in this chapter.

For related commands, see "Formatting Statements and Functions" in the section "WordBASIC Cross Reference," earlier in this chapter.

FormatDefineStylesPara

Dialog-box equivalent; defines the current style with the specified paragraph properties. This statement takes the same arguments as **FormatParagraph**. For more information, see **FormatParagraph**, later in this chapter.

For related commands, see "Formatting Statements and Functions" in the section "WordBASIC Cross Reference," earlier in this chapter.

FormatDefineStylesPosition

Dialog-box equivalent; defines the current style with the specified position properties. This statement takes the same arguments as **FormatPosition.** For more information, see **FormatPosition,** later in this chapter.

For related commands, see "Formatting Statements and Functions" in the section "WordBASIC Cross Reference," earlier in this chapter.

FormatDefineStylesTabs

Dialog-box equivalent; defines the current style with the specified tab properties. This statement takes the same arguments as **FormatTabs.** For more information, see **FormatTabs,** later in this chapter.

For related commands, see "Formatting Statements and Functions" in the section "WordBASIC Cross Reference," earlier in this chapter.

FormatDocument

FormatDocument *[PageWidth[$]], [PageHeight[$]], [DefTabs[$]], [TopMargin[$]], [BottomMargin[$]], [LeftMargin[$]], [RightMargin[$]], [Gutter[$]], [MirrorMargins], [FootnotesAt], [StartingNum[$]], [RestartNum], [Template$], [WidowControl]*

Equivalent to the Format Document dialog box. Applies document formatting properties.

The following table summarizes the arguments. Some arguments take measurements in points. Other arguments correspond to check boxes.

Argument	Description
PageWidth[$]	Width of page.
PageHeight[$]	Height of page.
DefTabs[$]	Distance between default tab stops.
TopMargin[$]	Width of top margin.
BottomMargin[$]	Width of bottom margin.
LeftMargin[$]	Width of left margin.
RightMargin[$]	Width of right margin.
Gutter[$]	Binding width.

(continued)

Continued

Argument	Description
MirrorMargins	If 1, *LeftMargin* becomes *InsideMargin* and *RightMargin* becomes *OutsideMargin*.
FootnotesAt	Where to place footnotes; can be 0 (zero) for end of section, 1 for bottom of page, 2 for beneath text, or 3 for end of document.
StartingNum[$]	Starting footnote number.
RestartNum	Corresponds to the Restart # Each Section check box.
Template$	Document template.
WidowControl	Corresponds to the Widow Control check box.

To set the global or template default, append the SetDefault command button name (**.SetDefault**) to this statement. This is a powerful argument that changes the default document properties to those specified in this statement.

For related commands, see "Formatting Statements and Functions" in the section "WordBASIC Cross Reference," earlier in this chapter.

FormatParagraph

FormatParagraph *[Alignment], [LeftIndent[$]], [RightIndent[$]], [FirstIndent[$]], [Before[$]], [After[$]], [LineSpacing[$]], [Style$], [KeepTogether], [KeepWithNext], [Border], [Pattern], [PageBreak], [NoLineNum]*

Equivalent to the Format Paragraph dialog box. Applies paragraph formatting.

Alignment argument	Paragraph formatting
0	Left
1	Centered
2	Right
3	Justified

The *LeftIndent[$]*, *RightIndent[$]*, and *FirstIndent[$]* arguments specify the amount of left, right, and first-line indents, respectively. The *Before[$]* and *After[$]* arguments specify the amount of spacing above and below a paragraph, respectively. The *LineSpacing[$]* argument specifies the amount of spacing for all lines in a paragraph. For these six arguments, you can omit quotation marks around the values only if the numbers are in points. The *Style$* argument specifies a style to be applied to a paragraph. The *KeepTogether* and *KeepWithNext* arguments prevent page breaks within a paragraph and between paragraphs, respectively.

***Border* argument**	**Paragraph formatting**
0	No border
1	Box
2	Outside bar; at left, unless alternating left and right pages, in which case, left on left pages and right on right pages
3	Bar above paragraph
4	Bar below paragraph

***Pattern* argument**	**Paragraph formatting**
0	None (default)
1	Single
2	Thick
3	Double
4	Shadow; available only if *Border* is below (4) or box (1)

The *PageBreak* argument inserts a page break before printing the paragraph. The *NoLineNum* argument turns off line numbering for the paragraph.

For related commands, see "Formatting Statements and Functions" in the section "WordBASIC Cross Reference," earlier in this chapter.

FormatPicture

FormatPicture *[Border], [ScaleY], [ScaleX], [CropTop[$]], [CropLeft[$]], [CropBottom[$]], [CropRight[$]]*

Equivalent to the Format Picture dialog box. Applies picture formatting properties.

The following table summarizes the arguments. Some arguments take measurements in points. Other arguments correspond to check boxes.

Argument	Description
Border	Same available values as *Pattern* for **FormatParagraph**.
ScaleY, ScaleX	Amount to scale the picture; the measurement is a percentage.
CropTop[$], CropLeft[$], CropBottom[$], CropRight[$]	Amount to crop the picture, in points; if a negative value is used, the picture is not cropped, but the amount of white space around the picture is increased. Measurements in units other than points must be enclosed in quotation marks.

For related commands, see "Formatting Statements and Functions" in the section "WordBASIC Cross Reference," earlier in this chapter.

FormatPosition

FormatPosition *[Horizontal[$]], [HRelativeTo], [Vertical[$]], [VRelativeTo], [DistanceFromText], [ParagraphWidth[$]]*

Equivalent to the Format Position dialog box. Applies position formatting to the selected paragraphs.

Argument	Description
Horizontal[$]	Absolute distance, in points; or can be Left, Center, Right, Inside, or Outside.
HRelativeTo	Indicates *Horizontal* is relative to specified item (margin, page, or column); can be 0 (zero) for Margin, 1 for Page, or 2 for Column.
Vertical[$]	Absolute distance, in points; or can be Inline, Normal, Top, Center, or Bottom.
VRelativeTo	Indicates *Vertical* is relative to specified item (margin or page); can be 0 (zero) for Margin, or 1 for Page.
DistanceFromText	Amount of white space between an object and text surrounding the object.
ParagraphWidth[$]	Total line width of the paragraph; if 0 (zero), use width between paragraph indents.

The Reset command button name (**.Reset**) can be appended to cancel the position formatting of the paragraphs.

For related commands, see "Formatting Statements and Functions" in the section "WordBASIC Cross Reference," earlier in this chapter.

FormatSection

FormatSection *[Columns], [ColumnSpacing[$]], [ColLine], [SectionStart], [Footnotes], [LineNum], [StartingNum[$]], [FromText[$]], [CountBy], [NumMode], [VertAlign]*

Equivalent to the Format Section dialog box. Applies section formatting properties to the selection. Some arguments take measurements in points or numbers. Other arguments correspond to check boxes.

Argument	Description
Columns	Number of columns.
ColumnSpacing[$]	Distance between columns.
ColLine	Corresponds to the Line Between check box.
SectionStart	Determines the type of the section break; can be 0 (zero) for no break, 1 for column, 2 for page, 3 for even page, or 4 for odd page.
Footnotes	Corresponds to the Include Footnotes check box.
LineNum	Corresponds to the Line Numbering check box.
StartingNum[$]	Number at which to begin line numbering.
FromText[$]	Distance from text; can be 0 (zero) for Auto, or a positive number.
CountBy	Numerical increment used to print line numbers.
NumMode	Determines how lines are numbered; can be 0 (zero) for per page, 1 for per section, or 2 for continuous.
VertAlign	Alignment of section to the page; can be 0 (zero) for top, 1 for center, or 2 for justify.

For related commands, see "Formatting Statements and Functions" in the section "WordBASIC Cross Reference," earlier in this chapter.

FormatStyles

FormatStyles *Name$, [Create]*

Equivalent to the Format Styles dialog box. Applies the style in *Name$* to the selected paragraphs. If the style does not exist and *Create* is not specified or is 0 (zero), an error is generated. If *Create* is 1, the style is created with the properties of the selection, if it doesn't already exist. If the style exists, *Create* is ignored.

For related commands, see "Formatting Statements and Functions" in the section "WordBASIC Cross Reference," earlier in this chapter.

FormatTable

FormatTable *[FromColumn], [Column], [ColumnWidth], [SpaceBetweenCols[$]], [IndentRows[$]], [MinimumRowHeight], [OutlineBorder], [TopBorder], [BottomBorder], [InsideBorder], [LeftBorder], [RightBorder], [AlignRows], [ApplyTo]*

Equivalent to the Format Table dialog box. When recording, pressing the Next or Prev Columns command button records a new **FormatTable** command.

Argument	Description
FromColumn, Column	Range of columns. For a single column, use only *Column.*
ColumnWidth	Width of columns, in points.
SpaceBetweenCols[$]	Space between columns, in points.
IndentRows[$]	Indent, in points.
MinimumRowHeight	Minimum row height, in points.
OutlineBorder, TopBorder, BottomBorder, InsideBorder, LeftBorder, RightBorder	Borders can be 0 (zero) for none, 1 for single, 2 for thick, or 3 for double. Outline border can also be 4 for Shadow.
AlignRows	Alignment can be 0 (zero) for left, 1 for center, or 2 for right.
ApplyTo	If 0 (zero), applies the formatting to the selection; if 1, applies the formatting to the entire table.

For related commands, see "Formatting Statements and Functions" in the section "WordBASIC Cross Reference," earlier in this chapter.

FormatTabs

FormatTabs *[Position], [Align], [Leader]*

Equivalent to the Format Tabs dialog box. The *Position* argument is a measurement, in points.

Align argument	Alignment
0	Left
1	Centered
2	Right
3	Decimal

Leader argument	Leader character
0	None
1	Dot
2	Dash
3	Underline

Set is the default action. You can also clear specified tabs or clear all tabs by appending the Clear (**.Clear**) or ClearAll (**.ClearAll**) command button name to the statement. Recording a set of tab actions generates new commands, as shown in the following example:

Statement	Result
`FormatTabs .ClearAll`	Clears all tabs.
`FormatTabs "1.5 in",2, .Set`	Positions a right-aligned tab at 1.5 inches.
`FormatTabs "3 in", .Clear`	Clears the tab at 3 inches.
`FormatTabs "4.5 in"`	Positions a tab at 4.5 inches.

For related commands, see "Formatting Statements and Functions" in the section "WordBASIC Cross Reference," earlier in this chapter.

Function...End Function

Function *Name [ParameterList]*

Statement(s)

End Function

Defines a function. A function returns a single value. If a function should return a string value, the function name must end with a $. *ParameterList* is a list of variables, separated by commas, for receiving arguments to the function. String variables must end with the $ character. *ParameterList* cannot include values. Constants should be declared as variables and passed to the function by variable name.

Example.

```
Sub MAIN
StartOfDocument               'Move insertion to start of document
Mark:                         'Beginning of loop
   If StartDot(1) Then        'Call StartDot with argument of 1
      EndOfLine 1             'Select to end of line
                              'Print message with line where found
      MsgBox"Period found at start of " + Chr$(34)\
      + Selection$() + Chr$(34)
                              'Note that "\" continues statement on
                              'next line
      StartOfLine             'Move insertion back to start of line
   End If
                              'If not at bottom of document, repeat
If LineDown() = -1 Then Goto Mark
End Sub                       'End Main Program
Function StartDot(Flag)       'Start function definition:
                              'Tests for period at beginning of
                              'current selection or in character to
                              'right of current selection point.
                              'If found, 1 is returned. If
                              'argument of 1 is passed to StartDot,
                              'beep sounds when period is found.
If Left$(Selection$(),1) = "." Then
   StartDot = 1               'If period is found, return value of 1.
   If Flag = 1 Then Beep      'If Flag is also 1, beep
End If
End Function                  'StartDot
```

For more information on user-defined functions, see Chapter 5, "The Word-BASIC Programming Language."

For related commands, see "BASIC Statements and Functions" in the section "WordBASIC Cross Reference," earlier in this chapter.

GetBookmark$( )

*A$* = **GetBookmark$(***BookmarkName$***)**

Returns the text without formatting at the specified bookmark. Operation is similar to **Selection$( )**.

For related commands, see "Bookmark Statements and Functions" in the section "WordBASIC Cross Reference," earlier in this chapter.

GetCurValues

GetCurValues *DialogRecord*

Stores in *DialogRecord* the current values for a previously dimensioned dialog box. For more information, see Chapter 2, "Introduction to Macros."

For related commands, see "Dialog Definition and Control Statements and Functions" in the section "WordBASIC Cross Reference," earlier in this chapter.

GetGlossary$( )

*A$* = **GetGlossary$(***Name$, [Context]***)**

Returns the text without formatting of the glossary entry in *Name$*. The *Context* is 0 (zero) for global (default), or 1 for document template.

Function	Result
`New$ = GetGlossary$("Disclaim", 1)` `Print New$`	Sets *New$* to the text in the document template glossary specified by the name `"Disclaim"` and displays the text on the status bar.

For related commands, see "Glossary Statements and Functions" in the section "WordBASIC Cross Reference," earlier in this chapter.

GetProfileString$( )

*A$* = **GetProfileString$(***[App$], Key$***)**

Gets a value from the current WIN.INI or OS2.INI file. *App$* is the name of the application. If the application is not specified, the string `"Microsoft Word"` is used. If the *Key$* is not found, the function returns a null string.

For related commands, see "Environment Statements and Functions" in the section "WordBASIC Cross Reference," earlier in this chapter.

GlossaryName$( )

*A$* = **GlossaryName$(***Count, [Context]***)**

Returns the name of the glossary defined in the given context (global or document template). *Count* can range from 1 to *CountGlossaries(Context)*. The name is taken from the list in the given context. *Context* is 0 (zero) for global, or 1 for document template.

For related commands, see "Glossary Statements and Functions" in the section "WordBASIC Cross Reference," earlier in this chapter.

GoBack

GoBack

Toggles among the last three selections where text or formatting has changed.

For related commands, see "Selection and Insertion Point Definition and Control Statements and Functions" in the section "WordBASIC Cross Reference," earlier in this chapter.

Goto

Goto *Label/LineNumber*

Branches unconditionally to a label. A label can be a line number of 32,000 or less, or it can be a string that consists of an initial letter followed by letters or numbers up to a total length of 40 characters.

Example.

```
.
.
.
If WordCount > 10000 Then Goto Novelette
.
.
.
Novelette:
.
.
.
```

For related commands, see "BASIC Statements and Functions" in the section "WordBASIC Cross Reference," earlier in this chapter.

GroupBox

GroupBox *x, y, dx, dy, Text$*

Creates a box with a title, often used to designate a group of option buttons or check boxes. A **GroupBox** does not have a result.

Example.

```
GroupBox 60, 29, 32, 37, "Status"
```

For related commands, see "Dialog Definition and Control Statements and Functions" in the section "WordBASIC Cross Reference," earlier in this chapter.

GrowFont

GrowFont

Increases the size of the selected font to the next available size supported by the assigned printer. Can be used either on the selection or at the insertion point. If more than one font size is included in the insertion point, each is increased to its next available size.

For related commands, see "Formatting Statements and Functions" in the section "WordBASIC Cross Reference," earlier in this chapter.

HangingIndent

HangingIndent

Sets the left indent of the selection to the next tab stop in the first paragraph. Keeps the first line of the paragraph indented at the current left position.

For related commands, see "Formatting Statements and Functions" in the section "WordBASIC Cross Reference," earlier in this chapter.

Help

Help

Activates Help. Equivalent to pressing F1.

For related commands, see "Help Statements" in the section "WordBASIC Cross Reference," earlier in this chapter.

HelpAbout

HelpAbout

Displays a dialog box that gives the Word version number and copyright information.

For related commands, see "Help Statements" in the section "WordBASIC Cross Reference," earlier in this chapter.

HelpActiveWindow

HelpActiveWindow

Activates Help for the active window.

For related commands, see "Help Statements" in the section "WordBASIC Cross Reference," earlier in this chapter.

HelpContext

HelpContext

Activates context-sensitive Help. Equivalent to pressing Shift+F1.

For related commands, see "Help Statements" in the section "WordBASIC Cross Reference," earlier in this chapter.

HelpIndex

HelpIndex

Displays the list of Help topics.

For related commands, see "Help Statements" in the section "WordBASIC Cross Reference," earlier in this chapter.

HelpKeyboard

HelpKeyboard

Displays the list of keyboard Help topics.

For related commands, see "Help Statements" in the section "WordBASIC Cross Reference," earlier in this chapter.

HelpTutorial

HelpTutorial

Starts the Tutorial.

For related commands, see "Help Statements" in the section "WordBASIC Cross Reference," earlier in this chapter.

HelpUsingHelp

HelpUsingHelp

Activates Help for using Help

For related commands, see "Help Statements" in the section "WordBASIC Cross Reference," earlier in this chapter.

Hidden

Hidden *[On]*

If *On* is omitted and View Preferences Hidden Text is on, toggles hidden text for the entire selection. If View Preferences Hidden Text is off and *On* is omitted, makes the entire selection hidden text. If *On* is nonzero, makes the entire selection hidden text. If *On* is 0 (zero), removes hidden text from the entire selection.

In the following table, hidden text is shown with a dotted underline:

Statement	If text is	New text is
`Hidden`	Trey Research Company	Trey Research Company
`Hidden (Hidden Text on)`	Trey Research Company	Trey Research Company
`Hidden (Hidden Text on)`	Trey Research Company	Trey Research Company
`Hidden 1`	Trey Research Company	Trey Research Company
`Hidden 0`	Trey Research Company	Trey Research Company

For related commands, see "Formatting Statements and Functions" in the section "WordBASIC Cross Reference," earlier in this chapter.

Hidden( )

Num = **Hidden( )**

Returns 0 (zero) if none of the selection is hidden text, 1 if all of the selection is hidden text, or –1 if part of the selection is hidden text.

For related commands, see "Formatting Statements and Functions" in the section "WordBASIC Cross Reference," earlier in this chapter.

HLine

HLine *[Count]*

Scrolls horizontally by *Count* lines. If *Count* is omitted, one line is the default. "Lines" are the amount the screen scrolls when clicking a horizontal scroll bar arrow with a mouse. A positive value for *Count* scrolls the screen to the right. A negative value for *Count* scrolls the screen to the left.

For related commands, see "Selection and Insertion Point Definition and Control Statements and Functions" in the section "WordBASIC Cross Reference," earlier in this chapter.

HPage

HPage *[Count]*

Scrolls horizontally by *Count* screens. If *Count* is omitted, one screen is the default. A positive value for *Count* scrolls the screen to the right. A negative value for *Count* scrolls the screen to the left.

For related commands, see "Selection and Insertion Point Definition and Control Statements and Functions" in the section "WordBASIC Cross Reference," earlier in this chapter.

HScroll

HScroll *Percentage*

Scrolls horizontally the specified percentage of the document width.

For related commands, see "Selection and Insertion Point Definition and Control Statements and Functions" in the section "WordBASIC Cross Reference," earlier in this chapter.

HScroll( )

Num = **HScroll( )**

Returns the current horizontal scroll position as a percentage of the document width.

For related commands, see "Selection and Insertion Point Definition and Control Statements and Functions" in the section "WordBASIC Cross Reference," earlier in this chapter.

IconBarMode

IconBarMode

Equivalent to pressing Shift+F10. Places the cursor in the icon bar, allowing a selection to be made using the cursor keys. Until a selection is made, the macro suspends operation, and the mouse pointer becomes an hourglass to indicate that the macro is still in operation. If a selection is not made, an error 102 (*Command Failed*) occurs.

For related commands, see "Mode Statements and Functions" in the section "WordBASIC Cross Reference," earlier in this chapter.

If...ElseIf...Else...End If

If *Condition* **Then** *Statement(s)* [**Else** *Statement(s)*]

If *Condition1* **Then**
    Statement(s)
[**ElseIf** *Condition2* **Then**
    Statement(s)]
[**Else**
    Statement(s)]
End If

Performs conditional execution or branching, depending on the expressions. The conditions in an **If...ElseIf...Else...End If** block can be any string, numeric, or Boolean expression in WordBASIC.

For more information, see Chapter 5, "WordBASIC Language." For related commands, see "BASIC Statements and Functions" in the section "WordBASIC Cross Reference," earlier in this chapter.

Indent

Indent

Indents the selected paragraphs. The indent is aligned with the next tab stop of the first paragraph in the selection. **Indent** does not change the setting of a first-line indent.

For related commands, see "Formatting Statements and Functions" in the section "WordBASIC Cross Reference," earlier in this chapter.

Input

Input *[#]StreamNumber, Variable, [Variable]*

Input *[Prompt$,] Variable, [Variable]*

Each input statement reads one line from the file specified by *#StreamNumber* into the variables listed. The line read from the file is separated into individual values by commas. In the source file, precede a comma with a space to avoid truncating the final character of each value. Spaces following a comma in the source file are input as a leading space for the value following. No more than 256 characters can be read in. Consequently, this statement should not be used on Word document or template files, or an error will be generated.

If a *StreamNumber* is not specified, the user is prompted in the status bar for keyboard input. The prompt ? is always displayed. An optional prompt string can also be supplied.

Examples.

Statement	Result
`Input#1, Name$, ZipCode`	Reads a line from stream #1 into the variables `Name$` and `ZipCode`.
`Input "File Search Mask", Mask$`	Displays the prompt `File Search Mask?` and loads the resulting keyboard input into the variable `Mask$`.

For related commands, see "BASIC Statements and Functions" and "File Statements and Functions" in the section "WordBASIC Cross Reference," earlier in this chapter.

Input$( )

*A$* = **Input$(***n, StreamNumber***)**

Reads *n* characters from the file specified by *StreamNumber*.

For related commands, see "BASIC Statements and Functions" and "File Statements and Functions" in the section "WordBASIC Cross Reference," earlier in this chapter.

InputBox$( )

*A$* = **InputBox$(***Prompt$, [Title$], [Default$]***)**

Displays a dialog box that can be edited. Returns the text that was in the box when OK was chosen. If *Title$* is omitted, `"Microsoft Word"` is used in the title bar. If you specified a default, it is loaded into the dialog box when it is displayed.

Example.

```
FilesPrn$ = InputBox$("File(s) to print?","Night Shift", "?????LTR.DOC")
```

For related commands, see "BASIC Statements and Functions" and "File Statements and Functions" in the section "WordBASIC Cross Reference," earlier in this chapter.

Insert

Insert *Text$*

Inserts the given text at the insertion point. Nonprinting characters are inserted as **Chr$(*n*)** statements, as shown in the following table:

Value	Character inserted
Chr$(9)	Tab
Chr$(11)	Linefeed (newline character)
Chr$(13)	Paragraph mark
Chr$(30)	Nonbreaking hyphen
Chr$(31)	Optional hyphen
Chr$(34)	Quotation marks
Chr$(160)	Nonbreaking space (Windows only)
Chr$(22)	Nonbreaking space (OS/2 only)

Statement	Result
`Insert "Hamlet"`	`Hamlet`
`Insert Chr$(34) + "Hamlet" + Chr$(34)`	`"Hamlet"`

For related commands, see "BASIC Statements and Functions" in the section "WordBASIC Cross Reference," earlier in this chapter.

InsertBookmark

InsertBookmark *Name$*

Equivalent to the Insert Bookmark dialog box. Creates or deletes the named bookmark. If the Delete command button name (**.Delete**) is appended, the bookmark is deleted. If the Delete command button name is not specified, the bookmark is created at the current selection. If you specify a nonexistent bookmark for deletion, an error is generated.

Statement	Result
`InsertBookmark "begin"`	Inserts the bookmark "`begin`" at the current selection or insertion point.
`InsertBookmark "begin", .Delete`	Deletes the bookmark "`begin`".

For related commands, see "Bookmark Statements and Functions" in the section "WordBASIC Cross Reference," earlier in this chapter.

InsertBreak

InsertBreak *Type*

Equivalent to the Insert Break dialog box. Inserts a page, section, or column break at the current selection.

Type argument	Break type
0	Page
1	Column

The following are section breaks:

Type argument	Break type
2	Next Page
3	Continuous
4	Even Page
5	Odd Page

For related commands, see "Formatting Statements and Functions" in the section "WordBASIC Cross Reference," earlier in this chapter.

InsertColumnBreak

InsertColumnBreak

Inserts a column break at the insertion point. If the insertion point is in a table, the break is inserted above the row in which the insertion point is located.

For related commands, see "Formatting Statements and Functions" and "Table Creation and Editing Statements and Functions" in the section "WordBASIC Cross Reference," earlier in this chapter.

InsertDateField

InsertDateField

Inserts a DATE field at the selection. If a header or footer pane is open, inserts the field in the header or footer. For more information on using fields, see Chapter 9, "Fields."

For related commands, see "Field Statements and Functions" in the section "WordBASIC Cross Reference," earlier in this chapter.

InsertField

InsertField *Field$*

Equivalent to the Insert Field dialog box. Inserts the specified field at the selection. Do not include the field characters in *Field$*, but follow all other syntax rules for field codes. To insert quotation marks in field codes, use Chr$(34). For more information on inserting fields, see Chapter 9, "Fields."

Examples.

```
InsertField "Author"
InsertField "Date \@" + Chr$(34) + "MMMM d, yyyy" + Chr$(34)
```

For related commands, see "Field Statements and Functions" in the section "WordBASIC Cross Reference," earlier in this chapter.

InsertFieldChars

InsertFieldChars

Inserts field characters ({ }) at the selection. For more information on inserting fields, see Chapter 9, "Fields."

For related commands, see "Field Statements and Functions" in the section "WordBASIC Cross Reference," earlier in this chapter.

InsertFile

InsertFile *Name$, [Range$], [Link]*

Equivalent to the Insert File dialog box. Inserts the named file at the current selection.

If *Name$* refers to a Word document, *Range$* refers to a bookmark. If *Name$* refers to another document type (for example, a Microsoft Excel worksheet), then *Range$* refers to a named range. Only that part of the file is inserted. If *Link* is nonzero, an INCLUDE field is inserted instead of the text of the file itself. If *Link* is nonzero, to link the entire file, specify a null *Range$* with quotation marks. For more information about fields, see Chapter 9, "Fields."

Statement	Result
`InsertFile "PRICES.TXT"`	Inserts the contents of the file PRICES.TXT into the current document.
`InsertFile "PRICES.DOC","sportscars"`	Inserts the portion of PRICES.DOC associated with the bookmark `"sportscars"` into the current document.
`InsertFile "PRICES.DOC", "sportscars", 1`	{INCLUDE PRICES.DOC sportscars}
`InsertFile "PRICES.DOC", "", -1`	{INCLUDE PRICES.DOC}

For related commands, see "Editing Commands and Statements" and "File Statements and Functions" in the section "WordBASIC Cross Reference," earlier in this chapter.

InsertFootnote

InsertFootnote *[Reference$]*

Equivalent to the Insert Footnote dialog box. Inserts a footnote at the current selection.

Reference$ is the footnote reference marker that you supply. If no marker is supplied, an automatically numbered footnote reference is inserted.

To insert a footnote separator, a continued footnote separator, or a notice for continued footnotes, append the Separator (**.Separator**), ContSeparator (**.ContSeparator**), or ContNotice (**.ContNotice**) command button name, respectively. These buttons open a pane for editing the specified separator and place the insertion point in that pane.

For related commands, see "Formatting Statements and Functions" in the section "WordBASIC Cross Reference," earlier in this chapter.

InsertIndex

InsertIndex *[Type], [HeadingSeparator], [Replace]*

Equivalent to the Insert Index dialog box. Inserts an INDEX field at the current selection.

Type is 0 (zero) for a normal index (default), or 1 for a run-in index. *HeadingSeparator* is 0 (zero) for none (default), 1 for a blank line, or 2 for a letter.

If *Replace* is 1, any existing index is overwritten. If *Replace* is omitted or 0 (zero), the user is prompted before an existing index is overwritten.

For more information about fields, see Chapter 9, "Fields." For related commands, see "Field Statements and Functions" in the section "WordBASIC Cross Reference," earlier in this chapter.

InsertIndexEntry

InsertIndexEntry *[Entry$], [Range$], [Bold], [Italic]*

Equivalent to the Insert Index Entry dialog box. Inserts an XE field at the current selection. If *Entry$* is omitted, the selection is the entry. *Range$* is the name of a bookmark that specifies the range of text to which the index entry applies. The *Bold* and *Italic* arguments correspond to check boxes.

For more information about fields, see Chapter 9, "Fields." For related commands, see "Field Statements and Functions" in the section "WordBASIC Cross Reference," earlier in this chapter.

InsertPageBreak

InsertPageBreak

Inserts a page break at the current selection.

For related commands, see "Formatting Statements and Functions" in the section "WordBASIC Cross Reference," earlier in this chapter.

InsertPageField

InsertPageField

Inserts a PAGE field at the current selection. If a header or footer pane is open, inserts the field in the header or footer.

For more information about fields, see Chapter 9, "Fields." For related commands, see "Field Statements and Functions" in the section "WordBASIC Cross Reference," earlier in this chapter.

InsertPageNumbers

InsertPageNumbers *[Type], [Position]*

Equivalent to the Insert Page Numbers dialog box. Inserts a PAGE field into the header or footer. Prompts to replace the current header or footer with a simple page-number header or footer.

Type is 0 (zero) for header, or 1 for footer. *Position* is 0 (zero) for left-aligned, 1 for centered, or 2 for right-aligned. Be aware that **InsertPageNumbers**, like the Insert Page Numbers command, turns on the Different First Page option and turns off the Different Odd and Even Pages option in the Edit Header/Footer dialog box.

For more information about fields, see Chapter 9, "Fields." For related commands, see "Field Statements and Functions" in the section "WordBASIC Cross Reference," earlier in this chapter.

InsertPara

InsertPara

Inserts a paragraph mark at the current selection.

For related commands, see "Formatting Statements and Functions" in the section "WordBASIC Cross Reference," earlier in this chapter.

InsertPicture

InsertPicture *[Filename$]*

Equivalent to the Insert Picture dialog box. Inserts an IMPORT field at the current selection. If *Filename$* is not supplied and the New Picture command button name (**.NewPicture**) is appended, a 1-inch graphic frame with a single border is inserted.

For more information about fields, see Chapter 9, "Fields." For related commands, see "Formatting Statements and Functions" in the section "WordBASIC Cross Reference," earlier in this chapter.

InsertTable

InsertTable *[NumColumns], [NumRows], [InitialColWidth[$]], [ConvertFrom]*

Equivalent to the Insert Table dialog box. Choosing the **Format** option is recorded with a **FormatTable** statement following **InsertTable**.

Argument	Description
NumColumns	Number of columns in table.
NumRows	Number of rows in table.
InitialColWidth[$]	Width of columns in points.
ConvertFrom	Can be 0 (zero) for paragraphs, 1 for tab-delimited text, or 2 for comma-delimited text.

For related commands, see "Formatting Statements and Functions" and "Table Creation and Editing Statements and Functions" in the section "WordBASIC Cross Reference," earlier in this chapter.

InsertTableOfContents

InsertTableOfContents *[Source], [From], [To], [Replace]*

Equivalent to the Insert Table Of Contents dialog box. Inserts a TOC field at the current selection. For more information about fields, see Chapter 9, "Fields."

Source is 0 (zero) for outline headings or 1 for table entry fields. *From* and *To* are numbers that refer to the outline levels used. If you omit *From* and *To* but include *Replace*, insert quoted null strings as position holders for *From* and *To*. If *Replace* is 1, any existing table of contents is overwritten. If *Replace* is omitted or 0 (zero), the user is prompted before an existing table of contents is overwritten.

For related commands, see "Field Statements and Functions" in the section "WordBASIC Cross Reference," earlier in this chapter.

InsertTableToText

InsertTableToText *[ConvertTo]*

Equivalent to Insert Table To Text dialog box. Converts the selected cells to normal text.

ConvertTo can be 0 (zero) for paragraphs, 1 for tab-delimited text, or 2 for comma-delimited text.

For related commands, see "Formatting Statements and Functions" and "Table Creation and Editing Statements and Functions" in the section "WordBASIC Cross Reference," earlier in this chapter.

InsertTimeField

InsertTimeField

Inserts a TIME field at the current selection. If a header or footer pane is open, inserts the field in the header or footer.

For more information about fields, see Chapter 9, "Fields." For related commands, see "Field Statements and Functions" in the section "WordBASIC Cross Reference," earlier in this chapter.

InStr( )

Num = **InStr(***[Index], Source$, Search$***)**

Searches for *Search$* in *Source$*. Returns the number of the character where *Search$* started, or 0 (zero) if *Search$* is not found in *Source$*. If *Index* is supplied, the search starts at character *Index*.

Statement	Result
`InStr("Testing","ing")`	5
`InStr("Microsoft","o")`	5
`InStr(6,"Microsoft","o")`	7

For related commands, see "BASIC Statements and Functions" in the section "WordBASIC Cross Reference," earlier in this chapter.

Int( )

Num = **Int(***n***)**

Returns the integer part of *n*.

Function	Return value
`Int(98.6)`	98
`Int(-9.6)`	–9

For related commands, see "BASIC Statements and Functions" in the section "WordBASIC Cross Reference," earlier in this chapter.

IsDirty( )

Log = **IsDirty( )**

Returns –1 if the document has been changed (made "dirty") since the last time it was saved, or 0 (zero) if the document has not changed.

For related commands, see "Environment Statements and Functions" in the section "WordBASIC Cross Reference," earlier in this chapter.

Italic

Italic *[On]*

If *On* is omitted, toggles italic for the entire selection. If *On* is nonzero, makes the entire selection italic. If *On* is 0 (zero), removes italic from the entire selection.

Statement	If text is	New text is
`Italic`	Trey Research Company	*Trey Research Company*
`Italic`	Trey *Research* Company	*Trey Research Company*
`Italic`	*Trey Research Company*	Trey Research Company
`Italic 1`	Trey Research Company	*Trey Research Company*
`Italic 0`	Trey *Research* Company	Trey Research Company

For related commands, see "Formatting Statements and Functions" in the section "WordBASIC Cross Reference," earlier in this chapter.

Italic( )

Num = **Italic( )**

Returns 0 (zero) if none of the selection is italic, 1 if all of the selection is italic, or –1 if part of the selection is italic.

If selected text is	Function returns
Trey Research	0 (zero); the selection is not italic
Trey Research	1; the entire selection is italic
Trey Research	–1; only part of the selection is italic

For related commands, see "Formatting Statements and Functions" in the section "WordBASIC Cross Reference," earlier in this chapter.

JustifyPara

JustifyPara

Justifies the selected paragraphs.

For related commands, see "Formatting Statements and Functions" in the section "WordBASIC Cross Reference," earlier in this chapter.

JustifyPara( )

Num = **JustifyPara( )**

Returns 0 (zero) if none of the selected paragraphs is justified, 1 if all of the selected paragraphs are justified, or –1 if more than one kind of paragraph alignment is used.

For related commands, see "Formatting Statements and Functions" in the section "WordBASIC Cross Reference," earlier in this chapter.

Kill

Kill *Name$*

Deletes the file specified by *Name$*.

Example.

```
Kill "C:\OS2\WORD\LETTERS\DRAFT.DOC"
```

For related commands, see "BASIC Statements and Functions" and "File Statements and Functions" in the section "WordBASIC Cross Reference," earlier in this chapter.

LCase$( )

*A$* = **LCase$(***Source$***)**

Returns *Source$* converted to lowercase.

For related commands, see "Formatting Statements and Functions" in the section "WordBASIC Cross Reference," earlier in this chapter.

Left$( )

*A$* = **Left$(***Source$*, *n***)**

Returns the leftmost *n* characters of *Source$*.

Function	Return value
`A$ = "Legal File List"` `Print Left$(A$,5)`	`Legal`
`A$ = "Legal File List"` `Print Left$(A$,10)`	`Legal File`

For related commands, see "BASIC Statements and Functions" in the section "WordBASIC Cross Reference," earlier in this chapter.

LeftPara

LeftPara

Left-aligns the selected paragraphs.

For related commands, see "Formatting Statements and Functions" in the section "WordBASIC Cross Reference," earlier in this chapter.

LeftPara( )

Num = **LeftPara( )**

Returns 0 (zero) if none of the selected paragraphs is left-aligned, 1 if all of the selected paragraphs are left-aligned, or –1 if more than one kind of paragraph alignment is used.

For related commands, see "Formatting Statements and Functions" in the section "WordBASIC Cross Reference," earlier in this chapter.

Len( )

Num = **Len(***Source$***)**

Returns the number of characters in *Source$*.

Function	Return value
`A$ = "Trey Research"`	
`Print Len(A$)`	13

For related commands, see "BASIC Statements and Functions" in the section "WordBASIC Cross Reference," earlier in this chapter.

Let

[**Let**] *Var* = *Expression*

Assigns the value of an expression to a variable. **Let** is optional and not commonly used. The following assignment statements are all valid.

Example.

```
Let A = 100
Let Discount = Gross - (Gross * .10)
Let StockNum$ = "AB4100-2"
A = 100
Discount = Gross - (Gross * .10)
StockNum$ = "AB4100-2"
```

For related commands, see "BASIC Statements and Functions" in the section "WordBASIC Cross Reference," earlier in this chapter.

LineDown

LineDown *[Repeat], [Select]*

Moves the insertion point down by *Repeat* lines. If *Repeat* is omitted, 1 is assumed. If *Select* is nonzero, the selection is extended down by *Repeat* lines.

Statement	Result
`LineDown 1, 1`	Extends the selection down one line from the insertion point.

For related commands, see "Selection and Insertion Point Definition and Control Statements and Functions" in the section "WordBASIC Cross Reference," earlier in this chapter.

LineDown( )

Log = **LineDown(***[Repeat], [Select]***)**

Moves the insertion point down by *Repeat* lines. If *Repeat* is omitted, 1 is assumed. If *Select* is nonzero, the selection is extended down by *Repeat* lines. Returns 0 (zero) if the action cannot be completed.

Function	Result
`While LineDown(,1)` `Wend`	Extends the selection one line at a time until the end of the document is reached.

For related commands, see "Selection and Insertion Point Definition and Control Statements and Functions" in the section "WordBASIC Cross Reference," earlier in this chapter.

Line Input

Line Input *[#]StreamNumber, Variable$*

Line Input *[Prompt$,]*

Reads an entire line from the file specified by *StreamNumber* and puts the result in the specified string variable. No more than 256 characters can be read in. Consequently, this statement should not be used on Word document or template files, or an error will be generated.

If *StreamNumber* is omitted, the user is prompted with a question mark (**?**) in the status bar for keyboard input. An optional prompt string can also be supplied. If *Prompt$* is supplied, **?** is not included.

Line Input is similar to the **Input** statement, but **Line Input** does not break the line into separate values at commas, places its result in a single string variable, and does not include a question mark with a supplied prompt string.

Statement	Result
`Line Input #1, Sample$`	Loads one line from the file attached to stream #1 into the variable `Sample$`.
`Line Input Key$`	Places the prompt **?** in the status bar and places the resulting keyboard input into the string variable `Key$`.
`Line Input "Search text:", Target$`	Places the prompt `Search text:` in the status bar and loads the resulting keyboard input into the string variable `Target$`.
`Line Input "", Code$`	Accepts keyboard input in the status bar but displays no prompt. Loads the resulting keyboard input into the string variable `Code$`.

For related commands, see "BASIC Statements and Functions" in the section "WordBASIC Cross Reference," earlier in this chapter.

LineUp

LineUp *[Repeat], [Select]*

Moves the insertion point up by *Repeat* lines. If *Repeat* is omitted, 1 is assumed. If *Select* is nonzero, the selection is extended up by *Repeat* lines. If *Select* is 0 (zero) or omitted, the selection is not extended.

Statement	Result
`LineUp 20`	Moves the selection point up 20 lines from the insertion point, and collapses any selection.

For related commands, see "Selection and Insertion Point Definition and Control Statements and Functions" in the section "WordBASIC Cross Reference," earlier in this chapter.

LineUp( )

Log = **LineUp(***[Repeat], [Select]***)**

Moves the insertion point up by *Repeat* lines. Returns 0 (zero) if the action cannot be completed. If *Repeat* is omitted, 1 is assumed. If *Select* is nonzero, the selection is extended up by *Repeat* lines. If *Select* is 0 (zero) or omitted, the selection is not extended. For example, the function returns 0 (zero) if the insertion point is at the beginning of the document.

For related commands, see "Selection and Insertion Point Definition and Control Statements and Functions" in the section "WordBASIC Cross Reference," earlier in this chapter.

ListBox

ListBox *x, y, dx, dy, ArrayVariable$, .Field*

Creates a list box filled with the strings in *ArrayVariable$*. After the dialog box is used, the value returned from *.Field* becomes the index in *ArrayVariable$* of the user's selection.

Example.

```
ListBox 6, 31, 49, 33, Arr$(), .LB
```

For related commands, see "Dialog Definition and Control Statements and Functions" in the section "WordBASIC Cross Reference," earlier in this chapter.

LockFields

LockFields

Prevents the fields within the selection from being updated.

For related commands, see "Field Statements and Functions" in the section "WordBASIC Cross Reference," earlier in this chapter.

Lof( )

Num = **Lof(***StreamNumber***)**

Returns the length of the file, in bytes.

Example.

```
Sub MAIN                              'Start "How Big?"
   Dim HowBig As FileOpen             'Create dialog record
                                      'File Open dialog equivalent used
   GetCurValues HowBig                'Move dialog record to dialog box
   Dialog HowBig                      'Display dialog box for input
                                      'User selects file
   Open Howbig.Name For Input As #1'Open selects file as sequential file
                                      'Connect to stream number one
      Size = Lof(1)                   'Load file size into variable "Size"
      Print Size                      'Display file size in status bar
   Close                              'Close file
End Sub                               'End program
```

For related commands, see "BASIC Statements and Functions" and "File Statements and Functions" in the section "WordBASIC Cross Reference," earlier in this chapter.

MacroAssignToKey

MacroAssignToKey *[Name$], [KeyCode], [Context]*

Equivalent to the Macro Assign To Key dialog box. You can assign a macro to a key or key combination.

Assigns the macro *Name$* to the specified *KeyCode*. *KeyCode* is a number representing the exact key. The numbers are not equivalent to those in the **SendKeys** syntax. *Context* is 0 (zero) for global, or 1 for document template.

Assign is the default action. The ResetAll command button name (**.ResetAll**) can be appended to return the key assignments to the default state. Appending the UnAssign command button name (**.UnAssign**) removes a macro connection to a specific key. To reset an assigned key to its original assignment, first use a **MacroAssignToKey** statement with the UnAssign button appended. Then, use a **MacroAssignToKey** statement to reassign the key to its original assignment.

Add this	For this key
256	Ctrl+
512	Shift+
1024	Alt+

Key code	Produces
8	Backspace
9	Tab
12	5 on numeric keypad when NumLock is off
13	Enter
27	Esc
32	Space
33	PgUp
34	PgDn
35	End
36	Home
45	Ins
46	Del
48	0
49	1
50	2
51	3
52	4
53	5
54	6
55	7
56	8

(continued)

Continued

Key code	Produces
57	9
65	A
66	B
67	C
68	D
69	E
70	F
71	G
72	H
73	I
74	J
75	K
76	L
77	M
78	N
79	O
80	P
81	Q
82	R
83	S
84	T
85	U
86	V
87	W
88	X
89	Y
90	Z
96	0 on numeric keypad
97	1 on numeric keypad
98	2 on numeric keypad
99	3 on numeric keypad
100	4 on numeric keypad
101	5 on numeric keypad

(continued)

Continued

Key code	Produces
102	6 on numeric keypad
103	7 on numeric keypad
104	8 on numeric keypad
105	9 on numeric keypad
106	* on numeric keypad
107	+ on numeric keypad
108	' on numeric keypad
109	– on numeric keypad
110	. on numeric keypad
111	/ on numeric keypad
112	F1
113	F2
114	F3
115	F4
116	F5
117	F6
118	F7
119	F8
120	F9
121	F10
122	F11 (Alt+F11 = Alt+F1; Windows limitation)
123	F12 (Alt+F12 = Alt+F2; Windows limitation)
124	F13 (Alt+F13 = Alt+F3; Windows limitation)
125	F14 (Alt+F14 = Alt+F4; Windows limitation)
126	F15 (Alt+F15 = Alt+F5; Windows limitation)
127	F16 (Alt+F16 = Alt+F6; Windows limitation)

Examples.

Statement	Result
`MacroAssignToKey "", 322, .Unassign`	Unassigns Ctrl+B from its current assignment.
`MacroAssignToKey "Bold", 322`	Assigns Bold to Ctrl+B.

For related commands, see "Macro Control, Creation, and Editing Statements and Functions" in the section "WordBASIC Cross Reference," earlier in this chapter.

MacroAssignToMenu

MacroAssignToMenu *Name$, Menu$, MenuText$, [Context]*

Equivalent to the Macro Assign To Menu dialog box. Assigns the macro *Name$* to the specified *Menu$* with *MenuText$*. *Menu$* can be &File, &Edit, &View, &Insert, Forma&t, &Utilities, &Macro, or &Window. *Menu$* must match the menu name in the menu bar, with & in front of the underlined character. *Context* is 0 (zero) for global, or 1 for document template.

Assign is the default action. You can append the ResetAll (**.ResetAll**) command button name to return the menu assignments to the default state or UnAssign (**.UnAssign**) to remove a macro from a menu.

For related commands, see "Macro Control, Creation, and Editing Statements and Functions" in the section "WordBASIC Cross Reference," earlier in this chapter.

MacroEdit

MacroEdit *Name$, [Context], [Description$], [ShowAll], [NewName$]*

Equivalent to the Macro Edit dialog box. Displays the *Name$* macro for editing. *Context* is 0 (zero) for global (default), or 1 for document template. The *Description$* refers to the text that appears in the status bar if the macro is assigned to a menu.

The *ShowAll* argument lists all Word commands as well as the macros you have created.

If the command button name Rename, Delete, or Set is used and followed by another action, multiple **MacroEdit** commands are recorded.

The *NewName$* argument specifies a new name for the macro; this argument is used with the Rename command button.

For related commands, see "Macro Control, Creation, and Editing Statements and Functions" in the section "WordBASIC Cross Reference," earlier in this chapter.

MacroName$( )

*A$* = **MacroName$(***Count, [Context], [All]***)**

Returns the name of the macro defined in the given context. *Count* can range from *1* to *CountMacros(Context)*. The name is taken from the list in the given context. **MacroName$(0)** gives the name of the current macro window, if any. *Context* is 0 (zero) for global, or 1 for document template. If *All* is True, built-in commands are included and are numbered before macros you created. Word contains over 230 built-in commands.

For related commands, see "Macro Control, Creation, and Editing Statements and Functions" in the section "WordBASIC Cross Reference," earlier in this chapter.

MacroRecord

MacroRecord *[Name$], [Context], [Description$]*

Equivalent to the File Record macro and the Macro Record dialog boxes. Starts the macro recorder. If *Name$* is not given, the next default recording name (Macro*n*) is used. *Context* is 0 (zero) for global (default), or 1 for document template. The *Description$* is the text that appears in the status bar if the macro is assigned to a menu.

For related commands, see "Macro Control, Creation, and Editing Statements and Functions" in the section "WordBASIC Cross Reference," earlier in this chapter.

MacroRun

MacroRun *Name$, [ShowAll]*

Equivalent to the Macro Run dialog box. Runs the named macro or command. If *ShowAll* is 1, built-in commands are included. In every case, *ShowAll* is optional.

For related commands, see "Macro Control, Creation, and Editing Statements and Functions" in the section "WordBASIC Cross Reference," earlier in this chapter.

MenuMode

MenuMode

Activates menu mode. Equivalent to pressing Alt or F10.

For related commands, see "Mode Statements and Functions" in the section "WordBASIC Cross Reference," earlier in this chapter.

Mid$( )

Num = **Mid$(***Source$, Index, [Count]***)**

Returns *Count* characters from *Source$*, starting at character *Index*. If *Count* is not supplied, the rest of the string is returned.

Function	Return value
`Print Mid$("ABCDEFGH", 2, 3)`	`BCD`
`Print Mid$("ABCDEFGH", 2)`	`BCDEFGH`

For related commands, see "BASIC Statements and Functions" in the section "WordBASIC Cross Reference," earlier in this chapter.

MkDir

MkDir *Name$*

Creates the directory specified by *Name$*.

Example.

```
MkDir"E:\PROGRAMS\EXCEL"
```

For related commands, see "BASIC Statements and Functions" and "File Statements and Functions" in the section "WordBASIC Cross Reference," earlier in this chapter.

MoveText

MoveText

Moves text. Equivalent to pressing F2. To use this statement, include in the macro statements for the following series of steps:

1. Make a selection.
2. Run **MoveText**.
3. Position the insertion point where you want to move the text.
4. Run **OK** (or press Enter).

For related commands, see "Editing Commands and Functions" in the section "WordBASIC Cross Reference," earlier in this chapter.

MsgBox

MsgBox *Message$, [Title$], [Type]*

Creates a message box that displays *Message$*.

Title$* is the title of the message box. If *Title$ is omitted, `"Microsoft Word"` is the title of the message box. *Type* determines the symbol and buttons displayed in the box. It is the sum of values from the following groups:

Type of argument	Argument value	Result
Button	0	OK button (default).
	1	OK and Cancel buttons.
	2	Abort, Retry, Ignore buttons.
	3	Yes, No, Cancel buttons.
	4	Yes and No buttons.
	5	Retry and Cancel buttons.
Icons	0	No icon (default).
	16	Stop icon.
	32	Question icon.
	48	Attention icon.
	64	Information icon.
Button action	0	First button is the default (default).
	256	Second button is the default.
	512	Third button is the default.

If you include a nonzero *Type*, you must include a *Title$*, even if you want the title to be "Microsoft Word." If you omit *Title$*, you see a *Type* zero message box.

Examples.

Statement	Result
`MsgBox "Unable to find file", "Microsoft Word", 16`	Message box with title of `"Microsoft Word"`, message of `"Unable to find file"`, OK button, and Stop icon (0 + 16 + 0 = 16).
`MsgBox "Delete File?", "Librarian", 289`	Message box with title of `"Librarian"`, message of `"Delete File?"`, OK button, Cancel button, Question icon, and second (Cancel) button as the default (1 + 32 + 256 = 289).

If *Type* is a negative value, the message is displayed in the status bar and *Type* must be –1 (display the message until another message replaces it), –2 (display until a mouse or key event occurs), or –8 (use the entire status bar width until a mouse or key event occurs).

Because **MsgBox** does not return a value, the use of button values other than 0 (zero) is not recommended. To make use of buttons other than the OK button, use the **MsgBox( )** function.

For related commands, see "Dialog Definition and Control Statements and Functions" in the section "WordBASIC Cross Reference," earlier in this chapter.

MsgBox( )

Num = **MsgBox(***Message$, [Title$], [Type]***)**

Message$*, *Title$, and *Type* are used the same way they are used in **MsgBox**.

Returns one of the following values:

Return value	Button pressed	Button text
–1	Leftmost button	OK
		Yes
		Abort
0	Next button	Cancel
		No
		Retry
1	Next button	Cancel
		Ignore

If *Type* is a negative value, **MsgBox( )** always returns 0 (zero).

For related commands, see "Dialog Definition and Control Statements and Functions" in the section "WordBASIC Cross Reference," earlier in this chapter.

Name

Name *OldName$* **As** *NewName$*

Renames a file. If the file name specified by *NewName$* already exists, an error is generated.

Statement	Result
`Name "COGS.DOC" As "COGS88.DOC"`	Renames the file COGS.DOC as COGS88.DOC.
`Name "COGS.DOC" As "JSY_R2.DOC"`	Renames the file COGS.DOC as JSY_R2.DOC.

For related commands, see "BASIC Statements and Functions" and "File Statements and Functions" in the section "WordBASIC Cross Reference," earlier in this chapter.

NextCell

NextCell

Selects the next cell in a table. If more than one cell is already selected, selects contents of first cell in selection. If there is no next cell, a new row is added to the table.

For related commands, see "Selection and Insertion Point Definition and Control Statements and Functions" and "Table Creation and Editing Statements and Functions" in the section "WordBASIC Cross Reference," earlier in this chapter.

NextCell( )

Log = **NextCell( )**

Selects the contents of the next cell. If more than one cell is already selected, selects contents of first cell in selection. Returns 0 (zero) if there is no next cell.

For related commands, see "Selection and Insertion Point Definition and Control Statements and Functions" and "Table Creation and Editing Statements and Functions" in the section "WordBASIC Cross Reference," earlier in this chapter.

NextField

NextField

Moves the selection to the next field that has a result. Skips over marker fields, such as Index Entry (XE) fields.

For more information about fields, see Chapter 9, "Fields." For related commands, see "Selection and Insertion Point Definition and Control Statements and Functions" and "Field Statements and Functions" in the section "WordBASIC Cross Reference," earlier in this chapter.

NextField( )

Log = **NextField( )**

Moves to the next field. Returns 0 (zero) if there is no next field.

For related commands, see "Selection and Insertion Point Definition and Control Statements and Functions" and "Field Statements and Functions" in the section "WordBASIC Cross Reference," earlier in this chapter.

NextObject

NextObject

Selects the next object in print preview or moves to the next text area in page view.

For related commands, see "Selection and Insertion Point Definition and Control Statements and Functions" in the section "WordBASIC Cross Reference," earlier in this chapter.

NextObject( )

Log = **NextObject( )**

Selects the next object in print preview or moves to the next text area in page view. Returns 0 (zero) if there is no next object.

For related commands, see "Selection and Insertion Point Definition and Control Statements and Functions" and "View Control Statements and Functions" in the section "WordBASIC Cross Reference," earlier in this chapter.

NextPage

NextPage

Moves the insertion point to the beginning of the next page in page view.

For related commands, see "Selection and Insertion Point Definition and Control Statements and Functions" and "View Control Statements and Functions" in the section "WordBASIC Cross Reference," earlier in this chapter.

NextPage( )

Log = **NextPage( )**

Moves the insertion point to the beginning of the next page in page view. Returns 0 (zero) if there is no next page.

For related commands, see "Selection and Insertion Point Definition and Control Statements and Functions" and "View Control Statements and Functions" in the section "WordBASIC Cross Reference," earlier in this chapter.

NextTab( )

Num = **NextTab(***Pos***)**

Returns the position of the next tab stop to the right of the position given by *Pos*. *Pos* is a floating-point number given in points. If more than one paragraph is selected and the tabs do not all match, –1 is returned.

For related commands, see "Selection and Insertion Point Definition and Control Statements and Functions" in the section "WordBASIC Cross Reference," earlier in this chapter.

NextWindow

NextWindow

Activates the next window.

For related commands, see "Selection and Insertion Point Definition and Control Statements and Functions" and "Window Control Statements and Functions" in the section "WordBASIC Cross Reference," earlier in this chapter.

NormalStyle

NormalStyle

Formats the selection with Normal style.

For related commands, see "Formatting Statements and Functions" in the section "WordBASIC Cross Reference," earlier in this chapter.

NormalStyle( )

Num = **NormalStyle( )**

Returns 1 if all of the selection has the Normal style, 0 (zero) if none of the selection has the Normal style, and –1 if part of the selection has the Normal style.

For related commands, see "Formatting Statements and Functions" in the section "WordBASIC Cross Reference," earlier in this chapter.

OK

OK

Terminates a copy or move operation and performs its action.

For related commands, see "Editing Commands and Functions" in the section "WordBASIC Cross Reference," earlier in this chapter.

OKButton and CancelButton

OKButton *x, y, dx, dy*

CancelButton *x, y, dx, dy*

Used as part of a user dialog definition, these commands create OK and Cancel buttons that the user chooses to terminate the dialog box. If the user chooses the OK button, the macro continues. If the user chooses the Cancel button, an error is generated. This error can be trapped with **On Error**. For more information on error handling, see Chapter 6, "More WordBASIC Programming Concepts" and individual entries for **On Error, Error** and **Err** in this chapter.

For related commands, see "Dialog Definition and Control Statements and Functions" in the section "WordBASIC Cross Reference," earlier in this chapter.

On Error

On Error Goto *Label*

On Error Resume Next

On Error Goto 0

The **On Error** control structure sets an error "trap" that causes a specific action to execute when an error occurs. The influence of an **On Error** statement is local to the portion of the program in which it occurs. It is possible (and necessary, if you want to trap all errors) for the main line and each subroutine of a program to have their own **On Error** statement and error-handling routine. When a subroutine is called, the local **On Error** statement (if any) is in effect. After control is returned to the main program, the main **On Error** statement is again in effect. It is not necessary to repeat the main **On Error** statement after calling a subroutine.

The form **On Error Goto** *Label* jumps from the line where the error occurred to the specified label. The statements following this label can then determine the nature of the error (using the special **Err** variable) and take some appropriate action to correct or resolve the problem. For more information, see the individual listing for **Err**, earlier in this chapter.

The form **On Error Resume Next** is the simplest type of error handling possible. If an error occurs, the program continues from the line that follows the line where the error occurred. In effect, the error is ignored. This statement should be used with caution because no error message is displayed and the condition that caused the error may still exist.

On Error Goto 0 disables the error trapping established by an earlier **On Error Goto** or **On Error Resume Next** statement.

Once an error trap is sprung by an error, no further error trapping occurs until the trap is reset. This is done using an **Err = 0** statement (for more information, see the individual entry for **Err**, earlier in this chapter). An **Err = 0** statement usually should be placed at the exit points of your error-handling routine. Such placement means that if an error occurs in the error routine, a message will be displayed and the macro will halt; this prevents the possibility of an endless loop. Any **OnError** statement will reset **Err** to 0.

Such a loop would happen in a macro where **Err = 0** is located at the beginning of the error routine and is followed by an error. The error causes a jump to the beginning of the error-handling routine where the error trap is reset and the error occurs again. This cycle could go on indefinitely, until the macro is interrupted by the user.

Errors with numbers 1000 or greater are generated by Word and not the macro language itself. If such an error occurs, an error message box is displayed, and the user must respond before the macro can continue. If the user chooses OK, control of the program then passes to the error-handling routine.

For more information on **On Error**, see Chapter 6, "More WordBASIC Programming Concepts."

For related commands, see "BASIC Statements and Functions" in the section "WordBASIC Cross Reference," earlier in this chapter.

OnTime

OnTime *When$, Name$, [Tolerance]*

Sets up a background timer that runs the macro specified by *Name$* at the time specified by *When$*. *When$* is a text representation of the time for execution in a

24-hour format. *When$* can also include a date string that precedes the time string. If the date is not specified, the macro runs at the first occurrence of the specified time. The macro is executed the next time Word is idle after the specified *When$*. Word does not run the macro if more than *Tolerance* seconds have elapsed since *When$*, and the macro has not yet run. If *Tolerance* is 0 (zero) or omitted, Word always runs the macro, regardless of how many seconds elapse before Word is idle and available to run the macro. Word can run only one OnTime macro at a time. If you start a second, it replaces the first as the background macro, and the first stops running without completing.

Example. The following example uses two macros to set up a simple alarm clock function in Word. The first macro is run to set up the background timer:

```
Sub MAIN                  'Alarm program
                          'Prompts user to input time for alarm to
                          'sound. Current time appears in title
                          'bar of input box.
   Alarm$ = InputBox$("Time? (HH:MM:SS), 24hr", "Alarm " + Time$())
   OnTime Alarm$, "Beeper"   'Set background timer to run macro
                          'called Beeper. No tolerance is set,
                          'so alarm will always sound.
End Sub                   'Alarm program
```

Example. The following macro sounds an alarm and an alert message in response to the timer set up by the preceding macro. This macro must be named `Beeper` to work properly.

```
Sub MAIN                  'Beeper program
   For Count = 1 To 7     'Seven series of beeps
      Beep                'Beep once
      Beep                'Beep twice
      For TL = 1 To 100   'Timer loop to wait a while
      Next                'Next timer loop
   Next                   'Next Count
   MsgBox "Preset alarm sounded", "Beeper " + Time$(), 48
                          'Print a message box with
                          'current time in title bar
End Sub                   'Beeper Program
```

For related commands, see "BASIC Statements and Functions" and "Macro Control, Creation, and Editing Statements and Functions" in the section "WordBASIC Cross Reference," earlier in this chapter.

Open

Open *Name$* **For** *Mode$* **As** *[#]StreamNumber*

Opens the file or device specified by *Name$*. *Name$* can be a device, such as Com1 or Lpt1, and must be enclosed in quotation marks. Do not include the colon following the device name. *Mode$* can be Input, Output, or Append. *StreamNumber* can be an integer from 1 to 4.

For related commands, see "BASIC Statements and Functions" and "File Statements and Functions" in the section "WordBASIC Cross Reference," earlier in this chapter.

OpenUpPara

OpenUpPara

Changes the Space Before option (in the Format Paragraph dialog box) to one line for the current paragraph(s).

For related commands, see "Formatting Statements and Functions" in the section "WordBASIC Cross Reference," earlier in this chapter.

OptionGroup and OptionButton

OptionGroup *.Field*

OptionButton *x, y, dx, dy, Text$*

OptionGroup begins the definition of a series of related option buttons. Within the group, only one button can be active (that is, on) at a time. *Field* is set to a value between 0 (zero) and *n*, which represents the value of the currently active button.

Example.

```
.
.
.
OptionGroup .brk
OptionButton 63, 36, 24, 12, "&PageBreak"
OptionButton 63, 47, 24, 12, "&LineBreak"
.
.
.
```

For more information on programming custom dialog boxes, see Chapter 6, "More WordBASIC Programming Concepts."

For related commands, see "Dialog Definition and Control Statements and Functions" in the section "WordBASIC Cross Reference," earlier in this chapter.

OtherPane

OtherPane

Activates the other pane of the current window.

For related commands, see "Window Control Statements and Functions" and "Selection and Insertion Point Definition and Control Statements and Functions" in the section "WordBASIC Cross Reference," earlier in this chapter.

OutlineCollapse

OutlineCollapse

Collapses the lowest level of subtext levels under the selected heading.

For related commands, see "Outlining Statements and Functions" in the section "WordBASIC Cross Reference," earlier in this chapter.

OutlineDemote

OutlineDemote

Applies the next higher-numbered heading level style to the selected paragraphs.

For related commands, see "Outlining Statements and Functions" in the section "WordBASIC Cross Reference," earlier in this chapter.

OutlineExpand

OutlineExpand

Expands the lowest level of subtext under the selected heading.

For related commands, see "Outlining Statements and Functions" in the section "WordBASIC Cross Reference," earlier in this chapter.

OutlineLevel( )

Num = **OutlineLevel( )**

In outline view, returns the heading level of the specified paragraph. Returns 0 (zero) if the specified paragraph has no defined level (for example, if the specified paragraph is body text). If multiple paragraphs are selected, returns the level of the first paragraph in the selection.

For related commands, see "Outlining Statements and Functions" in the section "WordBASIC Cross Reference," earlier in this chapter.

OutlineMoveDown

OutlineMoveDown

Moves the selection below the next visible heading.

For related commands, see "Outlining Statements and Functions" in the section "WordBASIC Cross Reference," earlier in this chapter.

OutlineMoveUp

OutlineMoveUp

Moves the selection above the next visible heading.

For related commands, see "Outlining Statements and Functions" in the section "WordBASIC Cross Reference," earlier in this chapter.

OutlinePromote

OutlinePromote

Applies the next lower-numbered heading level style to the selected paragraphs.

For related commands, see "Outlining Statements and Functions" in the section "WordBASIC Cross Reference," earlier in this chapter.

OutlineShowFirstLine

OutlineShowFirstLine *[On]*

Changes the view of nonheading text between all text shown and only the first line of text shown. If *On* is omitted, toggles the state. If *On* is nonzero, only the first line of text is shown. If *On* is 0 (zero), all nonheading text is shown.

For related commands, see "Outling Statements and Functions"and "View Control Statements and Functions" in the section "WordBASIC Cross Reference," earlier in this chapter.

Overtype

Overtype *[On]*

If *On* is omitted, toggles overtyping mode. If *On* is nonzero, overtype mode is activated and the letters OVR are displayed in the status bar. If *On* is 0 (zero), overtype mode is deactivated.

For related commands, see "Mode Statements and Functions" in the section "WordBASIC Cross Reference," earlier in this chapter.

Overtype( )

Log = **Overtype( )**

Returns –1 if overtype mode is on, or 0 (zero) if overtype mode is off.

For related commands, see "Mode Statements and Functions" in the section "WordBASIC Cross Reference," earlier in this chapter.

PageDown

PageDown *[Repeat], [Select]*

Moves the insertion point down by *Repeat* screens. If the *Repeat* argument is omitted, 1 is assumed. If *Select* is nonzero, the selection is extended down by *Repeat* screens. Equivalent to the PgDn key. If *Select* is 0 (zero) or omitted, the selection is not extended.

Statement	Result
`PageDown 1, 1`	Extends the selection down one screen from the insertion point.

For related commands, see "Selection and Insertion Point Definition and Control Statements and Functions"in the section "WordBASIC Cross Reference," earlier in this chapter.

PageDown( )

Log = **PageDown(***[Repeat], [Select]***)**

Moves the insertion point down by *Repeat* pages. If the *Repeat* argument is omitted, 1 is assumed. If *Select* is nonzero, the selection is extended down by *Repeat* screens. Returns –1 if operation was successful or 0 (zero) if not.

For related commands, see "Selection and Insertion Point Definition and Control Statements and Functions" in the section "WordBASIC Cross Reference," earlier in this chapter.

PageUp

PageUp *[Repeat], [Select]*

Moves the insertion point up by *Repeat* screens. If the *Repeat* argument is omitted, 1 is assumed. If *Select* is nonzero, the selection is extended up by *Repeat* screens. Equivalent to the PgUp key. If *Select* is 0 (zero) or omitted, the selection is not extended.

Statement	Result
`PageUp 20`	Moves the insertion point up 20 screens, but does not extend the selection.

For related commands, see "Selection and Insertion Point Definition and Control Statements and Functions" in the section "WordBASIC Cross Reference," earlier in this chapter.

PageUp( )

Log = **PageUp(***[Repeat], [Select]***)**

Moves the insertion point up by *Repeat* pages. If the *Repeat* argument is omitted, 1 is assumed. If *Select* is nonzero, the selection is extended up by *Repeat* screens. Returns –1 if operation was successful or 0 (zero) if not.

For related commands, see "Selection and Insertion Point Definition and Control Statements and Functions" in the section "WordBASIC Cross Reference," earlier in this chapter.

ParaDown

ParaDown *[Repeat], [Select]*

Moves the insertion point down by *Repeat* paragraphs. If *Repeat* is omitted, 1 is assumed. If *Select* is nonzero, the selection is extended down by *Repeat* paragraphs.

For related commands, see "Selection and Insertion Point Definition and Control Statements and Functions" in the section "WordBASIC Cross Reference," earlier in this chapter.

ParaDown( )

Log = **ParaDown(***[Repeat], [Select]***)**

Moves the insertion point down by *Repeat* paragraphs. If *Repeat* is omitted, 1 is assumed. If *Select* is nonzero, the selection is extended down by *Repeat* paragraphs. Returns 0 (zero) if the action cannot be performed. For example, the function returns 0 if the insertion point is at the end of the document.

Statement	Result
`While ParaDown(,1)` `Wend`	Extends the selection one paragraph at a time until the end of the document is reached.

For related commands, see "Selection and Insertion Point Definition and Control Statements and Functions" in the section "WordBASIC Cross Reference," earlier in this chapter.

ParaUp

ParaUp *[Repeat], [Select]*

Moves the insertion point up by *Repeat* paragraphs. If *Repeat* is omitted, 1 is assumed. If *Select* is nonzero, the selection is extended up by *Repeat* paragraphs.

For related commands, see "Selection and Insertion Point Definition and Control Statements and Functions" in the section "WordBASIC Cross Reference," earlier in this chapter.

ParaUp( )

Log = **ParaUp(***[Repeat], [Select]***)**

Moves the insertion point up by *Repeat* paragraphs. If *Repeat* is omitted, 1 is assumed. If *Select* is nonzero, the selection is extended up by *Repeat* paragraphs. Returns 0 (zero) if the action cannot be performed. For example, the function returns 0 if the insertion point is at the beginning of the document.

For related commands, see "Selection and Insertion Point Definition and Control Statements and Functions" in the section "WordBASIC Cross Reference," earlier in this chapter.

PauseRecorder

PauseRecorder

Stops macro recording until **PauseRecorder** is executed again.

For related commands, see "Macro Control, Creation, and Editing Statements and Functions" in the section "WordBASIC Cross Reference," earlier in this chapter.

PrevCell

PrevCell

Moves the selection to the previous cell. If the selection is more than one cell, selects the first cell in the selection.

For related commands, see "Selection and Insertion Point Definition and Control Statements and Functions" and "Table Creation and Editing Statements and Functions" in the section "WordBASIC Cross Reference," earlier in this chapter.

PrevCell( )

Log = **PrevCell( )**

Moves the selection to the previous cell. If the selection is more than one cell, selects the first cell in the selection. Returns 0 (zero) when the selection is in the first cell.

For related commands, see "Selection and Insertion Point Definition and Control Statements and Functions" and "Table Creation and Editing Statements and Functions" in the section "WordBASIC Cross Reference," earlier in this chapter.

PrevField

PrevField

Moves the selection to the previous field.

For related commands, see "Selection and Insertion Point Definition and Control Statements and Functions" and "Field Statements and Functions" in the section "WordBASIC Cross Reference," earlier in this chapter.

PrevField( )

Log = **PrevField( )**

Moves the selection to the previous field. Returns 0 (zero) when the selection is in the first field.

For related commands, see "Selection and Insertion Point Definition and Control Statements and Functions" and "Field Statements and Functions" in the section "WordBASIC Cross Reference," earlier in this chapter.

PrevObject

PrevObject

Selects the previous object in print preview or moves to the previous text area in page view.

For related commands, see "Selection and Insertion Point Definition and Control Statements and Functions" and "View Control Statements and Functions" in the section "WordBASIC Cross Reference," earlier in this chapter.

PrevObject( )

Log = **PrevObject( )**

Selects the previous object in print preview or moves to the previous text area in page view. Returns 0 (zero) when the first object or text area is selected.

For related commands, see "Outling Statements and Functions"and "View Control Statements and Functions" in the section "WordBASIC Cross Reference," earlier in this chapter.

PrevPage

PrevPage

In page view, moves the insertion point to the beginning of the previous page.

For related commands, see "Selection and Insertion Point Definition and Control Statements and Functions"and "View Control Statements and Functions" in the section "WordBASIC Cross Reference," earlier in this chapter.

PrevPage( )

Log = **PrevPage( )**

In page view, moves the insertion point to the beginning of the previous page. Returns 0 (zero) when the first page is selected.

For related commands, see "Selection and Insertion Point Definition and Control Statements and Functions"and "View Control Statements and Functions" in the section "WordBASIC Cross Reference," earlier in this chapter.

PrevTab( )

Log = **PrevTab(***Pos***)**

Returns the position of the next tab to the left of *Pos*. *Pos* is a floating-point number given in points. If more than one paragraph is selected and the tabs do not all match, –1 is returned.

For related commands, see "Selection and Insertion Point Definition and Control Statements and Functions" in the section "WordBASIC Cross Reference," earlier in this chapter.

PrevWindow

PrevWindow

Activates the previous window.

For related commands, see "Selection and Insertion Point Definition and Control Statements and Functions"and "Window Control Statements and Functions" in the section "WordBASIC Cross Reference," earlier in this chapter.

Print

Print *[[#]StreamNumber], Expression*

Writes *Expression* to the file specified by *StreamNumber*. With no *StreamNumber* specified, output goes to the status bar. For more information on BASIC sequential files, see Chapter 6, "More WordBASIC Programming Concepts."

Examples.

Statement	Effect
`Print #1, Record$`	Writes contents of `Record$` to file opened as #1.
`Print "Total is "; TotalSales`	Displays `"Total is"` followed by the value of `TotalSales` in the status bar.

For related commands, see "BASIC Statements and Functions," "File Statements and Functions" and "Dialog Definition and Control Statements and Functions" in the section "WordBASIC Cross Reference," earlier in this chapter.

Read

Read *[#]StreamNumber, Variable(s)*

Similar to the **Input** statement as used for file access, but removes quotation marks from strings. This statement is used with the **Write** statement.

For related commands, see "BASIC Statements and Functions"and "File Statements and Functions" in the section "WordBASIC Cross Reference," earlier in this chapter.

RecordNextCommand

RecordNextCommand

Records the next command at the insertion point in the current macro window.

For related commands, see "Macro Control, Creation, and Editing Statements and Functions"in the section "WordBASIC Cross Reference," earlier in this chapter.

Redim

Redim [**Shared**] *Var [(Size)] [, Var [(Size)]...]*

Reallocates storage space for a previously defined variable array. May be used to enlarge an array, but array contents will be lost.

Redim can also be employed to reuse a previously defined dialog record. For information on dialog records, see Chapter 6, "More WordBASIC Programming Concepts."

For related commands, see "BASIC Statements and Functions" and "Dialog Definition and Control Statements and Functions" in the section "WordBASIC Cross Reference," earlier in this chapter.

Rem

Rem *Remarks*

'Remarks

Inserts explanatory text into the macro. You can use an apostrophe (') instead of a **Rem** statement. If a **Rem** statement follows other statements on a line, it must be separated from those statements by a colon (:). A colon is not required before a remark introduced by an apostrophe.

For related commands, see "BASIC Statements and Functions" in the section "WordBASIC Cross Reference," earlier in this chapter.

RenameMenu

RenameMenu *MenuNumber, NewText$*

Renames the top-level menu of *MenuNumber* to *NewText$*. *MenuNumber* represents the name of a menu. *NewText$* replaces the menu name. An ampersand (&) preceding a character makes it the keyboard equivalent for selecting from the menu. For example, "&Programs" becomes Programs when this statement is executed.

The *MenuNumber* argument values are:

***MenuNumber* argument**	**Menu**
0	File
1	Edit
2	View
3	Insert
4	Format
5	Utilities
6	Macro
7	Window

Statement	**Result**
`RenameMenu 5, "&Other Tasks"`	Changes `Utilities` to `Other Tasks`

For related commands, see "Utility Statements and Functions" and "View Control Statements and Functions" in the section "WordBASIC Cross Reference," earlier in this chapter.

RepeatSearch

RepeatSearch

Repeats the most recent search. Equivalent to the REPEATSEARCH key (Shift+F4).

For related commands, see "Editing Commands and Functions" in the section "WordBASIC Cross Reference," earlier in this chapter.

ResetChar

ResetChar

Removes manual character formatting from the selected text. Manual character formatting is formatting that is not applied as a style. For example, you manually format a word or phrase in a paragraph as bold text and the paragraph style is normal text. **ResetChar** would return the bold text to the character format dictated by the style.

For related commands, see "Formatting Statements and Functions" in the section "WordBASIC Cross Reference," earlier in this chapter.

ResetChar( )

Num = **ResetChar( )**

Returns 1 if the selected text contains no manual character formatting. Returns 0 (zero) if any manual character formatting is present.

For related commands, see "Formatting Statements and Functions" in the section "WordBASIC Cross Reference," earlier in this chapter.

ResetFootnoteContNotice

ResetFootnoteContNotice

Resets the footnote continuation notice to the default value. Works only in the Footnote Cont. Notice editing pane (see **InsertFootnote**) and only if the contents of the pane are "dirty" (that is, changes have been made since the last save).

For related commands, see "Formatting Statements and Functions" in the section "WordBASIC Cross Reference," earlier in this chapter.

ResetFootnoteContSep

ResetFootnoteContSep

Resets the footnote continuation separator to the default value. Works only in the Footnote Cont. Separator editing pane (see **InsertFootnote**) and only if the contents of the pane are "dirty" (that is, changes have been made since the last save).

For related commands, see "Formatting Statements and Functions" in the section "WordBASIC Cross Reference," earlier in this chapter.

ResetFootnoteSep

ResetFootnoteSep

Resets the footnote separator to the default value. Works only in the Footnote Separator editing pane (see **InsertFootnote**) and only if the contents of the pane are "dirty" (that is, changes have been made since the last save).

For related commands, see "Formatting Statements and Functions" in the section "WordBASIC Cross Reference," earlier in this chapter.

ResetPara

ResetPara

Removes manual paragraph formatting from the selected text. The text is left with the paragraph formatting of the current style.

For related commands, see "Formatting Statements and Functions" in the section "WordBASIC Cross Reference," earlier in this chapter.

ResetPara( )

Num = **ResetPara( )**

Returns –1 if the selected text contains no manual paragraph formatting. Returns 0 (zero) if any manual paragraph formatting is present.

For related commands, see "Formatting Statements and Functions" in the section "WordBASIC Cross Reference," earlier in this chapter.

Right$( )

*A$* = **Right$(***Source$*, *Count***)**

Returns the rightmost *Count* characters of *Source$*.

Function	Result
`A$ = "Legal File List"` `Print Right$(A$,4)`	List
`A$ = "Legal File List"` `Print Right$(A$,9)`	File List

For related commands, see "BASIC Statements and Functions" in the section "WordBASIC Cross Reference," earlier in this chapter.

RightPara

RightPara

Right-aligns the selected paragraphs.

For related commands, see "Formatting Statements and Functions" in the section "WordBASIC Cross Reference," earlier in this chapter.

RightPara( )

Num = **RightPara( )**

Returns 0 (zero) if none of the selected paragraphs are right-aligned, 1 if all of the selected paragraphs are right-aligned, or –1 if more than one kind of paragraph alignment is used.

For related commands, see "Formatting Statements and Functions" in the section "WordBASIC Cross Reference," earlier in this chapter.

RmDir

RmDir *Name$*

Removes the specified directory or subdirectory. Files must first be removed from the subdirectory for this statement to work.

Example.

```
.
.
.
Kill "C:\WORD\FCCPROJ\*.*"        'Delete all files in chosen directory
RmDir "C:\WORD\FCCPROJ"           'Remove empty directory
.
.
.
```

For related commands, see "BASIC Statements and Functions" and "File Statements and Functions" in the section "WordBASIC Cross Reference," earlier in this chapter.

Rnd( )

Num = **Rnd(***[Expression]***)**

Returns a random fractional value between 0 (zero) and 1. The *Expression* is not used by WordBASIC, but is provided for compatibility with other forms of BASIC.

Function	Result
`A = Rnd()`	The variable A is loaded with a random value between 0 (zero) and 1.
`A = Int(Rnd() * 10))`	The variable A is loaded with a random integer between 0 (zero) and 10.

For related commands, see "BASIC Statements and Functions" in the section "WordBASIC Cross Reference," earlier in this chapter.

RulerMode

RulerMode

Switches to ruler mode. Ruler mode allows setting of tabs from the keyboard.

For related commands, see "Mode Statements and Functions" in the section "WordBASIC Cross Reference," earlier in this chapter.

SaveTemplate

SaveTemplate

Saves the document's template. If the document has no template, saves NORMAL.DOT

For related commands, see "File Statements and Functions" in the section "WordBASIC Cross Reference," earlier in this chapter.

Seek

Seek *[#]StreamNumber, Count*

Positions a file pointer at character *Count* in the file attached to the stream specified by *StreamNumber*.

For related commands, see "BASIC Statements and Functions" and "File Statements and Functions" in the section "WordBASIC Cross Reference," earlier in this chapter.

Seek( )

Num = **Seek(***[#]StreamNumber***)**

Returns the current file pointer for the specified *StreamNumber*.

For related commands, see "BASIC Statements and Functions" and "File Statements and Functions" in the section "WordBASIC Cross Reference," earlier in this chapter.

Select Case...Case...Case Else...End Select

Select Case *Expression*
    Case *CaseExpression*
        Statement(s)
    [**Case Else**
        Statement(s)]
End Select

The *Expression* is compared with all the values given in each *CaseExpression* until a match is found. If a match is found, the *Statement(s)* following the *CaseExpression* are executed. If there is no match and there is a **Case Else** statement, those *Statement(s)* are executed.

For more information on **Select Case**, see Chapter 4, "Interlude—WordBASIC for Beginners," and Chapter 5, "The WordBASIC Programming Language."

For related commands, see "BASIC Statements and Functions" in the section "WordBASIC Cross Reference," earlier in this chapter.

Selection$( )

*A$* = **Selection$( )**

Returns the plain, unformatted text of the selection. The selection can contain up to 32,000 characters, or the maximum that memory can hold. If the selection is too large, **Selection$( )** is filled with as much of the selection as possible, and an error is generated. If the selection is an insertion point, the character following the insertion point is returned.

Example.

```
Sub MAIN                                     'Begin AllUpper
   On Error Goto TooBig                      'Set up error trap
   EditSelectAll                             'Select entire document
   All$ = Selection$()                       'Store text of selection as All$
   EditCut                                   'Delete selected text
   Upper$ = UCase$(All$)                     'Convert text to all uppercase
   Insert Upper$                             'Insert text back into document
   Goto Finish
TooBig:
   If Err = 513 Then                         'If error is "String too long"
      MsgBox "Sorry, document too big"       '"Too big" error message
   Else                                      'Otherwise...
      Error Err                              'Unknown error. Print error
                                             'message and quit.
   End If
Finish:                                      'End label
End Sub                                      'End AllUpper
```

For related commands, see "Editing Commands and Functions" and "Selection and Insertion Point Definition and Control Statements and Functions" in the section "WordBASIC Cross Reference," earlier in this chapter.

SelectTable

SelectTable

Selects the table that contains the insertion point or selection. If the insertion point or selection is not in a table, an error occurs. If the selection contains more than one table, the first table is selected.

For related commands, see "Table Creation and Editing Statements and Functions" and "Selection and Insertion Point Definition and Control Statements and Functions" in the section "WordBASIC Cross Reference," earlier in this chapter.

SelType

SelType *Type*

Changes the selection highlighting to the form specified by *Type*. *Type* is one of the following:

Type argument	Type
0	Hidden
1	Solid insertion point
2	Solid selection
4	Dotted selection or insertion point (whichever is current)
5	Dotted insertion point
6	Dotted selection

For related commands, see "Formatting Statements and Functions" and "Selection and Insertion Point Definition and Control Statements and Functions" in the section "WordBASIC Cross Reference," earlier in this chapter.

SelType( )

Num = **SelType( )**

Returns the type of the selection highlighting.

If selection is	Function returns
Hidden	0
Solid insertion point	1
Solid selection	2
Dotted insertion point or selection (whichever is current)	4
Dotted insertion point	5
Dotted selection	6

For related commands, see "Formatting Statements and Functions" and "Selection and Insertion Point Definition and Control Statements and Functions" in the section "WordBASIC Cross Reference," earlier in this chapter.

SendKeys

SendKeys *Keys$, Wait*

Sends the keys specified by *Keys$* to the active application, just as if they were typed at the keyboard. If Word is not the active application and *Wait* is –1, Word waits for all keys to be processed before proceeding.

SendKeys must be executed before the program or command that receives the keystrokes so that those keystrokes are in the buffer when the macro pauses.

Keys$ is represented by one or more characters, such as a for the letter *a*, {enter} for the Enter key, and {pgup} for the PgUp key.

Syntax examples.

```
SendKeys "{break}"
```

```
Key$ = "{delete 5}"
SendKeys Key$, -1
```

To specify characters that aren't displayed when you press the key, use the codes shown in the following table:

Key	Code
Backspace	{backspace} or {bs} or {bksp}
Break	{break}
CapsLock	{capslock}
Clear	{clear}
Del	{delete} or {del}
Down	{down}
End	{end}
Enter	{enter}
Esc	{escape} or {esc}
Help	{help}
Home	{home}
Ins	{insert}
Left	{left}
NumLock	{numlock}
PgDn	{pgdn}
PgUp	{pgup}
PrtSc	{prtsc}

(continued)

Continued

Key	Code
Right	{right}
Tab	{tab}
Up	{up}
F1	{F1}
F2	{F2}
F3	{F3}
F4	{F4}
F5	{F5}
F6	{F6}
F7	{F7}
F8	{F8}
F9	{F9}
F10	{F10}
F11	{F11}
F12	{F12}
F13	{F13}
F14	{F14}
F15	{F15}
F16	{F16}

The plus sign (+), the percent sign (%), and the caret (^) have special meanings:

To combine with	Precede the key code by
Shift	+ (plus sign)
Alt	% (percent sign)
Ctrl	^ (caret)

For example, %{enter} sends the code for Alt+Enter. You can group keys with parentheses and precede the group with the key code for a Shift, Alt, or Ctrl key. The code +(eb) specifies EB.

To repeat a key sequence, use the syntax {*Keys$ Number*}. For example, `{pgdn 20}` means "press the PgDn key 20 times." Remember to put a space between the key and the number.

> **NOTE:** *Use great care when applying* **SendKeys** *to operate other programs. Word has no way to detect or correct errors generated by the other program and always sends the programmed series of keystrokes. Be sure to test your macros with the other progam under a variety of conditions to ensure that the keystrokes required by the other program remain exactly the same. If the other program requires different keystrokes than programmed, data could be lost. If more keystrokes are required than are programmed (as in an {enter} to respond to an error message box) the macro freezes, waiting for the missing input. If there are too many keystrokes in the programmed sequence, any extra are passed to Word itself, and the results are unpredictable.*
>
> *Use* **SendKeys** *to operate other applications only when there is no alternative, and then use it with caution. In general, DDE (Dynamic Data Exchange) is a better way for Word to interact with other programs, because DDE provides a channel for two-way communication between programs and provides a path for detecting and dealing with errors in the other application.*

For related commands, see "Utility Statements and Functions" and "DDE (Dynamic Data Exchange) Statements and Functions" in the section "WordBASIC Cross Reference," earlier in this chapter.

SentLeft

SentLeft *[Repeat], [Select]*

Moves the insertion point left by *Repeat* number of sentences. If *Repeat* is omitted, 1 is assumed. If *Select* is nonzero, the selection is extended up by *Repeat* sentences.

For related commands, see "Selection and Insertion Point Definition and Control Statements and Functions" in the section "WordBASIC Cross Reference," earlier in this chapter.

SentLeft ( )

Log = **SentLeft(***[Repeat], [Select]***)**

Moves the insertion point left by *Repeat* number of sentences. If *Repeat* is omitted, 1 is assumed. If *Select* is nonzero, the selection is extended up by *Repeat* sentences. Returns 0 (zero) if the action cannot be performed. For example, the function returns 0 (zero) if the insertion point is at the beginning of the document.

For related commands, see "Selection and Insertion Point Definition and Control Statements and Functions" in the section "WordBASIC Cross Reference," earlier in this chapter.

SentRight

SentRight *[Repeat], [Select]*

Moves the insertion point right by *Repeat* number of sentences. If *Repeat* is omitted, 1 is assumed. If *Select* is nonzero, the selection is extended down by *Repeat* sentences.

For related commands, see "Selection and Insertion Point Definition and Control Statements and Functions" in the section "WordBASIC Cross Reference," earlier in this chapter.

SentRight ( )

Log = **SentRight(***[Repeat], [Select]***)**

Moves the insertion point right by *Repeat* number of sentences. If *Repeat* is omitted, 1 is assumed. If *Select* is nonzero, the selection is extended down by *Repeat* sentences. Returns 0 (zero) if the action cannot be performed. For example, the function returns 0 (zero) if the insertion point is at the end of the document.

For related commands, see "Selection and Insertion Point Definition and Control Statements and Functions" in the section "WordBASIC Cross Reference," earlier in this chapter.

SetDirty

SetDirty *[Dirty]*

Causes Word to recognize the current document as "dirty" (that is, changed since the last time the document was saved). The dirty flag is used by Word functions such as **FileClose** and **FileSaveAll**. If *Dirty* is omitted or 1, the document is recognized as dirty. If *Dirty* is 0 (zero), the document is treated as not dirty (that is, unchanged).

For related commands, see "Environment Statements and Functions" and "File Statements and Functions" in the section "WordBASIC Cross Reference," earlier in this chapter.

SetEndOfBookmark

SetEndOfBookmark *Bookmark1$, [Bookmark2$]*

Sets *Bookmark2$* to the end point of *Bookmark1$*. If *Bookmark2$* is omitted, *Bookmark1$* is set to its own end.

For related commands, see "Bookmark Statements and Functions" in the section "WordBASIC Cross Reference," earlier in this chapter.

SetGlossary

SetGlossary *Name$, Text$, [Context]*

Defines a glossary entry called *Name$* that contains the text *Text$*. *Context* is 0 (zero) for global or 1 for document template.

The variables can be set prior to calling the statement, as shown in the second example. Using variables makes it easier to change the definition if necessary.

Statement	Result
`SetGlossary "Disclaim", "No warranty, either express or implied, is made by Trey Research.", 1`	Defines the glossary entry `Disclaim`, with the template context, containing the specified text.
`Text$ ="No warranty, either express or implied, is made by Trey Research."` `SetGlossary "Disclaim", Text$, 1`	Defines the same glossary entry as in the preceding example, but uses the variable `Text$`.

For related commands, see "Glossary Statements and Functions" in the section "WordBASIC Cross Reference," earlier in this chapter.

SetProfileString

SetProfileString *[App$], Key$, Value$*

Sets a value in the current WIN.INI or OS2.INI file.

App$* is the name of the Microsoft Windows or OS/2 application. If the application is not specified, the string `"Microsoft Word"` is used. If *Key$ does not yet appear in the file, this statement inserts it.

For related commands, see "Utility Statements and Functions" in the section "WordBASIC Cross Reference," earlier in this chapter.

SetStartOfBookmark

SetStartOfBookmark *Bookmark1$, [Bookmark2$]*

Sets *Bookmark2$* to the starting point of *Bookmark1$*. If *Bookmark2$* is omitted, *Bookmark1$* is set to its own starting point.

For related commands, see "Bookmark Statements and Functions" in the section "WordBASIC Cross Reference," earlier in this chapter.

Sgn( )

Num = **Sgn(***n***)**

Returns the sign of *n*. Returns 1 for a positive number, –1 for a negative number, or 0 for zero.

Function	Return value
`Sgn(4)`	1
`Sgn(-14)`	–1
`Sgn(0)`	0

For related commands, see "BASIC Statements and Functions" in the section "WordBASIC Cross Reference," earlier in this chapter.

Shell

Shell *App$, [WindowStyle]*

Starts another program under Microsoft Windows or OS/2. *App$* should include the exact name of the program file and the extension and path required to find the file, as well as any switches or arguments that the program accepts. If *App$* is the name of a file with an extension specific to an installed application that is specified in the current WIN.INI or OS2.INI file (for example, .DOC for a Word document), the statement starts the application and loads that file.

WindowStyle specifies how the window containing the program should appear, as follows:

Mode	Window type
0	Minimized window
1	Normal window
2	Minimized window (for Microsoft Excel compatibility)
3	Maximized window
4	Deactivated window

Statement	Result
`Shell "EXCEL.EXE", 2`	Starts Microsoft Excel and minimizes the window.
`Shell "TRENDS.XLC", 1`	Starts Microsoft Excel and loads the document TRENDS.XLC in a normal window.
`Shell "NOTEPAD.EXE TORT.TXT"`	Starts Notepad and loads the document TORT.TXT.

For related commands, see "BASIC Statements and Functions" in the section "WordBASIC Cross Reference," earlier in this chapter.

ShowAll

ShowAll *[On]*

If *On* is omitted, toggles the ShowAll option of the View Preferences command. If *On* is nonzero, shows all invisible objects such as hidden text, tabs, spaces, paragraph marks, and so on. If *On* is 0 (zero), the ShowAll option is turned off.

For related commands, see "View Control Statements and Functions" in the section "WordBASIC Cross Reference," earlier in this chapter.

ShowAllHeadings

ShowAllHeadings

Shows all text in outline view.

For related commands, see "Outlining Statements and Functions" in the section "WordBASIC Cross Reference," earlier in this chapter.

ShowHeading1

ShowHeading1

In outline view, shows all Level 1 headings and hides subordinate headings and body text.

For related commands, see "Outlining Statements and Functions" in the section "WordBASIC Cross Reference," earlier in this chapter.

ShowHeading2

ShowHeading2

In outline view, shows all Level 2 headings and hides subordinate headings and body text.

For related commands, see "Outlining Statements and Functions" in the section "WordBASIC Cross Reference," earlier in this chapter.

ShowHeading3

ShowHeading3

In outline view, shows all Level 3 headings and hides subordinate headings and body text.

For related commands, see "Outlining Statements and Functions" in the section "WordBASIC Cross Reference," earlier in this chapter.

ShowHeading4

ShowHeading4

In outline view, shows all Level 4 headings and hides subordinate headings and body text.

For related commands, see "Outlining Statements and Functions" in the section "WordBASIC Cross Reference," earlier in this chapter.

ShowHeading5

ShowHeading5

In outline view, shows all Level 5 headings and hides subordinate headings and body text.

For related commands, see "Outlining Statements and Functions" in the section "WordBASIC Cross Reference," earlier in this chapter.

ShowHeading6

ShowHeading6

In outline view, shows all Level 6 headings and hides subordinate headings and body text.

For related commands, see "Outlining Statements and Functions" in the section "WordBASIC Cross Reference," earlier in this chapter.

ShowHeading7

ShowHeading7

In outline view, shows all Level 7 headings and hides subordinate headings and body text.

For related commands, see "Outlining Statements and Functions" in the section "WordBASIC Cross Reference," earlier in this chapter.

ShowHeading8

ShowHeading8

In outline view, shows all Level 8 headings and hides subordinate headings and body text.

For related commands, see "Outlining Statements and Functions" in the section "WordBASIC Cross Reference," earlier in this chapter.

ShowHeading9

ShowHeading9

In outline view, shows all Level 9 headings and hides subordinate headings and body text.

For related commands, see "Outlining Statements and Functions" in the section "WordBASIC Cross Reference," earlier in this chapter.

ShowVars

ShowVars

Displays the list of variables (and their values) currently in use. Equivalent to using the Vars button on the macro-editing icon bar. This statement is useful for debugging macros.

For related commands, see "Macro Control, Creation, and Editing Statements and Functions" in the section "WordBASIC Cross Reference," earlier in this chapter.

ShrinkFont

ShrinkFont

Decreases the size of the selected font to the next available size supported by the assigned printer. Can be used either for the selection or at the insertion point. If the selection contains more than one font size, each is reduced to its next available size.

For related commands, see "Formatting Statements and Functions" in the section "WordBASIC Cross Reference," earlier in this chapter.

ShrinkSelection

ShrinkSelection

Shrinks the selection to the next smaller unit (word, sentence, paragraph, and so forth).

For related commands, see "Selection and Insertion Point Definition and Control Statements and Functions" in the section "WordBASIC Cross Reference," earlier in this chapter.

SmallCaps

SmallCaps *[On]*

If *On* is omitted, toggles small caps for the entire selection. If *On* is nonzero, makes the entire selection small caps. If *On* is 0 (zero), removes small caps from the entire selection.

Statement	If text is	New text is
`SmallCaps`	Trey Research Company	TREY RESEARCH COMPANY
`SmallCaps`	Trey RESEARCH Company	TREY RESEARCH COMPANY
`SmallCaps`	TREY RESEARCH COMPANY	Trey Research Company
`SmallCaps 1`	Trey Research Company	TREY RESEARCH COMPANY
`SmallCaps 0`	Trey RESEARCH Company	Trey Research Company

For related commands, see "Formatting Statements and Functions" in the section "WordBASIC Cross Reference," earlier in this chapter.

SmallCaps( )

Num = **SmallCaps( )**

Returns 0 (zero) if none of the selection is small caps, 1 if all of the selection is small caps, or –1 if part of the selection is small caps.

If selected text is	Function returns
Trey Research	0; the selection is not small caps
TREY RESEARCH	1; the entire selection is small caps
TREY Research	–1; only part of the selection is small caps

For related commands, see "Formatting Statements and Functions" in the section "WordBASIC Cross Reference," earlier in this chapter.

SpacePara1

SpacePara1

Formats the selected paragraphs with single spacing (12 points).

For related commands, see "Formatting Statements and Functions" in the section "WordBASIC Cross Reference," earlier in this chapter.

SpacePara1( )

Num = **SpacePara1( )**

Returns 0 (zero) if none of the selected paragraphs is single spaced, 1 if all of the selected paragraphs are single spaced, or –1 if more than one kind of paragraph spacing is used.

For related commands, see "Formatting Statements and Functions" in the section "WordBASIC Cross Reference," earlier in this chapter.

SpacePara2

SpacePara2

Formats the selected paragraphs with double spacing.

For related commands, see "Formatting Statements and Functions" in the section "WordBASIC Cross Reference," earlier in this chapter.

SpacePara2( )

Num = **SpacePara2( )**

Returns 0 (zero) if none of the selected paragraphs is double spaced, 1 if all of the selected paragraphs are double spaced, or –1 if more than one kind of paragraph spacing is used.

For related commands, see "Formatting Statements and Functions" in the section "WordBASIC Cross Reference," earlier in this chapter.

SpacePara15

SpacePara15

Formats the selected paragraphs with one-and-one-half line spacing.

For related commands, see "Formatting Statements and Functions" in the section "WordBASIC Cross Reference," earlier in this chapter.

SpacePara15( )

Num = **SpacePara15( )**

Returns 0 (zero) if none of the selected paragraphs has one-and-one-half line spacing, 1 if all of the selected paragraphs have one-and-one-half line spacing, or –1 if more than one kind of paragraph spacing is used.

For related commands, see "Formatting Statements and Functions" in the section "WordBASIC Cross Reference," earlier in this chapter.

Spike

Spike

Copies the selection to a special glossary called the Spike and then deletes the selection. For more information on using the Spike, see *Word User's Reference.*

For related commands, see "Editing Commands and Functions" and "Glossary Statements and Functions" in the section "WordBASIC Cross Reference," earlier in this chapter.

StartOfColumn

StartOfColumn *[Select]*

Moves the insertion point to the topmost position in the first selected table column. If *Select* is nonzero, the selection is extended.

For related commands, see "Selection and Insertion Point Definition and Control Statements and Functions" and "Table Creation and Editing Statements and Functions" in the section "WordBASIC Cross Reference," earlier in this chapter.

StartOfDocument

StartOfDocument *[Select]*

Moves the insertion point to the beginning of the document. If *Select* is nonzero, the selection is extended.

For related commands, see "Selection and Insertion Point Definition and Control Statements and Functions" in the section "WordBASIC Cross Reference," earlier in this chapter.

StartOfLine

StartOfLine *[Select]*

Moves the insertion point to the beginning of the line. If *Select* is nonzero, the selection is extended.

For related commands, see "Selection and Insertion Point Definition and Control Statements and Functions" in the section "WordBASIC Cross Reference," earlier in this chapter.

StartOfRow

StartOfRow *[Select]*

Moves the insertion point to the leftmost position in the first selected table row. If *Select* is nonzero, the selection is extended.

For related commands, see "Selection and Insertion Point Definition and Control Statements and Functions" in the section "WordBASIC Cross Reference," earlier in this chapter.

StartOfWindow

StartOfWindow *[Select]*

Moves the insertion point to the upper left corner of the window. If *Select* is nonzero, the selection is extended.

For related commands, see "Selection and Insertion Point Definition and Control Statements and Functions" and "Window Control Statements and Functions" in the section "WordBASIC Cross Reference," earlier in this chapter.

StartUpOptions

StartUpOptions *AppNumber, Option$, Value$ [,ActionButton]*

Available in Word for OS/2 only. Edits Word entries in the OS2.INI file. Equivalent to the Startup Option dialog box under the Utilities Customize command. The *AppNumber* is 0 (zero) for Microsoft Word, or 1 for MSGraphicsFilters. *Option$* is the option to be changed under the given application. *Value$* is the value to be passed to the specified option. *.ActionButton* is the default Set (**.Set**) to add or change the specified file entry, or Delete (**.Delete**) to remove the specified entry from the file.

Example.

```
StartUpOptions 0, "Conversions", "No", .Set
```

Stop

Stop

Stops a running macro and displays a message that says the macro was interrupted.

For related commands, see "BASIC Statements and Functions" and "Macro Control, Creation, and Editing Statements and Functions" in the section "WordBASIC Cross Reference," earlier in this chapter.

Str$( )

*A$* = **Str$(***n***)**

Returns the string representation of the value *n*. Positive numbers have a leading space character.

For related commands, see "BASIC Statements and Functions" in the section "WordBASIC Cross Reference," earlier in this chapter.

String$( )

*A$* = **String$(***Count, Source$***)**

Returns the first character in *Source$*, repeated *Count* times. Replacing *Source$* with the number *m* representing the ASCII value of *Source$* returns the character with ANSI code *m*, repeated *Count* times.

Function	Return value
`A$ = "Persistence of Vision"`	
`Print String$(5, A$)`	`PPPPP`
`Print String$(5,100)`	`ddddd`

For related commands, see "BASIC Statements and Functions" in the section "WordBASIC Cross Reference," earlier in this chapter.

StyleName$( )

*A$* = **StyleName$(***[Count], [Context], [All]***)**

Returns the name of the style defined in the given context (document or document template). *Count* can range from 1 to *CountStyles(Context)*. If *Count* is

0 (zero), the name of the current style is returned; otherwise, the name is taken from the list in the given context. *Context* is 0 (zero) for document, or 1 for document template. If *All* is specified, all built-in styles are included at the beginning of the list.

For related commands, see "Formatting Statements and Functions" in the section "WordBASIC Cross Reference," earlier in this chapter.

Sub...End Sub

Sub *Name [ParameterList]*
Statement(s)
End Sub

Defines a subroutine. For more information on subroutines, see Chapter 4, "Interlude—WordBASIC for Beginners," and Chapter 5, "The WordBASIC Programming Language."

For related commands, see "BASIC Statements and Functions" in the section "WordBASIC Cross Reference," earlier in this chapter.

SubScript

SubScript *[On]*

If *On* is omitted, toggles subscript for the entire selection. If *On* is nonzero, makes the entire selection subscript. If *On* is 0 (zero), removes subscript from the entire selection.

For related commands, see "Formatting Statements and Functions" in the section "WordBASIC Cross Reference," earlier in this chapter.

SubScript( )

Num = **SubScript( )**

Returns 0 (zero) if none of the selection is subscript, 1 if all of the selection is subscript, or –1 if part of the selection is subscript or superscript.

For related commands, see "Formatting Statements and Functions" in the section "WordBASIC Cross Reference," earlier in this chapter.

Super

Super *Statement*

Directs Word to run the named macro at the next context level. For macros with the same name, Word runs the template macro before a global macro and a global macro before a built-in command. Super overrides this order. If, for example, you have a macro named FilePrint, a **Super FilePrint** statement runs the built-in command.

SuperScript

SuperScript *[On]*

If *On* is omitted, toggles superscript for the entire selection. If *On* is nonzero, makes the entire selection superscript. If *On* is 0 (zero), removes superscript from the entire selection.

For related commands, see "Formatting Statements and Functions" in the section "WordBASIC Cross Reference," earlier in this chapter.

SuperScript( )

Num = **SuperScript( )**

Returns 0 (zero) if none of the selection is superscript, 1 if all of the selection is superscript, or –1 if part of the selection is superscript or subscript.

For related commands, see "Formatting Statements and Functions" in the section "WordBASIC Cross Reference," earlier in this chapter.

TabLeader$( )

*A$* = **TabLeader$(***Pos***)**

Returns the leader character of the tab at the position *Pos*, which is given in points. If more than one paragraph is selected and all the tabs do not match, an empty string is returned.

The leader characters returned are blank space ( ), period (.), hyphen (-), and underscore (_).

For related commands, see "Formatting Statements and Functions" in the section "WordBASIC Cross Reference," earlier in this chapter.

TabType( )

Num = **TabType(***Pos***)**

Returns the type of tab at the position *Pos*, which is given in points. Returns -1 if more than one paragraph is selected and all the tabs do not match. If the tabs match, the tab type is returned, as follows:

If function returns	Tab type is
0	Left-aligned
1	Centered
2	Right-aligned
3	Decimal

For related commands, see "Formatting Statements and Functions" in the section "WordBASIC Cross Reference," earlier in this chapter.

Text

Text *x, y, dx, dy, Text$*

Creates a box of static text. **Text** does not have a result. The **Text** statement must precede the dialog-box control it is associated with. An ampersand (&) preceding a character makes it the keyboard equivalent to selecting in the dialog box. For example, `"&Programs"` becomes `Programs` when this statement is executed.

Statement	Result
`Text 7, 10, 21, 9, "Format &Options:"`	`Format Options`

For more information on creating custom dialog boxes, see Chapter 6, "More WordBASIC Programming Concepts."

For related commands, see "Dialog Definition and Control Statements and Functions" in the section "WordBASIC Cross Reference," earlier in this chapter.

TextBox

TextBox *x, y, dx, dy, .Field*

Creates an edit control, which is a box into which the user can type a response.

Example.

```
TextBox 32, 8, 65, 12, .TB
```

For more information on creating custom dialog boxes, see Chapter 6, "More WordBASIC Programming Concepts."

For related commands, see "Dialog Definition and Control Statements and Functions" in the section "WordBASIC Cross Reference," earlier in this chapter.

Time$( )

*A$* = **Time$( )**

Returns the current time in the default format specified in the WIN.INI or OS2.INI file.

For related commands, see "BASIC Statements and Functions" in the section "WordBASIC Cross Reference," earlier in this chapter.

ToggleFieldDisplay

ToggleFieldDisplay

Toggles the display of the current selection between the field codes and the field results.

For related commands, see "Field Statements and Functions" and "View Control Statements and Functions" in the section "WordBASIC Cross Reference," earlier in this chapter.

UCase$( )

*A$* = **UCase$(***A$***)**

Returns *A$* converted to uppercase.

For related commands, see "BASIC Statements and Functions" in the section "WordBASIC Cross Reference," earlier in this chapter.

Underline

Underline *[On]*

If *On* is omitted, toggles underlining for the entire selection. If *On* is nonzero, makes the entire selection underlined. If *On* is 0 (zero), removes underlining from the entire selection.

Statement	If text is	New text is
`Underline`	Trey Research Company	Trey Research Company
`Underline`	Trey Research Company	Trey Research Company
`Underline`	Trey Research Company	Trey Research Company
`Underline 1`	Trey Research Company	Trey Research Company
`Underline 0`	Trey Research Company	Trey Research Company

For related commands, see "Formatting Statements and Functions" in the section "WordBASIC Cross Reference," earlier in this chapter.

Underline( )

Num = **Underline( )**

Returns 0 (zero) if none of the selection is underlined, 1 if all of the selection is underlined, or –1 if part of the selection is underlined or more than one kind of underlining is used.

If selected text is	Function returns
Trey Research	0; the selection is not underlined.
Trey Research	1; the entire selection is underlined.
Trey Research	–1; only part of the selection is underlined.

For related commands, see "Formatting Statements and Functions" in the section "WordBASIC Cross Reference," earlier in this chapter.

UnHang

UnHang

Reduces the left indent in a hanging indent to the left by one tab stop. Keeps the first line of the paragraph indented at the current position.

For related commands, see "Formatting Statements and Functions" in the section "WordBASIC Cross Reference," earlier in this chapter.

UnIndent

UnIndent

Reduces the indent of the selected paragraphs. The indent is aligned with the previous tab stop of the first paragraph in the selection. **Unindent** does not change the setting of a first-line indent.

For related commands, see "Formatting Statements and Functions" in the section "WordBASIC Cross Reference," earlier in this chapter.

UnLinkFields

UnLinkFields

Converts the selected fields to plain text and uses the last result.

Example.

```
Sub MAIN                          'Begin "OutField"
   Box = MsgBox \
   ("Are you sure that you want to convert all fields to text?", \
   "OutField", 33)                'Verify action with user
   If Box = 0 Then Goto Finish    'If "Cancel" selected then end
   EditSelectAll                  'Select entire document
   UnLinkFields                   'Convert all fields in document to text
```

If there are no fields in the document, an error is generated. Certain kinds of fields cannot be unlinked. For more information, see Chapter 9, "Fields."

For related commands, see "Field Statements and Functions" in the section "WordBASIC Cross Reference," earlier in this chapter.

UnLockFields

UnLockFields

Unlocks fields in the current selection, for updating.

For related commands, see "Field Statements and Functions" in the section "WordBASIC Cross Reference," earlier in this chapter.

UnSpike

UnSpike

Empties the Spike glossary and inserts all contents into the document at the selection. For more information on using the Spike, see *Word User's Reference.*

For related commands, see "Editing Commands and Functions" and "Glossary Statements and Functions" in the section "WordBASIC Cross Reference," earlier in this chapter.

UpdateFields

UpdateFields

Updates the fields in the selection.

For related commands, see "Field Statements and Functions" in the section "WordBASIC Cross Reference," earlier in this chapter.

UpdateSource

UpdateSource

Sends changes in the result of an INCLUDE field back to the source document. The source document must be in Word Normal file format. For more information on the INCLUDE field, see Chapter 9, "Fields."

For related commands, see "Field Statements and Functions" in the section "WordBASIC Cross Reference," earlier in this chapter.

UtilCalculate

UtilCalculate

Equivalent to the Calculate command on the Utilities menu. The selection is evaluated as a mathematical expression. The result of the evaluation is placed on the Clipboard and displayed on the status bar.

For related commands, see "Utility Statements and Functions" in the section "WordBASIC Cross Reference," earlier in this chapter.

UtilCalculate( )

Num = **UtilCalculate(***[Expression$]***)**

Evaluates *Expression$*. If *Expression$* is given, this function is equivalent to the = field. Values in *Expression$* can be table cell references. For more information on the = field, see Chapter 9, "Fields." If *Expression$* is omitted, performs the same operation as the **UtilCalculate** statement, but returns the result rather than placing it on the Clipboard.

For related commands, see "Utility Statements and Functions" in the section "WordBASIC Cross Reference," earlier in this chapter.

UtilCompareVersions

UtilCompareVersions *Name$*

Equivalent to the Utilities Compare Versions dialog box. Compares the current document with the document specified by *Name$*.

For related commands, see "Utility Statements and Functions" in the section "WordBASIC Cross Reference," earlier in this chapter.

UtilCustomize

UtilCustomize *[AutoSave], [Units], [Pagination], [SummaryPrompt], [ReplaceSelection], [Name$], [Initials$], [ButtonFieldClicks]*

Equivalent to the Utilities Customize dialog box. Some arguments take measurements in points or numbers. Other arguments correspond to check boxes.

Argument	Description
AutoSave	Specifies automatic save frequency; can be 0 (zero) for High, 1 for Medium, 2 for Low, or 3 for Never.
Units	Units of measure used in the ruler; can be 0 (zero) for inches, 1 for centimeters, 2 for points, or 3 for picas.
Pagination	Corresponds to the Background Pagination check box.
SummaryPrompt	Corresponds to the Prompt For Summary Info check box.
ReplaceSelection	Corresponds to the Typing Replaces Selection check box.
Name$	Your name.
Initials$	Your initials.
ButtonFieldClicks	1 if one mouse click activates a MACROBUTTON or GOTOBUTTON field; 2 if two clicks are required.

For related commands, see "Utility Statements and Functions," "Environment Statements and Functions," "Formatting Statements and Functions," "Field Statements and Functions," and "Macro Control, Creation, and Editing Statements and Functions" in the section "WordBASIC Cross Reference," earlier in this chapter.

UtilGetSpelling

UtilGetSpelling *FillArray$( ), [Word$], [MainDic$], [SuppDic$]*

Fills the string array *FillArray$* with all available spellings for a word. If *Word$* is supplied, that word is used. If *Word$* is omitted, Word uses the word closest to the insertion point. The *MainDic$* argument specifies a two-letter key that represents the main dictionary (for example, "AM" for LEX-AM.DLL). The *SuppDic$* argument specifies the supplemental dictionary. The spellings for each definition are appended in the order they appear in the spelling checker.

```
Sub MAIN
   Dim Spell$(10)                        'Set up array to hold spellings
   UtilGetSpelling Spell$(), "color"  'Load spellings for color into array
   For Count = 1 To 10                   'Start loop Count
      MsgBox Spell$(Count)               'Display spelling number Count
   Next                                  'End loop Count
End Sub
```

For related commands, see "Utility Statements and Functions" in the section "WordBASIC Cross Reference," earlier in this chapter.

UtilGetSpelling( )

Log = **UtilGetSpelling(***FillArray$( ), [Word$], [MainDic$], [SuppDic$]***)**

Fills the string array *FillArray$* with all available spellings of a word. If *Word$* is supplied, that word is used. If *Word$* is omitted, Word uses the word closest to the insertion point. The *MainDic$* argument specifies a two-letter key that represents the main dictionary (for example, "AM" for LEX_AM.DLL). The *SuppDic$* argument specifies the supplemental dictionary. The spellings for each definition are appended in the order they appear in the spelling checker. Returns 0 (zero) if the word is spelled correctly.

For related commands, see "Utility Statements and Functions" in the section "WordBASIC Cross Reference," earlier in this chapter.

UtilGetSynonyms

UtilGetSynonyms *FillArray$( ), [Word$]*

Fills the string array *FillArray$* with all available synonyms for *Word$*. If *Word$* is omitted, Word uses the word nearest the insertion point.

For related commands, see "Utility Statements and Functions" in the section "WordBASIC Cross Reference," earlier in this chapter.

UtilGetSynonyms( )

Log = **UtilGetSynonyms(***FillArray$( ), [Word$]***)**

Fills the string array *FillArray$* with all available synonyms for *Word$*. If *Word$* is omitted, Word uses the word nearest the insertion point. Returns 0 (zero) if there are no synonyms available, or –1 if one or more synonyms are available.

For related commands, see "Utility Statements and Functions" in the section "WordBASIC Cross Reference," earlier in this chapter.

UtilHyphenate

UtilHyphenate *[HyphenateCaps], [Confirm], [HotZone[$]]*

Equivalent to the Utilities Hyphenate dialog box. The following table summarizes the arguments:

Argument	Description
HyphenateCaps	Corresponds to Hyphenate Caps check box.
Confirm	Corresponds to Confirm check box.
HotZone[$]	Measurement for hyphenation hot zone.

For related commands, see "Utility Statements and Functions" in the section "WordBASIC Cross Reference," earlier in this chapter.

UtilRenumber

UtilRenumber *[NumParas], [Type], [StartAt], [ShowAllLevels], [Format$]*

Equivalent to the Utilities Renumber dialog box. The following table summarizes the arguments:

Argument	Description
NumParas	Specifies which paragraphs to renumber; can be 0 (zero) for all (default), 1 for numbered paragraphs only, or 2 for remove.
Type	0 (zero) for automatic (default) or 1 for manual.
StartAt	Number at which to start paragraph numbering. Applies only if *Type* is 1 (manual).
ShowAllLevels	Corresponds to Show All Levels check box. Applies only if *Type* is 1 (manual).
Format$	Numbering format; can be Legal, Outline, or Sequence. If *Type* is 1 (manual), *Format$* can also be Learn.

For related commands, see "Utility Statements and Functions, " "Formatting Statements and Functions," and "Outlining Statements and Functions" in the section "WordBASIC Cross Reference," earlier in this chapter.

UtilRepaginateNow

UtilRepaginateNow

Equivalent to the Repaginate Now command on the Utilities menu. Forces repagination of the entire document.

For related commands, see "Utility Statements and Functions" and "Formatting Statements and Functions" in the section "WordBASIC Cross Reference," earlier in this chapter.

UtilRevisionMarks

UtilRevisionMarks *[MarkRevisions], [RevisionBar], [NewText]*

Equivalent to the Utilities Revision Marks dialog box. The following table summarizes the arguments:

Argument	Description
MarkRevisions	Corresponds to Mark Revisions check box.
RevisionBar	Specifies type of revision bar; can be 0 (zero) for none (default), 1 for outside, or 2 for inside.
NewText	Specifies how to mark new text; can be 0 (zero) for none (default), 1 for bold, 2 for italic, 3 for underline, or 4 for double underline.

The Search for next text with revision marking (**.Search**), Accept Revisions (**.AcceptRevisions**), or Undo Revisions (**.UndoRevisions**) command button name can be appended.

UtilSort

UtilSort *[Order], [Type], [Separator], [FieldNum[$]], [SortColumn], [CaseSensitive]*

Equivalent to the Utilities Sort dialog box. The following table summarizes the arguments:

Argument	Description
Order	Sorting order; can be 0 (zero) for ascending, or 1 for descending.
Type	Sort type; can be 0 (zero) for alphanumeric, 1 for numeric, or 2 for date.
Separator	Can be 0 (zero) for comma, or 1 for tab.
FieldNum[$]	Field number (column) to use as sort key.
SortColumn	Corresponds to the Sort Column Only check box. Requires column selection.
CaseSensitive	Corresponds to the Case Sensitive check box.

For related commands, see "Utility Statements and Functions" in the section "WordBASIC Cross Reference," earlier in this chapter.

UtilSpelling

UtilSpelling *[Word$], [MainDic$], [SuppDic$], [IgnoreCaps], [AlwaysSuggest]*

Equivalent to the Utilities Spelling dialog box. The following table summarizes the arguments:

Argument	Description
Word$	If *Word$* is supplied, that word is used; if *Word$* is omitted, Word searches forward from the insertion point for the next unmatched word.
MainDic$	The main dictionary, a two-letter key; for example, `"AM"` for LEX-AM.DLL.
SuppDic$	The supplemental dictionary.
IgnoreCaps	Corresponds to the Ignore ALL CAPS check box.
AlwaysSuggest	Corresponds to the Always Suggest check box.

The Delete command button name (**.Delete**) can be appended to remove the word from the current supplemental dictionary.

For related commands, see "Utility Statements and Functions" in the section "WordBASIC Cross Reference," earlier in this chapter.

UtilSpellSelection

UtilSpellSelection

Checks the selection. If the selection is only part of a word, the selection is expanded to include the whole word. The default supplemental dictionary is used.

For related commands, see "Utility Statements and Functions" in the section "WordBASIC Cross Reference," earlier in this chapter.

UtilThesaurus

UtilThesaurus

Lists alternative words for the selection. Equivalent to the Thesaurus command on the Utilities menu.

For related commands, see "Utility Statements and Functions" in the section "WordBASIC Cross Reference," earlier in this chapter.

Val( )

Num = **Val(***A$***)**

Returns the numeric value of *A$*. Strings that begin with characters other than a digit return 0 (zero).

Examples.

String	Resulting value
`10`	10
`ten`	0
`10 Apples`	10
`Apartment 10`	0

Statement	Result

`A$ = InputBox$("How many dozen apples?")`
`Total = Val(A$) * 12`
`Print A$ + " dozen equals" + Total`
	If user types `12` in the dialog box, `12 dozen equals 144` appears in the status bar.

For related commands, see "BASIC Statements and Functions" in the section "WordBASIC Cross Reference," earlier in this chapter.

ViewAnnotations

ViewAnnotations *[On]*

If *On* is omitted, toggles the annotations pane on and off. If *On* is nonzero, turns on the annotations pane; if *On* is 0 (zero), turns off the annotations pane. If no window is open, an error is generated.

For related commands, see "View Control Statements and Functions" in the section "WordBASIC Cross Reference," earlier in this chapter.

ViewAnnotations( )

Log = **ViewAnnotations( )**

Returns –1 if annotations view mode is on or 0 (zero) if annotations view mode is off.

For related commands, see "View Control Statements and Functions" in the section "WordBASIC Cross Reference," earlier in this chapter.

ViewDraft

ViewDraft *[On]*

If *On* is omitted, toggles draft view mode. If *On* is nonzero, turns on draft view mode. If *On* is 0 (zero), turns off draft view mode. If no window is open, an error is generated.

For related commands, see "View Control Statements and Functions" in the section "WordBASIC Cross Reference," earlier in this chapter.

ViewDraft( )

Log = **ViewDraft( )**

Returns –1 if draft view mode is on or 0 (zero) if draft view mode is off.

For related commands, see "View Control Statements and Functions" in the section "WordBASIC Cross Reference," earlier in this chapter.

ViewFieldCodes

ViewFieldCodes *[On]*

If *On* is omitted, toggles field codes view mode. If *On* is nonzero, turns on field codes view mode. If *On* is 0 (zero), turns off field codes view mode. If no window is open, an error is generated.

For related commands, see "View Control Statements and Functions" and "Field Statements and Functions" in the section "WordBASIC Cross Reference," earlier in this chapter.

ViewFieldCodes( )

Log = **ViewFieldCodes( )**

Returns –1 if field codes view mode is on or 0 (zero) if field codes view mode is off.

For related commands, see "View Control Statements and Functions" and "Field Statements and Functions" in the section "WordBASIC Cross Reference," earlier in this chapter.

ViewFootnotes

ViewFootnotes *[On]*

If *On* is omitted, toggles footnotes view mode. If *On* is nonzero, turns on footnotes view mode. If *On* is 0 (zero), turns off footnotes view mode. If no window is open, an error is generated.

For related commands, see "View Control Statements and Functions" in the section "WordBASIC Cross Reference," earlier in this chapter.

ViewFootnotes( )

Log = **ViewFootnotes( )**

Returns –1 if footnotes view mode is on or 0 (zero) if footnotes view mode is off.

For related commands, see "View Control Statements and Functions" in the section "WordBASIC Cross Reference," earlier in this chapter.

ViewFullMenus

ViewFullMenus

Turns on full menus.

For related commands, see "View Control Statements and Functions" in the section "WordBASIC Cross Reference," earlier in this chapter.

ViewMenus( )

Num = **ViewMenus( )**

Returns the menu state, as follows:

Return value	Menu state
0	Normal short menus
1	Normal full menus
2	No document short menus
3	No document full menus

For related commands, see "View Control Statements and Functions" in the section "WordBASIC Cross Reference," earlier in this chapter.

ViewOutline

ViewOutline *[On]*

If *On* is omitted, toggles outline view mode. If *On* is nonzero, turns on outline view mode. If *On* is 0 (zero), turns off outline view mode. If no window is open, an error is generated.

For related commands, see "View Control Statements and Functions" and "Outlining Statements and Functions" in the section "WordBASIC Cross Reference," earlier in this chapter.

ViewOutline( )

Log = **ViewOutline( )**

Returns –1 if outline view mode is on or 0 (zero) if outline view mode is off.

For related commands, see "View Control Statements and Functions" and "Outlining Statements and Functions" in the section "WordBASIC Cross Reference," earlier in this chapter.

ViewPage

ViewPage *[On]*

If *On* is omitted, toggles page view mode. If *On* is nonzero, turns on page view mode. If *On* is 0 (zero), turns off page view mode. If no window is open, an error is generated.

For related commands, see "View Control Statements and Functions" in the section "WordBASIC Cross Reference," earlier in this chapter.

ViewPage( )

Log = **ViewPage( )**

Returns –1 if page view mode is on or 0 (zero) if page view mode is off.

For related commands, see "View Control Statements and Functions" in the section "WordBASIC Cross Reference," earlier in this chapter.

ViewPreferences

ViewPreferences *[Tabs], [Spaces], [Paras], [Hyphens], [Hidden], [ShowAll], [DisplayAsPrinted], [Pictures], [TextBoundaries], [HScroll], [VScroll], [TableGridlines], [StyleAreaWidth[$]]*

Equivalent to the View Preferences dialog box. The following table summarizes the arguments:

Argument	Description
Tabs	Corresponds to the Tabs check box.
Spaces	Corresponds to the Spaces check box.
Paras	Corresponds to the Paragraph Marks check box.
Hyphens	Corresponds to the Optional Hyphens check box.
Hidden	Corresponds to the Hidden Text check box.
ShowAll	Corresponds to the Show All check box.
DisplayAsPrinted	Corresponds to the Display As Printed check box.
Pictures	Corresponds to the Pictures check box.
TextBoundaries	Corresponds to the Text Boundaries check box.
HScroll	Corresponds to the Horizontal Scroll Bar check box.
VScroll	Corresponds to the Vertical Scroll Bar check box.
TableGridlines	Corresponds to the Table Gridlines check box.
StyleAreaWidth[$]	Size occupied by style name area in the document window.

For related commands, see "View Control Statements and Functions," "Field Statements and Functions," "Formatting Statements and Functions," and "Table Creation and Editing Statements and Functions" in the section "WordBASIC Cross Reference," earlier in this chapter.

ViewRibbon

ViewRibbon *[On]*

If *On* is omitted, toggles the ribbon. If *On* is nonzero, turns on the ribbon. If *On* is 0 (zero), turns off the ribbon.

For related commands, see "View Control Statements and Functions" and "Formatting Statements and Functions" in the section "WordBASIC Cross Reference," earlier in this chapter.

ViewRibbon( )

Log = **ViewRibbon( )**

Returns –1 if the ribbon is on or 0 (zero) if the ribbon is off.

For related commands, see "View Control Statements and Functions" and "Formatting Statements and Functions" in the section "WordBASIC Cross Reference," earlier in this chapter.

ViewRuler

ViewRuler *[On]*

If *On* is omitted, toggles the ruler. If *On* is nonzero, turns on the ruler. If *On* is nonzero, turns off the ruler. If no window is open, the first window opened is opened with the ruler.

For related commands, see "View Control Statements and Functions" and "Formatting Statements and Functions" in the section "WordBASIC Cross Reference," earlier in this chapter.

ViewRuler( )

Log = **ViewRuler( )**

Returns –1 if the ruler is on or 0 (zero) if the ruler is off.

For related commands, see "View Control Statements and Functions" and "Formatting Statements and Functions" in the section "WordBASIC Cross Reference," earlier in this chapter.

ViewShortMenus

ViewShortMenus

Turns on short menus.

For related commands, see "View Control Statements and Functions" in the section "WordBASIC Cross Reference," earlier in this chapter.

ViewStatusBar

ViewStatusBar *[On]*

If *On* is omitted, toggles the status bar. If *On* is nonzero, turns on the status bar. If *On* is 0 (zero), turns off the status bar .

For related commands, see "View Control Statements and Functions" in the section "WordBASIC Cross Reference," earlier in this chapter.

ViewStatusBar( )

Log = **ViewStatusBar( )**

Returns –1 if the status bar is on or 0 (zero) if the status bar is off.

For related commands, see "View Control Statements and Functions" in the section "WordBASIC Cross Reference," earlier in this chapter.

VLine

VLine *[Count]*

Scrolls down vertically by *Count* number of lines. If *Count* is omitted, one line is the default. A negative *Count* value scrolls up.

For related commands, see "View Control Statements and Functions" in the section "WordBASIC Cross Reference," earlier in this chapter.

VPage

VPage *[Count]*

Scrolls down vertically by *Count* number of screens. If *Count* is omitted, one screen is the default. A negative *Count* value scrolls up.

For related commands, see "View Control Statements and Functions" in the section "WordBASIC Cross Reference," earlier in this chapter.

VScroll

VScroll *Percentage*

Scrolls vertically to the place in the document that is the specified percentage of the document's length.

For related commands, see "View Control Statements and Functions" in the section "WordBASIC Cross Reference," earlier in this chapter.

VScroll( )

Num = **VScroll( )**

Returns the current vertical scroll position as a percentage of the document's size.

For related commands, see "View Control Statements and Functions" in the section "WordBASIC Cross Reference," earlier in this chapter.

While...Wend

While *Condition*
    Statement(s)
Wend

Repeats the statements in the block while the *Condition* is True. If the *Condition* is initially False, the loop is never executed.

For related commands, see "BASIC Statements and Functions" in the section "WordBASIC Cross Reference," earlier in this chapter.

Window( )

Num = **Window( )**

Returns the number of the active window. The number can range from 0 (zero) to the number of open windows. The number corresponds to the number on the Window menu. A value of 0 indicates no window is open.

For related commands, see "Window Control Statements and Functions" in the section "WordBASIC Cross Reference," earlier in this chapter.

Window1

Window1

Activates Window 1. This number corresponds to the number on the Window menu. If you select a nonexistent window, an error is generated.

For related commands, see "Window Control Statements and Functions" in the section "WordBASIC Cross Reference," earlier in this chapter.

Window2

Window2

Activates Window 2. This number corresponds to the number on the Window menu. If you select a nonexistent window, an error is generated.

For related commands, see "Window Control Statements and Functions" in the section "WordBASIC Cross Reference," earlier in this chapter.

Window3

Window3

Activates Window 3. This number corresponds to the number on the Window menu. If you select a nonexistent window, an error is generated.

For related commands, see "Window Control Statements and Functions" in the section "WordBASIC Cross Reference," earlier in this chapter.

Window4

Window4

Activates Window 4. This number corresponds to the number on the Window menu. If you select a nonexistent window, an error is generated.

For related commands, see "Window Control Statements and Functions" in the section "WordBASIC Cross Reference," earlier in this chapter.

Window5

Window5

Activates Window 5. This number corresponds to the number on the Window menu. If you select a nonexistent window, an error is generated.

For related commands, see "Window Control Statements and Functions" in the section "WordBASIC Cross Reference," earlier in this chapter.

Window6

Window6

Activates Window 6. This number corresponds to the number on the Window menu. If you select a nonexistent window, an error is generated.

For related commands, see "Window Control Statements and Functions" in the section "WordBASIC Cross Reference," earlier in this chapter.

Window7

Window7

Activates Window 7. This number corresponds to the number on the Window menu. If you select a nonexistent window, an error is generated.

For related commands, see "Window Control Statements and Functions" in the section "WordBASIC Cross Reference," earlier in this chapter.

Window8

Window8

Activates Window 8. This number corresponds to the number on the Window menu. If you select a nonexistent window, an error is generated.

For related commands, see "Window Control Statements and Functions" in the section "WordBASIC Cross Reference," earlier in this chapter.

Window9

Window9

Activates Window 9. This number corresponds to the number on the Window menu. If you select a nonexistent window, an error is generated.

For related commands, see "Window Control Statements and Functions" in the section "WordBASIC Cross Reference," earlier in this chapter.

WindowArrangeAll

WindowArrangeAll

Arranges all open windows so that windows do not overlap.

For related commands, see "Window Control Statements and Functions" in the section "WordBASIC Cross Reference," earlier in this chapter.

WindowName$( )

*A$* = **WindowName$(***n***)**

Returns the title of the *n*th open window. The *n* corresponds to the number on the Window menu. If *n* is 0 (zero) or not supplied, the name of the active window is returned.

For related commands, see "Window Control Statements and Functions" in the section "WordBASIC Cross Reference," earlier in this chapter.

WindowNewWindow

WindowNewWindow

Equivalent to the New Window command on the Window menu. Creates a copy of the active window.

For related commands, see "Window Control Statements and Functions" in the section "WordBASIC Cross Reference," earlier in this chapter.

WindowPane( )

Num = **WindowPane( )**

Returns 1 if the window is not split or if the top pane of the active window is selected. Returns 3 if the bottom pane is selected.

For related commands, see "Window Control Statements and Functions" in the section "WordBASIC Cross Reference," earlier in this chapter.

WordLeft

WordLeft *[Repeat], [Select]*

Moves the insertion point left by *Repeat* number of words. If *Repeat* is omitted, 1 is assumed. If *Select* is nonzero, the selection is extended left by *Repeat* words.

For related commands, see "Selection and Insertion Point Definition and Control Statements and Functions" in the section "WordBASIC Cross Reference," earlier in this chapter.

WordLeft( )

Log = **WordLeft(***[Repeat], [Select]***)**

Moves the selection left by *Repeat* number of words. If *Repeat* is omitted, 1 is assumed. If *Select* is nonzero, the selection is extended left by *Repeat* words. Returns 0 (zero) if the action cannot be performed. For example, the function returns 0 (zero) if the insertion point is at the beginning of the document.

For related commands, see "Selection and Insertion Point Definition and Control Statements and Functions" in the section "WordBASIC Cross Reference," earlier in this chapter.

WordRight

WordRight *[Repeat], [Select]*

Moves the insertion point right by *Repeat* number words. If *Repeat* is omitted, 1 is assumed. If *Select* is nonzero, the selection is extended right by *Repeat* words.

For related commands, see "Selection and Insertion Point Definition and Control Statements and Functions" in the section "WordBASIC Cross Reference," earlier in this chapter.

WordRight( )

Log = **WordRight(***[Repeat], [Select]***)**

Moves the selection right by *Repeat* number words. If *Repeat* is omitted, 1 is assumed. If *Select* is nonzero, the selection is extended right by *Repeat* words. Returns 0 (zero) if the action cannot be performed.

Statement	Result
`While WordRight(,1)` `Wend`	Extends the selection one word at a time until the end of the document is reached.

For related commands, see "Selection and Insertion Point Definition and Control Statements and Functions" in the section "WordBASIC Cross Reference," earlier in this chapter.

WordUnderline

WordUnderline *[On]*

If *On* is omitted, toggles word underlining for the entire selection. If *On* is nonzero, makes the entire selection word underlined. If *On* is 0 (zero), removes word underlining from the entire selection.

Statement	If text is	New text is
`WordUnderline`	Trey Research Company	Trey Research Company
`WordUnderline`	Trey Research Company	Trey Research Company
`WordUnderline`	Trey Research Company	Trey Research Company
`WordUnderline 1`	Trey Research Company	Trey Research Company
`WordUnderline 0`	Trey Research Company	Trey Research Company

For related commands, see "Formatting Statements and Functions" in the section "WordBASIC Cross Reference," earlier in this chapter.

WordUnderline( )

Log = **WordUnderline( )**

Returns 0 (zero) if none of the selection is word underlined, 1 if all of the selection is word underlined, or –1 if part of the selection is word underlined or more than one kind of underlining is used.

If selected text is	Function returns
Trey Research Company	0; the selection is not word underlined.
Trey Research Company	1; the entire selection is word underlined.
Trey Research Company	–1; only part of the selection is word underlined.

For related commands, see "Formatting Statements and Functions" in the section "WordBASIC Cross Reference," earlier in this chapter.

Write

Write *[#]StreamNumber, Expressions*

Writes the arguments to the file associated with *StreamNumber*, including delimiters, so that the arguments can be read by the **Read** statement.

For more information on sequential files, see Chapter 6, "More WordBASIC Programming Concepts."

For related commands, see "BASIC Statements and Functions" in the section "WordBASIC Cross Reference," earlier in this chapter.

MACRO ERROR MESSAGES

NOTE: *If an untrapped error occurs in a macro while Word is minimized, the macro halts, Word remains minimized, and the Word icon flashes. When Word is maximized, an error message box that indicates the nature of the error is displayed.*

5 Illegal function call

The program tried to pass an out-of-parameter value to a math or a string function or statement. This can occur for the following reasons:

- An improper or out-of-range argument value was given to a function.
- Strings have been concatenated to create a string longer than 32,767 characters.

6 Overflow

The result of a calculation is too large to be represented within the range allowed for floating-point numbers, or the floating-point number is too large to convert to an integer.

7 Out of memory

There is not enough memory to perform the operation.

9 Subscript out of range

You have used an array element that has a subscript outside the dimensions of the array or that has the wrong number of subscripts.

11 Division by zero

The program contains an expression that is an attempt to divide by 0 (zero).

14 Out of string space

String variables exceed the allocated amount of string space (total of 65,535 characters).

16 String formula too complex

A string formula is too long. Break the formula into parts for correct execution.

39 Case Else expected

An expression in a **Select Case** statement has no matching case.

40 Variable required

A statement without a required variable was encountered.

51 Internal error

An internal error occurred in WordBASIC interpreter. Please report to Microsoft the error and the conditions under which it occurred.

52 Bad file name or number

A statement refers to a file with a file number that is not open or is out of range.

53 File not found

A statement refers to a file that does not exist or cannot be found because you moved it or removed the floppy disk the file is on.

54 Bad file mode

The program tried to execute an **Open** statement with a file mode other than I (input), O (output), or A (append); an attempt was made to read from a file opened for output or appending; or an attempt was made to write to a file opened for input.

55 File already opened

You specified an open file for an **Open** statement or **Kill** statement.

57 Device I/O error

An error occurred on a device I/O operation.

58 File already exists.

A file name specified in a **Name** statement is identical to a file name already in use on the disk.

61 Disk full

There is not enough room on the disk for the file.

62 Input past end of file

The program contains an **Input** statement that reads from an empty file or from a file in which all the data has already been read.

64 Bad file name

An illegal form was used for a file name.

67 Too many files

Four files have already been opened.

68 Device unavailable

The program is attempting to access a device that is not on-line or that does not exist.

70 Permission denied

The program tried to write to a write-protected disk or a read-only file.

71 Disk not ready

The disk drive door is open, or there is no disk in the drive.

72 Disk media error

The disk-drive hardware has detected a physical flaw on the disk.

73 Advanced features unavailable

The program tried to use a feature that is not available in this version of Word-BASIC.

74 Cannot rename across disks

The program tried to rename a file with a new drive designation.

75 Path/file access error

The operating system was unable to make the correct path-to-file name connection.

76 Path not found

The operating system was unable to find the specified path.

100 Syntax error

The program contains a line with an incorrect sequence of characters. If you run the program from the macro-editing window, Word highlights the line that contains the syntax error.

101 Comma missing

The macro interpreter expected a comma somewhere in the line.

102 Command failed.

A macro command failed to complete properly, usually because the user pressed the Esc key or the program contains a **Stop** statement.

103 Dialog record variable expected

A dialog record variable is missing. For example, you have a **Dialog** statement or **GetCurValues** statement without a dialog record variable.

104 Else without If

The macro interpreter encountered an **Else** statement without an **If** statement.

105 End If without If

The macro interpreter encountered an **End If** statement without an **If** statement.

109 Input missing

The **Input** keyword was expected.

110 No Resume Next

There is no **Next** keyword after **Resume** in the error handler.

111 Expression too complex

The expression is too complex. Try breaking up the expression into multiple expressions.

112 Identifier expected

An identifier such as a variable, **Sub** name, or **Function** name was expected.

113 Duplicate label

Two program lines are assigned the same label. Each label must be unique.

114 Label not found

A line label is referred to (for example, in a **Goto** statement) but does not occur in the program.

115 Right parenthesis missing

The interpreter expected a right (closing) parenthesis.

116 Argument-count mismatch

A statement or function has an incorrect number of arguments.

117 Missing Next or Wend

A **For** statement or a **While** statement is missing a corresponding **Next** statement or **Wend** statement.

118 Nested Sub or Function definitions

A **Sub** or **Function** definition appears inside another **Sub** or **Function** definition.

119 Next without For

A **Next** statement is missing a corresponding **For** statement.

120 Array already dimensioned

There is more than one **Dim** statement for the same array. Use the **ReDim** statement.

121 Duplicate definition

Two **Subs** or **Functions** have the same name.

122 Type mismatch

The argument types for a statement, function, or variable assignment are not compatible. This usually means a string was used where a number was required or a number was used where a string was needed.

123 Undefined dialog record field

A field that is not part of the dialog record was used.

124 Undefined Sub or Function

A **Sub** or **Function** cannot be found. This message also appears if you leave out the $ in the name of a string function, or for a variable name that has not been assigned a value.

125 Unexpected end of macro

The macro program ended unexpectedly.

126 Wend without While

A **Wend** statement is missing a corresponding **While** statement.

127 Wrong number of dimensions

An array reference contains a different number of dimensions than the **Dim** statement.

128 No current option button group

The **OptionGroup** statement must precede the **OptionButton** statement.

129 Too many nested control structures

While, For, or **If** statements are nested too deeply.

130 Select without End Select

A **Select** statement is missing a corresponding **End Select** statement.

500 Cannot initiate link

The program cannot initiate a DDE link. These are some possible reasons: The other application does not support DDE, or has too many links active; the other application is not running and cannot be started; there is not enough memory; the topic specified is not currently supported in the other application; Word has too many links active; the other application is busy.

501 Invalid channel number

The DDE channel number specified is invalid.

502 Application does not respond.

The application does not respond to a DDE request. These are some possible reasons: The other application does not support the specified item; there is not enough memory; the other application is busy.

503 Process failed in other application.

Instructions failed to pass to another application via a DDE link.

504 Window does not exist.

The specified application or document window cannot be found.

505 Cannot activate application

The specified application cannot be activated.

506 Cannot send keys

The string specified in the **SendKeys** statement cannot be sent to the other application.

508 Other application is busy.

The other application cannot respond to Word's requests.

509 Command is not available.

The operation cannot be performed at this time or in the current context. The command is grayed on the menu when it is unavailable.

511 No such macro

The macro called from within the program does not exist.

513 String too long

A string parameter is too long.

514 Document not open

The document referred to in the program is not open.

528 . Unable to load Speller
Word cannot load the spelling checker. Check the path to make sure it is correct.

529 Cannot open dictionary
Word cannot open the dictionary specified in the program. Check the name of the dictionary to make sure it is correct.

530 Dialog box description too complex
Too many controls have been included in the dialog box definition. Reduce the number of controls or create two dialog boxes for the program.

WORD ERROR MESSAGES

These error messages are generated outside WordBASIC, by Word itself. Unattended trapping of these errors is not possible, as the application always displays an error dialog box and waits for the user to respond. Once the user responds, Word's error routine returns control to the WordBASIC macro and, in most respects, the error can be trapped and handled like any other. The only exception is that the **Error** cannot create these error conditions nor can it be used to display these error messages. For a description of these error messages, see Word's on-line Help or the *Word User's Reference.*

1001 Low memory: save your document now.

1003 Line, footnote, and annotation are mutually exclusive.

1004 Undefined Go To operation

1005 Bookmark does not exist.

1006 Go To group character repeated.

1007 No previous Go To or Search

1008 Sections not allowed

1009 Bookmark name not valid

1011 Not enough memory to compile index

1012 Not enough memory to run Help

1013 Not enough memory to run DDE application

1014 Not enough memory to run application

1016 Not enough memory to complete operation

1017 Not enough memory to update display

1018 Not enough memory to define glossary

1019 Not enough memory to merge styles

1020 Not enough memory to display outline

1021 Not enough memory to display ruler

1022 No such glossary

1023 Serious disk error on file: (name)

1024 File is not available: (name).

1025 Cannot open document

1026 Style name does not exist.

1027 Low memory: cannot perform Replace

1028 Search text not found

1029 Not enough memory to display/print picture

1030 Dimensions after cropping are too small or too large.

1031 Dimensions after scaling are too small or too large.

1032 File too large to save; delete some text and try again.

1033 DOT-PATH specified in WIN.INI is not valid: ignoring (Word for Windows).
DOT-PATH specified in OS2.INI is not valid: ignoring (Word for OS/2).

1034 INI-PATH specified in WIN.INI is not valid: ignoring (Word for Windows).
INI-PATH specified in OS2.INI is not valid: ignoring (Word for OS/2).

1035 UTIL-PATH specified in WIN.INI is not valid: ignoring (Word for Windows).
UTIL-PATH specified in OS2.INI is not valid: ignoring (Word for OS/2).

1036 Cannot start converter: (name)

1037 Not enough memory to run converter

1038 Incorrect password

1039 Not a valid hot zone value

1040 Cannot open Word hyphenation file

1041 Not a valid document template

1042 Margins, column spacing, or paragraph indentations too large

1043 Tab position too large

1044 Cannot print; no printer installed

1045 Not a valid print range

1046 Cannot print

1047 Not enough memory to repaginate/print this document

1048 Not enough disk space to print this document

1049 Cannot open window; too many open

1050 Not a valid integer

1051 Not a valid measurement

1052 Number must be between nn and nn.

1053 Measurement must be between (size) and (size).

1054 Cannot write to file WINWORD.INI (Word for Windows).
Cannot write to file PMWORD.INI (Word for OS/2).

1055 Document name or path is not valid.

1056 Not a valid file name

1057 Cannot name a document the same as an open document

1058 Cannot write foreign format over open document

1059 File is read-only.

1060 Cannot save; cannot create file

1062 Fields nested too deeply.

1063 Low memory: run with background pagination off for better performance.

1064 Low memory: run with background pagination, ruler, ribbon, and status bar off for better performance.

1065 Low memory: use draft view for better performance.

1066 Not enough memory to run Word

1069 Cannot open existing NORMAL.DOT

1070 Not a valid date

1071 Not a valid style name

1072 Style sheet is full. Cannot define new style.

1073 Style cannot be based on itself.

1074 Based On style name does not exist.

1075 Next style name does not exist.

1076 Cannot merge the active style sheet

1077 Style name already exists.

1078 Document does not exist.

1079 Not enough memory for large Clipboard

1080 Indentation too large

1081 Paragraph too wide

1082 Full Windows required to run another application. (This error applies to Word for Windows running under Windows runtime version only.)

1083 Command name must have extension.

1084 Cannot open document template

1085 Document template is not valid.

1086 Cannot open file: has old file format. Opening as plain text.

1087 Cannot open file: do not understand file format. Opening as plain text.

1088 Cannot open file: saved in old template format. Opening as plain text.

1089 Cannot open file: fast saved in old format. Opening as plain text.

1090 Style sheet full. Style of some paragraphs may become Normal.

1091 Cannot insert file into itself

1093 Not enough memory to run Thesaurus

1094 Can't start Thesaurus

1095 Not enough memory to run Speller

1096 Cannot find Speller

1097 Can't start Speller

1098 Cannot create main update dictionary

1103 Cannot find WINWORD.CBT directory (Word for Windows).
Cannot find PMWORD.CBT directory (Word for OS/2).

1104 Not a valid tab position

1105 Too many tabs set

1106 Too many tabs to be cleared

1107 No index entries found

1108 Cannot create work file

1109 Not a valid WINWORD.INI file; using defaults (Word for Windows).
Not a valid PMWORD.INI file; using defaults (Word for OS/2).

1111 Cannot open a window for result: close some open windows and try again.

1112 DATA, NEXT, NEXTIF, and SKIPIF fields may not be nested in any other fields.

1113 DATA, NEXT, NEXTIF, and SKIPIF fields may not be in annotations, headers, footers, or footnotes.

1114 DATA field must precede NEXT, NEXTIF, or SKIPIF fields.

1115 DATA field does not contain a data file name.

1116 Syntax error in field condition

1117 Cannot open data file

1118 Cannot open header file

1119 Requested first record is beyond end of data file.

1120 Printer error

1121 Cannot change printer; no printers installed

1122 Not a valid number in Start At

1123 Not a valid number in Format

1124 Not valid numbers in Start At and Format

1125 No table of contents entry fields found

1126 No heading paragraphs found

1127 Make selection first.

1128 Not a valid selection

1129 Document is too large to be saved. Delete some text before trying to save.

1130 Serious problem: Your document is too big for Word to handle.

1132 Low memory: close an application.

1133 Not a valid search list

1134 Not a valid search expression

1135 Not a valid date range

1136 List may be incomplete.

1137 Cannot save; (name) is locked.

1138 Cannot save; (name) is read-only.

1139 Window is too small.

1142 Not a valid action for annotations

1143 Revision marks not found

1144 Style sheet definition is too large. Some styles discarded.

1145 Formatting too complex

1146 No footnotes to show

1147 No annotations to show

1148 Low memory: fonts in copied text may be incorrect.

1149 Can't move sections into headers/footers

1150 Can't move footnote references here

1151 Can't replace footnote references

1152 Cannot move sections into destination

1153 Cannot move footnote/annotation references into destination

1154 Cannot replace footnote/annotation references

1155 Too many edits; operation will be incomplete. Save your work.

1156 Not a valid action for end of row

1157 Not a valid action for footnotes

1158 Document not saved

1159 Original file may be damaged due to serious disk error. Save with a new name.

1160 System disk is locked or full and memory is nearly full. Save your work.

1161 System disk and memory are nearly full. Save your work.

1162 Maximum number of columns exceeded

1163 Maximum width exceeded

1164 Cannot delete end of row

1165 Illegal text in table

1166 Name refers to more than one style.

1167 Name is not a style name.

1168 Valid style name is required.

1169 Session too complex. Please close a window.

1170 Sections not allowed

1172 Illegal paste into table

1173 Maximum number of cells exceeded

1174 Text contains section mark; cannot paste.

1175 Cannot paste table into a table cell

1176 Copy and paste areas are different shapes.

1177 Low memory: close extra windows and save your work.

1178 Document name or path is not valid.

1179 Fields nested too deeply.

1180 Not a valid action for annotations

1181 Value is out of range.

1182 Warning: could not create work file. Check temp environment variable.

1183 Not enough memory to sort

1184 Cannot sort fields in selection

1185 No valid records to sort

1186 Style has too many Based On ancestors.

1190 Low memory: closing saved document

1191 Unrecoverable disk error on file: (filename)

1192 Disk is full trying to write (filename). Save document on a different disk.

1193 Macro is too big.

1194 Cannot change menu help text for built-in commands

1195 Cannot close a running macro

1196 No such macro

1197 Not enough memory to record command

1198 Word is already running.

1199 Cannot run Word: incorrect Windows or DOS version (Word for Windows).
Cannot run Word: incorrect OS/2 version (Word for OS/2).

1200 No visible text to convert

1202 Cannot start Tutorial

1203 Not enough memory to run Tutorial

1204 Not enough memory to encode macro

1205 Not enough memory to run macro

1206 Cannot replace end-of-cell mark

1207 Document is too large to be saved. Change aborted.

1208 Cannot rename or delete a built-in macro

1209 Cannot rename or delete a macro that is open for editing

1210 Cannot edit macro being recorded

1211 Macro line is too long.

1212 Cannot record over macro being edited

1213 Invalid selection to format cells

1214 Menu text is too long.

1215 Mixed table/text selection; shrinking replacement area

1216 Low memory: close extra windows and try again.

1217 Only whole rows may be converted to text.

1218 One or more rows are too wide to split.

1219 Recorded macro was too long and has been truncated.

1220 One or more rows are too wide for operation.

1221 Cannot find or run application

1222 Low memory: close extra windows and save your work.

1223 Cannot insert a table inside a table

1224 Table cannot be moved to end of document.

1226 Illegal selection for copy or move

1227 Low memory: cannot display requested font

1228 Cannot open data file

1230 Style has circular Based On list.

1231 Not a valid style name

1232 Word was not found.

1233 Cannot remove word from dictionary

1234 Cannot find Help application

1235 Skipping records with an incorrect number of fields

1236 Not enough memory to complete operation

1237 Low memory: list may be incomplete.

1238 Cannot quit Microsoft Word

1239 Document is too long to save using this version.

1240 Document is too long to print using this version.

1241 Cannot repaginate; no printer installed

1242 Opening PM Word document. (Documents may be fully converted by saving the document as a Windows Word document from within Word for OS/2).

Chapter 8

Dynamic Data Exchange

One of the most powerful facilities of Microsoft Windows and OS/2 is Dynamic Data Exchange (DDE). DDE allows intertask communication and the sharing of data between applications. This section provides examples of DDE used with Word and other Windows or OS/2 applications.

The primary method of communication is the passing of messages from one Windows or OS/2 application to another. Windows and OS/2 applications receive all information in the form of messages. For example, keyboard input, mouse activities, menu selections, and communications from peripherals are all sent to a Windows or OS/2 application as messages. The application is always receiving messages and processing them.

The most powerful way you can make use of DDE is to send and receive these messages. For example, assume you have been asked to prepare a complex report on productivity at your company. The report is to include the number of items produced, the percentage that passed quality control, the number of items shipped, the number of hours worked per employee, the number of items each employee produced, and the percentage of items each employee produced that passed quality-control standards. You compile this data in a Microsoft Excel worksheet with the following layout:

	A	B	C	D
1	Items Produced	4,000		
2	% Passing QC	97%		
3	Items Shipped	3,290		
4				
5	Employee	Hours	Items Produced	% Passing QC
6	W. Hobbes	39	763	99%
7	A. Jackson	45	883	99%
8	J. Morales	62	1,432	94%
9	G. Pederson	41	922	98%
10				

You could manually cut and paste the information from the worksheet to your Word document. However, if the information changes or if you update the information on a regular basis, DDE provides an automatic link to current values without your intervention. For example, you might be asked to provide this data on a weekly or biweekly basis. With DDE, you can set up a means of "conversation" between the server (Microsoft Excel) and the client (Word).

You can use fields or macro statements to set up the DDE interface between Word and other applications. To use DDE to import data into a Word document from a Microsoft Excel worksheet, you can use the DDE field, which has the following syntax:

{DDE *App, Topic, Item***}**

Word then updates the DDE field whenever you request updating. Word updates the DDEAUTO field whenever new information is available.

Here's an example:

```
{DDE excel cogs.xls COGS}
```

When you insert this field in a document, Word imports data from the area (or *Item*) with the defined name `COGS` in the Microsoft Excel worksheet with the file name (or *Topic*) COGS.XLS. When Word updates the field, DDE starts Microsoft Excel as the server (unless Microsoft Excel is already running and the topic is available), loads the topic, and transfers the data defined by the *Item* to the Word document.

For more information on the DDE and DDEAUTO fields and their usage, see Chapter 9, "Fields."

DDE applications can support a special System *Topic*. If you use System as the *Topic*, Word also recognizes three special *Item* arguments with which you can ask for specific information:

Item	Effect
SysItems	Returns a list of all items you can use with the System topic.
Topics	Returns a list of currently open documents, including full path names.
Formats	Returns a list of all the Clipboard formats supported by Word.

Word returns these values in CF_TEXT format (ASCII text), separating items in a list with Tab characters.

CREATING A LINK BETWEEN WORD AND ANOTHER APPLICATION

To create a DDE link between Word and another application, you must already be running both applications under Microsoft Windows, version 2.0 (or later), Microsoft Windows/386, or OS/2.

To create a link between the two applications:

1. Choose Insert Field (Alt+I+D).
2. Select the DDE or DDEAUTO field.
3. Type the name of the application; the name of the file (including the filename extension) containing the information you are requesting; and the bookmark, named range, or other *Item*; and then choose OK. If the information or application is not available, Word displays a message to that effect. Choose OK to continue.

You can also create a DDE link using macro statements. When you record a macro that uses DDE, Word records the actions as DDE fields, not as DDE macro statements. For more information about DDE statements, see Chapter 7, "Word-BASIC Command Reference."

DDE AND WORDBASIC

You can accomplish most DDE conversations with the DDE and DDEAUTO fields. If you want to perform complex actions involving DDE, you can use WordBASIC statements to construct special-purpose macros.

In a DDE conversation, each application opens one "channel," similar to a "stream" in file I/O, for every conversation that application is engaged in. After a DDE conversation is initiated, the client application interacts with the server by issuing transactions that ask the server to perform specific actions. DDE issues the transaction instructions as Windows messages.

DDE conversations are always one way. Only client applications can issue transaction requests. If a server application issues a transaction request, it initiates a new conversation and therefore becomes a client application as well as a server. Both the server and the client, however, can issue termination transactions to end the conversation.

You can use WordBASIC statements to write your own transactions. For the syntax of these statements and more information, see Chapter 7, "WordBASIC Command Reference."

INTERCHANGE TYPES

DDE fields link data to your document; DDE macro statements and functions allow you to access another application or information used by another application, by issuing the following transactions between Word and another application:

- Initiating a DDE conversation
- Transferring data
- Terminating a DDE conversation

Some simple examples follow.

Initiating a DDE Conversation Between Word and Another Application

To initiate a DDE conversation between two applications, the client application sends an initiate message to the server application. The server acknowledges only topics it can support.

Program listing	Effect
`ChanNum = DDEInitiate("EXCEL", "COGS.XLS")`	Initiates a channel. to Microsoft Excel and to the file COGS.XLS
`Print ChanNum`	Prints the channel number.
`DDETerminate ChanNum`	Closes the channel.

Transferring Data Between Word and Another Application

A client application can receive data from a server with a **DDERequest$()** function and post data to a server with a **DDEPoke** statement.

Program listing	Effect
`ChanNum = DDEInitiate("EXCEL", "COGS.XLS")`	Initiates a channel to Microsoft Excel and to the file COGS.XLS.
`Print DDERequest$(ChanNum,"payroll")`	Requests the information named `payroll`.
`DDETerminate ChanNum`	Closes the channel.

The following example uses DDE to copy the selected chart into a Word document:

```
Sub MAIN
   DisableInput
   On Error Goto LFinish
   If SelType() = 1 Then
      Beep
      MsgBox "Make a selection first", "Chart Selection", 16
      Goto LFinish
   End If
   EditCopy                         'Copy selection.
                                    'Only numeric data is charted.
   Print "Sending Macro Program to Excel..."  'Excel must be on your path
   ChanNum = DDEInitiate("Excel", "System")   'Get Data Channel to Excel
   DDEExecute ChanNum, "[New(1)]"           'Open new spreadsheet
   DDEExecute ChanNum, "[Paste()][New(2)]" 'Paste data/create new chart
   DDEExecute ChanNum, "[Select()]"        'Select chart
   DDEExecute ChanNum, "[Copy.Picture(1,1)]"  'Copy chart to Clipboard
   DDEExecute ChanNum, "[Close(0)][Close(0)]" 'Close chart/spreadsheet
   DDETerminate ChanNum
   Print "Excel Chart is on the Clipboard"
LFinish:
End Sub
```

Note that for this example to work, Microsoft Excel must be on your path. Only two numeric selections are converted into charts.

Terminating a DDE Conversation Between Word and Another Application

To terminate a DDE conversation, the client or server application issues a terminate message. This message tells the recipient that the sender will issue no more transactions. All applications are prepared to receive a terminate at any time. The recipient sends a terminate message in response.

Program listing	Effect
`ChanNum = DDEInitiate("EXCEL", "COGS.XLS")`	Opens a channel to Microsoft Excel and to the file COGS.XLS.
`Print ChanNum`	Displays the channel number in the status bar.
`DDETerminate ChanNum`	Closes the channel.

Chapter 9

Fields

Fields contain instructions for inserting special information into your document. These instructions tell Word how to display and print such items as text, pictures, charts, tables, indexes, tables of contents, and page numbers.

Fields provide a common structure for performing dissimilar functions. With this common structure, you can use features that seem unrelated in a common manner. For example, you can use Print Merge and other linked text functions in similar ways.

As a simple example, you can use fields in Microsoft Word to print the current date or time in the header of your document. As a more complex example, you can use fields to request information from another application, format the data, and insert it into your document.

FIELD CATEGORIES

Fields fall into one of the following three categories:

- Result fields
- Action fields
- Marker fields

Result Fields

A result field displays information in your document. Most result fields display information that can be converted to static text. A few result fields display information that is visible only as long as the field is intact. Word gets this information in several ways. Some fields, such as the DATE and AUTHOR fields, are updated by Word or by the operating system. Others, such as the REF field, refer to the document for information. Still others, such as the DDE and INCLUDE fields, perform high-level functions to get information.

The AUTONUM, AUTONUMOUT, and AUTONUMLGL fields are automatic result fields. Word updates these fields automatically.

Action Fields

You use action fields to tell Word to perform some action without inserting visible text in the document. Word performs the action either when you request that the field be updated, as with the ASK field, or automatically, as when you click the GOTOBUTTON field.

Marker Fields

A marker field produces no visible result and performs no action. It merely supplies information to other features of Word. The Index Entry (XE) field is an example of a marker field. An XE field provides a pointer for the index field. It has no result because no information is acted on; it is a reference for another field.

FIELD SYNTAX

All fields share a common syntax. Each field includes the *field characters* ({ }) and the *field type*, which identifies the field to Word. Some fields also have instructions that modify the field or control the display of the result of the field.

Field Characters

The field characters begin and end the field. You can't use the regular braces on the keyboard to insert field characters. You must use the INSERT FIELD key, Ctrl+F9, the Insert Field menu command, or the InsertFieldChars built-in command.

Selecting one of the field characters automatically selects the entire field. Therefore, you cannot delete or edit a single field character.

Field Type

The field type identifies the action or the effect the field has on the document. For example, the field type of `{date}` is date. You can precede the field type with any amount of white space, which can include spaces, tabs, newline characters, paragraph marks, column breaks, and section marks. You can precede a field type with a backslash. The backslash has no known effect on a field; it is entirely optional and usually omitted, as in all the examples in this chapter. If you precede a field type with much white space, you might insert a backslash as a visual reminder that the field type is part of a field and not a literal word in the text. If you use a field type that Word does not recognize, Word treats it as a bookmark reference.

Word field types are described in "Field Types and Instructions," later in this chapter. Bookmarks are also described later.

Instructions

Certain field types use additional instructions to define the specific procedure Word should use to update the field. A field's instructions consist of one or more arguments that modify the action or effect of the field. Arguments can be bookmarks, mathematical expressions, identifiers, text and graphics, or switches. These are described later in this section.

If you use a multiple-word argument, you must enclose it within quotation marks. It's a good idea to enclose single-word arguments in quotation marks as well. You won't cause an error, and if you add other instructions later, you won't need to add the quotation marks. If you want to use an argument that includes quotation marks as part of the argument string, you must precede the quotation marks with a backslash (\). If the argument includes a backslash, you must double the backslash (\\).

> **NOTE:** *Remember to use regular double quotation marks to enclose arguments. Single quotation marks have a different meaning in Word and are explained later in this chapter.*

Here are some examples of field instructions (refer to "Field Types and Instructions," later in this chapter, for a discussion of the field types used):

Field code	Field result	Remarks
`Although we started discussing large, flightless waterfowl, we only mentioned {subject penguins}.`	`Although we started discussing large, flightless waterfowl, we only mentioned penguins.`	Single-word argument can omit quotation marks.
`Our topic for discussion is {subject "penguins' behavior"}.`	`Our topic for discussion is penguins' behavior.`	Multiple-word argument needs quotation marks.
`Why are we writing about {subject \"behavior\"}?`	`Why are we writing about "behavior"?`	Argument that contains quotation marks needs backslashes.
`This document is stored in {keywords c:\\dreams\\penguin.doc}`	`This document is stored in c:\dreams\penguin.doc.`	Argument that contains backslashes needs double backslashes.

Instructions can be formatted as hidden text. Word ignores hidden instructions within the field during calculation. You can use this feature to insert comments into fields, just as you put comments into macros or other programs.

Bookmarks

A bookmark associates a selection with a name you specify. Once you have created a bookmark, you can use it as an argument in an instruction. Some fields use the contents of the selection associated with the bookmark as the argument; others use the location of the bookmark selection—for example, the page number. The REF field in the following example uses the text associated with the bookmark to insert a cross reference. The PAGEREF field in the following example uses the location of the bookmark selection to insert a page number.

Field code	Field result
`For more information on using automatic replies, see "{ref auto_r}."`	`For more information on using automatic replies, see "Sending Replies."`
`For more information on using automatic replies, see page {pageref auto_r}.`	`For more information on using automatic replies, see page 27.`

Expressions

An expression is a mathematical statement that evaluates to a single number. An expression can contain numbers, bookmark references, and the following operators and functions: +, –, *, /, ^, =, <, >, <=, >=, ( ), **Abs**, **Int**, **Sign**, **Defined**, **Mod**, **Round**, **And**, **Or**, and **Not**. The following is an example of a field containing an expression:

Field code	Field result
`The value of the shares is {=Sum (line_14,line_29) \# $000,000.00}.`	`The value of the shares is $011,540.45.`

Identifiers

Identifiers distinguish between fields that perform the same action for different parts of the document.

For example, the fields `{toc \f illus}` and `{toc \f line_art}` both perform the same type of action—collecting and organizing tables of contents. The identifiers `illus` and `line_art` specify that the first field generates a table of contents for illustrations and the second field generates a table of contents for line art.

Text

A text argument is words or graphics you want Word to insert into a document as part of the field's result or display on the screen as part of the field's action when the program updates the field. For example, a field that displays a message prompting the user to perform an action contains a *prompt text* argument.

Switches

A field can also contain *switches* which change the field's default actions or formatting. Switches always have a backslash (\) as their first character and a letter or nonalphabetic character as their second character. Some switches are followed by additional arguments that further define the effect of the switch.

Some switches can be used with more than one field type and are called *general switches*. Other switches can be used with only one field type and are called *field-specific switches*. A field can contain as many as 10 general switches and 10 field-specific switches. General and field-specific switches are described in more detail later in this chapter.

FIELD COMMANDS AND FUNCTION KEYS

Word provides a large set of menu commands and special keys for inserting, editing, and updating fields. The following sections describe each field command and key combination. The commands are Insert Field and View Field Codes. The keys are INSERT FIELD (Ctrl+F9), UPDATE FIELD (F9), TOGGLE FIELD CODES VIEW (Shift+F9), UNLINK FIELD (Ctrl+Shift+F9), LOCK FIELD (Ctrl+F11), UNLOCK FIELD (Ctrl+Shift+F11), NEXT FIELD (F11), PREVIOUS FIELD (Shift+F11), UPDATE SOURCE (Ctrl+Shift+F7), and DO FIELD CLICK (Alt+Shift+F9). For convenience and for users who do not want to deal with field codes directly, Word provides menu commands that insert fields for popular word-processing features, such as table of contents and index. The commands in this category (listed with their related fields) are:

Insert File (INCLUDE)
Insert Page Numbers (PAGE)
Insert Picture (IMPORT)
Insert Index Entry (XE)
Insert Index (INDEX)
Insert Table of Contents (TOC)
Edit Paste Link (DDE and DDEAUTO)
Utilities Renumber (AUTONUM, AUTONUMOUT, and AUTONUMLGL)

In addition, the Edit Header/Footer Pane command provides an icon bar for inserting PAGE, DATE, and TIME fields.

Insert Field Command/INSERT FIELD Key (Ctrl+F9)

This command inserts a field at the insertion point, just like typing. When you choose OK in the dialog box, Word updates the field as it is inserted. If you have the View Field Codes command and Show All option in the View Preferences dialog box turned off, you see the field's result. Otherwise, you see the field codes.

If you use the INSERT FIELD key to insert a field, Word inserts the field characters around the selection or insertion point if there is no selection. When you use the INSERT FIELD key, you must type the field codes and update the field yourself.

When you choose Insert Field from the command menu, Word displays a dialog box with the following elements.

Insert Field Type list box

Select the field type you want to insert from this list.

Instructions list box

Select additional instructions for the field type, if desired, from this list. Not all field types will have an accompanying list of instructions.

Field Code information

Check the syntax for the selected field type here. The text box below shows the field type and any instructions you have selected and typed. If necessary, you can edit the field code in this text box before choosing OK.

Prompt line

The prompt below the Field Code box gives instructions for defining the field you want to insert.

Add, OK, and Cancel buttons

Choose the Add button to add the selected instruction to the Field Code box, and then choose OK to insert the field in your document. Choose Cancel to cancel the Insert Field command.

Insert Index Entry Command

This command inserts an Index Entry (XE) field. When you choose Insert Index Entry, Word displays the following dialog box:

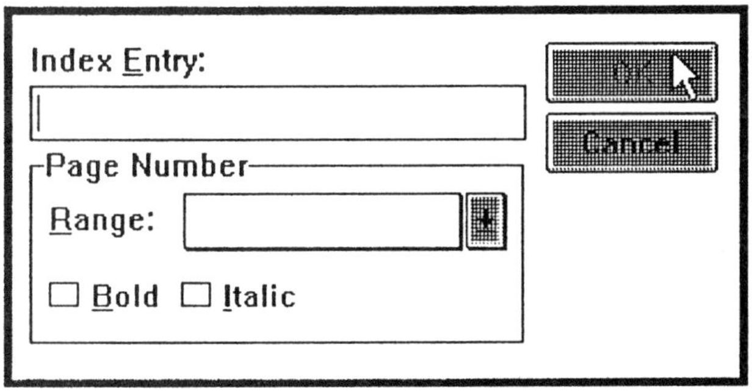

This dialog box has the following elements.

Index Entry text box

Type the text of the index entry here. If you have a selection when you choose the Index Entry command, Word inserts the first 64 characters as the proposed text of the index entry. You can edit or replace the proposed text. If the selection contains a picture within the first 64 characters, Word proposes the text from the beginning of the selection up to the picture. If the selection is only a picture or an insertion point, Word proposes nothing. If the selection is within the text of a single table cell, Word proposes the selection, up to 64 characters. If the selection is an entire cell (including the cell marker) or multiple cells, Word proposes the text of the first cell in the top row of the selection, even if the first cell in that row is not selected.

Page Number box

The following three options control the appearance of the page numbers for the index entry:

Range. Type or select a bookmark name for the page(s) of the index entry.

Bold. Makes the page number(s) bold in the index.

Italic. Makes the page number(s) italic in the index.

Insert Index Command

This command inserts an index field in your document. Word updates this field when you insert it with this command, thereby generating an index.

When you choose Insert Index, Word displays the following dialog box:

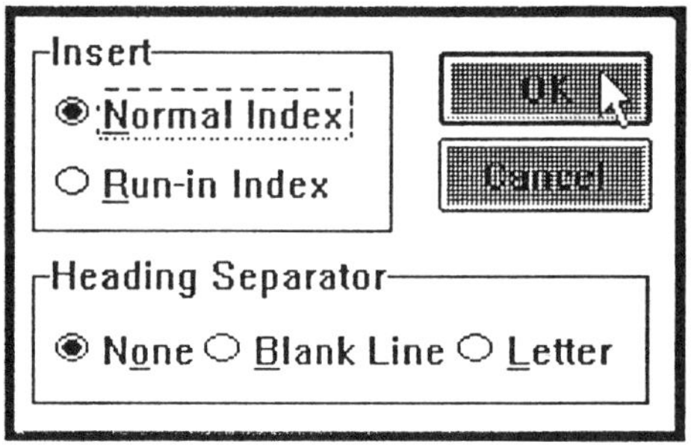

This dialog box has the following elements.

Normal Index button

Choose this button to indent subentries within main entries.

Run-in Index button

Choose this button to put all entries on the same line, wrapping to a new line if necessary. Subentries are separated by semicolons.

Heading Separator options

The following three options control how entries beginning with different letters are separated from each other:

None. Leaves no extra space or any other indication between letter sections.

Blank line. Leaves one blank line before each letter section.

Letter. Prints the appropriate letter at the beginning of each letter section.

Insert Table Of Contents Command

This command inserts a Table of Contents (TOC) field in your document. Word updates this field when you insert it with this command, thereby generating a table of contents.

When you choose Insert Table of Contents, Word displays the following dialog box:

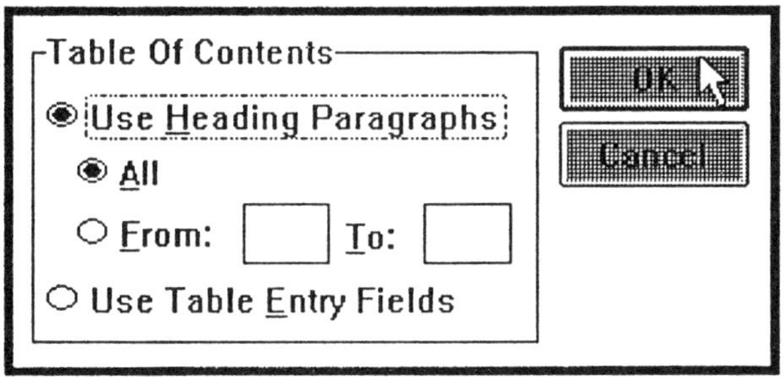

This dialog box has the following elements.

Use Heading Paragraphs button

Choose this button to create the table of contents from outline headings, which are paragraphs to which the styles heading 1 through heading 9 have been applied.

Outline Levels options

The following three options specify how many outline levels Word should use in the table of contents:

All. Uses all paragraphs with the styles heading 1 through heading 9.

From. Type the number of the highest outline level you want Word to use.

To. Type the number of the lowest outline level you want Word to use. To tell Word to use only one level, type that level number in both the To and From boxes.

Use Table Entry Fields button

Choose this button to create the table of contents from TOC Entry (TC) fields.

Edit Paste Link Command

This command inserts in your document a Dynamic Data Exchange (DDE) field with a link to the application and file you specify. When Word updates this field, the program inserts new information from the source.

When you choose Edit Paste Link, Word displays a dialog box with the following options.

Auto Update box

Turn on to create a link that inserts new data as soon as it is available. Turn off to create a link that inserts new data only when you update the field.

Link To line

Check this line to find out the source of the data currently on the Clipboard. You cannot edit this source to change a link; instead, you must cancel the old link and set up a new one.

UPDATE FIELD Key (F9)

Pressing this key updates the selected fields. A field is selected if the insertion point is in it, if any part of the field is selected, or if the field is within the selection. If the insertion point is anywhere within a field that contains nested fields, the nested fields are also considered to be selected. If the selection contains or is within a nested field, however, the enclosing field is not considered to be selected. When Word updates a field, it also updates all of the field's nested fields. Updated fields switch to the view set by the View Fields Codes command. Word does not update action, marker, or locked fields. Result fields that display a result that is not calculated (AUTONUM, AUTONUMOUT, AUTONUMLGL, and IMPORT) are also not affected by this key. Choosing the Edit Undo command restores the previous result.

UNLINK FIELD Key (Ctrl+Shift+F9)

Pressing this key replaces a field with its most recent result. If the field has no result or displays a result that is not calculated (AUTONUM, AUTONUMOUT, AUTONUMLGL, and, IMPORT), Word deletes the field. Choosing the Edit Undo command restores the field.

View Field Codes Command

This command switches the display of all fields between the field codes and the field results.

The View Field Codes command operates on a pane-by-pane basis. You can split a window containing a document and show the field codes in one window and the field results in another, as shown on the next page.

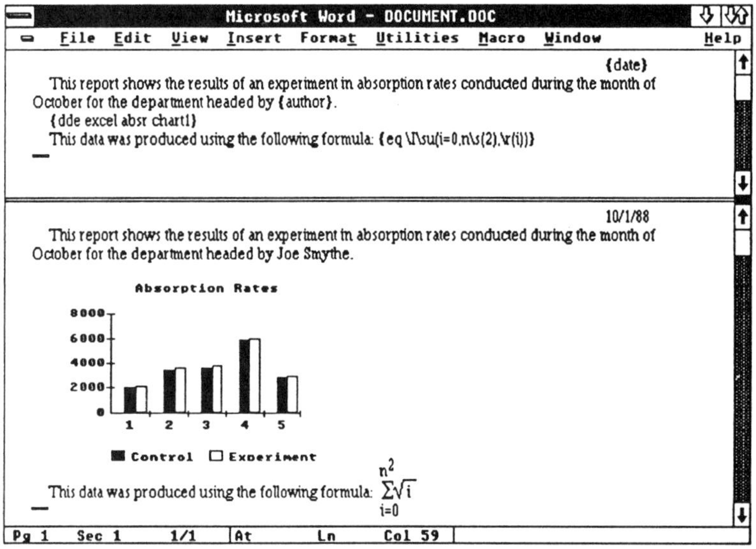

TOGGLE FIELD CODES VIEW Key (Shift+F9)

Pressing this key toggles the view of the selected fields between field codes and field results.

The TOGGLE FIELD CODES VIEW key operates on a document-wide basis. If you display the same field in multiple windows, pressing this key toggles the view of the selected fields in all windows.

LOCK FIELD Key (Ctrl+F11) and UNLOCK FIELD Key (Ctrl+Shift+F11)

Pressing one of these keys locks or unlocks any fields in the current selection. Word cannot update locked fields.

When you lock a field, you also lock all its nested fields. However, you can update a field that is nested within a locked field by selecting the nested field, unlocking it, and then updating. The enclosing field and other nested fields will not be updated.

NEXT FIELD Key (F11)

Pressing this key selects the next result field or action field. If a field that contains nested fields is selected when you press the NEXT FIELD key, the first nested field is selected. When you have cycled to the bottom layer of nesting, pressing the key then selects the field at the next layer up.

PREVIOUS FIELD Key (Shift+F11)

Pressing this key selects the previous result field or action field. For nested fields, pressing the PREVIOUS FIELD key selects the opposite of the NEXT FIELD key.

UPDATE SOURCE Key (Ctrl+Shift+F7)

If the result of an INCLUDE field comes from a Word document, selecting the INCLUDE field and pressing this key writes any change made to the field result back to the source file. This key does not work for any other type of field or any other file format.

DO FIELD CLICK Key (Alt+Shift+F9)

When you have an action field (GOTOBUTTON or MACROBUTTON) selected, pressing this key causes the field to perform its action. This key is equivalent to double-clicking the fields with the mouse.

EDITING AND FORMATTING FIELDS

You can edit and format all parts of a field including the field characters ({ }). How you edit and format a field depends on the category of the field and the view mode. When field codes are displayed, you can change the field type and instruction arguments, and you can select and delete the whole field. When field results are displayed, you can modify field results as you do any document text. To delete a field, you must first select the entire field.

If you have turned off the Hidden Text and Show All options of the View Preferences command, you cannot select fields that have hidden format by default (XE and TC). If you formatted other types of fields as hidden, you can select them with the NEXT FIELD and PREVIOUS FIELD keys.

There are two ways to format a field's result. By default for most fields, formatting is taken from the first character following the opening field character, so if you format the field codes, the field result will have the same formatting, as shown in the following example:

Field code	Field result
`Today's date is {date}.`	`Today's date is` *8/2/90.*

The field result is printed in italic, the formatting of the first character of the field following the opening field character.

Although this method is simple and fast, using general switches is a more powerful way of formatting the result of a field. In addition, a few fields—REF, GLOSSARY, and INCLUDE—format the results as they appear in the source. Formatting the field codes does not affect the result unless you add a general switch to make it so. There are four general switches:

- Format switch (*): Applies formatting specified by the argument
- Numeric picture switch (\#): Formats a floating-point numeric result according to the argument
- Date-time picture switch (\@): Formats a date or time according to the argument
- Lock result switch (\!): Prevents fields that are part of a result from being updated

Format Switch (*)

The format switch (*) applies a predefined function or formatting to the active result, overriding the formatting based by default on the first character of the field code or the source of the result. The general syntax for this switch is:

* *FormatName*

where *FormatName* is an argument that falls into one of the following categories:

- Case conversion
- Number conversion
- Character formatting

Case conversion

The following *FormatName* arguments change the case of text:

- The **upper** argument: Converts all characters to uppercase.
- The **lower** argument: Converts all characters to lowercase.
- The **firstcap** argument: Capitalizes the first letter of the first word.
- The **caps** argument: Capitalizes the first letter of all words.

The following table shows examples of these arguments:

Argument	Field code	Field result
upper	`{quote \* upper "trey research"}`	`TREY RESEARCH`
lower	`{quote \* lower "TREY RESEARCH"}`	`trey research`
firstcap	`{quote \* firstcap "trey research"}`	`Trey research`
caps	`{quote \* caps "trey research"}`	`Trey Research`

Number conversion

The following *FormatName* arguments format the integer of the most recent field result:

- The **arabic** argument: Converts the result to an arabic cardinal number.
- The **ordinal** argument: Converts the result to an arabic ordinal number.
- The **roman** argument: Converts the result to a roman numera.l
- The **alphabetic** argument: Converts a numeric result to corresponding alphabetic characters.
- The **cardtext** argument: Converts the result to cardinal text; that is, to the name of the cardinal number of the result.
- The **ordtext** argument: Converts the result to ordinal text; that is, to the name of the ordinal number of the result.
- The **hex** argument: Converts the result to a hexadecimal number.
- The **dollartext** argument: Converts the result to cardinal text with a fraction and the word *dollars*.

If the result is not a number, the *FormatName* is ignored. If the result is alphabetic or a roman numeral, the result has the case of the first character of the argument. The following table shows examples of these arguments:

Argument	Field code	Field result
arabic	`{= 100 + 100 \* arabic}`	`200`
ordinal	`{= 40.5 + 17 \* ordinal}`	`57th`
roman	`{= 110 \* Roman}`	`CX`
alphabetic	`{= 26 + 5 \* alphabetic}`	`ee`
cardtext	`{= 5.25 + 4 \* cardtext}`	`Nine`
ordtext	`{= 5 + 4 \* ordtext}`	`Ninth`
hex	`{= 16 + 31 \* hex}`	`2F`
dollartext	`{= 11.55 + 2.17 \* dollartext}` `dollars`	`Thirteen and 72/100 dollars`

Character formatting

The following *FormatName* arguments control character formatting:

- The **charformat** argument: Replaces previous formatting with the format of the first character of the field type. This argument is especially useful for fields that use the format of their sources to format the results.
- The **mergeformat** argument: Preserves character format applied to the result when the field is updated; new text not in the previous result has the default format for the field type.

The following table shows examples of these arguments:

Argument	Field code	Field result
charformat	`{quote \* charformat` *`window`*`}`	*`window`*
mergeformat	`{ref title}`	`Titles are Dangerous`
	Apply italic to `are` in result and insert `Very` in source	`Titles` *`are`* `Dangerous`
	`{ref title \* mergeformat}`	`Titles` *`are`* `Very Dangerous`

Numeric Picture Switch (\#)

The numeric picture switch (\#) specifies how Word displays a numeric field result. If the result of the field is not a number, the switch has no effect. The general syntax for this switch is:

\# *NumericPicture*

where the result has the format specified in the *NumericPicture*, which is a string of predefined characters and literal text enclosed in apostrophes. For example, a numeric picture switch can format a numeric result as dollars and cents:

```
{=3279.4 * 1.81 \#$,0.00}
```

The result of this field appears as $5,935.71. Without the numeric picture switch, the result would appear as 5935.71.

The predefined characters are described below. Word copies all other characters in the switch argument into the result.

Digit placeholder: Zero (0)

If the result has fewer digits on either side of the decimal point than there are zeros in the *NumericPicture*, Word adds zeros to the result. If the result has more digits to the right of the decimal point, Word rounds the result so that the number of digits in the result equals the number of zeros in the *NumericPicture*. If the result has more digits to the left of the decimal point, Word displays all the digits in the result.

Digit placeholder: Number sign (#)

This digit placeholder is similar to the preceding one, except that Word adds spaces instead of zeros if there are fewer digits in the result than in the *NumericPicture*. If the result is zero, a space is displayed.

Truncating digit placeholder (x)

The predefined character is similar to the second digit placeholder (#), except that if this character is to the left of the decimal point in the *NumericPicture* and if there are more digits to the left of the decimal point in the result than in the *Numeric-Picture*, then Word does not display the extra digits.

If the truncating digit placeholder is to the right of the decimal point in the *NumericPicture* and if there are more digits to the right of the decimal point in the result than in the *NumericPicture*, then Word rounds the last digit specified by the placeholder and truncates the extra digits. If there are fewer digits to the right of the decimal point in the result than in the *NumericPicture*, then Word does not add digits.

Decimal point (.)

This character determines which digits make up the integer and fractional parts of the result. The character Word uses as the decimal point in both the *NumericPicture* and the field result is specified in your WIN.INI or OS2.INI file. You can change this character in the Control Panel.

Thousands separator (,)

Word displays the separator character specified in your WIN.INI or OS2.INI file when the numeric picture switch contains the separator and the result is large enough to require a thousands separator. If the separator is not needed, Word ignores it. You can change this character in the Control Panel.

Negative sign (–)

When the *NumericPicture* contains this predefined character, Word displays a minus sign if the number is negative. If the number is positive or zero, Word displays a space.

Required sign (+)

When the *NumericPicture* contains this predefined character, Word displays the sign of the number if the number is nonzero. If the number is zero, Word displays a space.

Negative variant (Expr1;Expr2)

If the number is positive or zero, Word uses *Expr1* to format the number. If the number is negative, Word uses *Expr2*.

Full variant (Expr1;Expr2;Expr3)

If the number is positive, Word uses *Expr1*. If the number is negative, Word uses *Expr2*. If the number is zero, Word uses *Expr3*.

Text ('Text')

Word displays the text typed between apostrophes.

Sequence name (`SequenceName`)

Word substitutes the current value of the sequence in arabic format. The *SequenceName* is enclosed by grave accent marks (input by pressing Alt+0+96 on the numeric keypad with the NumLock key on). For more information, see the SEQ field in "Field Types and Instructions," later in this chapter.

The following examples show different uses of the numeric picture switch (`total` and `number` are bookmarks that include a number or a calculation resulting in a number):

Field code	Input data	Field result
`{total \# $00.00}`	254.63	`$254.63`
`{total \# $##0.00}`	.49	`$  0.49 (two blank spaces)`
`{number \# x#}`	109	`09`
	29	`29`
	9	` 9 (one blank space)`
`{number \# ##0.00}`	109	`109.00`
	8.933	`  8.93 (two blank spaces)`
`{total \# #,##0}`	233	`  233 (two blank spaces)`
	25062	`25,062`
`{total \# - #0}`	–19	`-19`
	19	` 19 (one blank space)`
`{total \# +#0.00}`	–50	`-50.00`
	50	`+50.00`
	0	`  0.00 (two blank spaces)`
`{total \# $#0.00; ($#0.00)}`	14.50	`$14.50`
	0	`$ 0.00`
	–14.50	`($14.50)`
`{total \# $0.00; ($0.00);'-0-'}`	22.87	`$22.87`
	–22.87	`($22.87)`
	0	`-0-`

Date-Time Picture Switch (\@)

This switch tells Word how to format and display a date or time. Without this switch, fields that result in a date or time display their results in the default format set up in WIN.INI or OS2.INI. The general syntax for this switch is:

\@ *DatePicture, TimePicture*

The result has the same format as the characters in the *DatePicture* or *TimePicture*. If the result of a field is not a date or time, this switch has no effect. Word parses the result of the field, if necessary, to obtain a date.

If a date or time field cannot yet have a real result because the event has yet to take place, the program substitutes zeros for numbers and X's for text. For example, the PRINTDATE field does not have a result until Word has printed the document once. If you set up the date-time picture switch as follows:

```
{printdate \@ "HHmm AM/PM dd MMMM yyyy"}
```

the result of the field appears before the first printing as:

```
0000 AM 00 XXXX 0000
```

After Word has printed the document, the correct date or time appears the next time the field is updated.

You can use any date-time picture switch with any field that results in a date or time. For example, the DATE field normally displays a date, but if you use a switch such as `\@HAM/PM`, the result is not a date, but a time.

Following are three examples of the date-time picture switch used with the DATE and FILLIN field types:

Field code	Field result
`This study was completed on {date \@ "d MMMM, yyyy"}.`	`This study was completed on 12 November, 1990.`
`This study was completed on {date \@ "d MMMM, yyyy 'at' h:mm AM/PM "}.`	`This study was completed on 12 November, 1990 at 11:29 AM.`
`This study was completed on {fillin "Date for letter:" \@ "dddd, MMMM d, yyyy"}.`	`This study was completed on Monday, November 12, 1990.`

The picture must be enclosed in quotation marks if the picture includes spaces. Word evaluates the result in the second example as a date and time. Note that Word prints the `'at'` as literal text because the text is enclosed in apostrophes. In the third example, Word prompts you with a dialog box to fill in the date. You can type the date in any format, and Word prints the date in the date format specified by the switch.

The predefined characters that can be used in the *DatePicture* or *TimePicture* are described below. Word copies as literal text all characters not falling into one of the following categories.

Month (M, MM, MMM, MMMM)

Word displays the month as a number without a leading zero, as a number with a leading zero, as an abbreviation, or as a full name. Uppercase M's are used to distinguish the month from the minute, which is described later.

Date or day of the week (d, dd, ddd, dddd)

Word displays the result as a date without a leading zero, as a date with a leading zero, as an abbreviation for the day of the week, or as a full day name.

Year (yy, yyyy)

Word displays the year as two or four digits.

Hour (h, hh, H, HH)

Word displays the hour on a 12-hour clock without a leading zero or with a leading zero, or on a 24-hour clock without a leading zero or with a leading zero.

Minute (m, mm)

Word displays the minute with or without a leading zero.

AM/PM (AM/PM, am/pm, A/P, a/p)

Word displays *AM*, *am*, *A*, or *a* before noon and *PM*, *pm*, *P*, or *p* from noon until midnight. Word uses the morning and evening strings specified in the WIN.INI or OS2.INI file. You can change these strings in International Settings in the Control Panel.

Literal text ('Text')

Word displays all text enclosed in apostrophes.

Sequence name ('SequenceName')

Word substitutes the current value of the sequence in arabic format. The *Sequence-Name* is enclosed by grave accent marks (input with Alt+0+96 on the numeric keypad with the NumLock key on).

The following table summarizes the result of using predefined characters with the date-time picture switch:

Argument	Field code	Range of results
M	`{date \@ M}`	1–12
MM	`{date \@ MM}`	01–12
MMM	`{date \@ MMM}`	Jan–Dec
MMMM	`{date \@ MMMM}`	January–December
d	`{date \@ d}`	1–31
dd	`{date \@ dd}`	01–31
ddd	`{date \@ ddd}`	Mon–Sun
dddd	`{date \@ dddd}`	Monday–Sunday
yy	`{date \@ yy}`	00–99
yyyy	`{date \@ yyyy}`	1900–2040
h	`{time \@ h}`	1–12
hh	`{time \@ hh}`	01–12
H	`{time \@ H}`	0–23
HH	`{time \@ HH}`	00–23
m	`{time \@ m}`	0–59
mm	`{time \@ mm}`	00–59

Lock-Result Switch (\!)

Insert a lock-result switch into fields that will include fields in their results, if you do not want the fields in the result updated. For example, suppose you are writing a long document and storing the parts in separate files. To compile the final document, you create a document with an INCLUDE field for each part, as follows:

```
{INCLUDE C:\\REPORTS\\PART1.DOC \!}
{INCLUDE C:\\REPORTS\\PART2.DOC \!}
{INCLUDE C:\\REPORTS\\PART3.DOC \!}
{INCLUDE C:\\REPORTS\\PART4.DOC \!}
```

By inserting the lock-result switch, you tell Word not to update each field in the source file before displaying the result of the INCLUDE field. Using this switch can save you much time. Moreover, if you have already updated the fields in the source, you might not want them updated again. The results might change and be incorrect because of the influence of the larger "environment" of the combined document.

NESTING FIELDS

Nesting means putting one field inside another, either as part of the field's instructions or as part of its result. You can nest fields up to 20 fields deep. You cannot nest the field type. If you include a nested field in the instructions for a field, Word uses the result of the nested field to evaluate the enclosing field. Word always treats a field that is nested in another field's instructions as a single argument, even if the result of the nested field contains spaces or quotation marks. For example:

Field code	Field result
`The average word length is {={numchars}/{numwords}} characters.`	`The average word length is 12 characters.`

Here, the final result is the evaluation of the results of the two nested fields. In this case, the total number of words divided by the total number of characters yields the average word length in characters.

Nesting fields is an advanced technique that increases their power. You can insert fields that branch to different results and fields that require certain conditions to be met before evaluation. For example:

Field code	Remarks
`{fillin {if addressee = {author} "Salutation to yourself" "Salutation to {addressee}"}}`	If the addressee is the author, you are prompted for the salutation to yourself. If the addressee is someone else, you are prompted for a salutation to that person.
`{if addressee = {author} {fillin "Salutation to yourself"} {fillin "Salutation to {addressee}"}}`	You are prompted with both FILLIN field prompts at update time, but Word uses only one in the final result.

Both of these examples have the same result, but in the second example you must respond to both FILLIN field prompts. This is because Word updates the nested fields first (by showing the FILLIN field dialog boxes) and then selects one of the two responses, based on the addressee and author.

In the first example, the IF field is the nested field, so Word first selects from the two prompts. Word then uses the correct prompt text in the dialog box and there is only one result text (the response to the dialog box).

In the second example, Word first updates the two nested FILLIN fields (by showing two dialog boxes). Only after you have responded to both dialog boxes does Word evaluate the condition and select the correct text.

FIELD TYPES AND INSTRUCTIONS

This section assumes that you are familiar with the basics of both Word and field usage. Field types are listed alphabetically. The field's syntax, its category, exceptions to general rules, and cross references are summarized under each field type.

= (Expression) Field

{=*Expression*}

Field category: Result

Updated by: UPDATE FIELD key (F9); File Print Merge command. If in header or footer, updated once per printed copy.

You use an Expression field to have Word calculate the result of an expression. An expression can contain numbers, bookmark references, and the following operators and functions: +, –, *, /, ^, =, <, >, <=, >=, ( ), **Abs**, **Int**, **Sign**, **Defined**, **Mod**, **Round**, **And**, **Or**, and **Not**. (The operators perform as normal mathematical operators. The functions are explained later.) The expression can also contain the following reduction functions: **Average**, **Count**, **Max**, **Min**, **Sum**, and **Product**.

The following examples show the use of the Expression field:

Field code	Remarks
`{=Abs ((Average(5,10,15)) * (Sum (1,2,3)))}`	Result is 60, the absolute value of **Average** times **Sum**.
`{=if {{gross_income} >= $45000 20% 30%} * annual_rate}`	If the bookmark `gross_income` is greater than or equal to $45,000, Word multiplies the bookmark `annual_rate` by 20%. If `gross_income` is less than $45,000, Word multiplies `annual_rate` by 30%.
`{={if {=Sum ([R1C3])} >= 250 {=10% * {=Sum ([R1C3])}} {=15% * {=Sum ([R1C3])}}} +{cost}}`	This field is in a table. R1C3 is a reference to a location in that table. If the value of R1C3 is greater than or equal to 250, Word adds 10% of this value to the `cost` bookmark; otherwise, Word adds 15% of this value to the `cost` bookmark.

Composing table references

You can use table references only with reduction functions in Expression fields—Average, Count, Max, Min, Sum, and Product; they do not work anywhere else. Table references can be table rows, columns, or cells, or they can be a range of rows, columns, or cells.

If the field is inside a table, you can reference a cell like this:

```
{=Sum ([R3C5])}
```

If the field is outside a table, you have to set a bookmark in the table and then reference the cell through the bookmark like this:

```
{=Sum (table1[R3C5])}
```

You can reference a whole row:

```
{=Sum (table1[R3])}
```

or a whole column:

```
{=Sum (table1[C5])}
```

or a range:

```
{=Sum (table1[R3C5:R6C5])}
```

Here are some more examples:

This table reference	Refers to
`tax_table[R3]`	A specific row in the table associated with the bookmark `tax_table`.
`Schedule_D[C7]`	A specific column in the table associated with the bookmark `Schedule_D`.
`AMT_table[R3C5]`	A specific row and column in the table associated with the bookmark `AMT_table`.
`DEP_table ([R3:R8])`	A range of values from row 3 through row 8 in the table associated with the bookmark `DEP_table`.

Operators and functions

Abs. Returns the absolute value of *Expression.*

Syntax	Field code	Remarks
Abs (*Expression*)	`{=Abs -2}`	Result is 2.
	`{=Abs 2}`	Result is 2.

And. Returns 1 if all the arguments are True; returns 0 (zero) if one or more arguments are False.

Syntax	Field code	Remarks
And (*Logical1*, *Logical2*)	`{=And (6 + 6 = 12, 1 + 1 = 2)}`	Result is 1.
	`{=And (6 - 3 = 4, 3 + 8 = 11)}`	Result is 0.

Average. Returns the average of the arguments.

Syntax	Field code	Remarks
Average (*Expression1*, *Expression2*,...)	`{=Average (2, 4, 9)}`	Result is 5.
	`{=Average ([R1C1:R3C1])}`	If the values in R1C1, R2C1, and R3C1 are 2, 4, and 9, the result is 5. This field must be in a table.

Count. Counts the numbers in a list of arguments.

Syntax	Field code	Remarks
Count (*Value1*, *Value2*,,...)	`{=Count (9, 5, 6.63, 87)}`	Result is 4.
	`{=Count ([R23:R40])}`	Result is the count of numbers in rows 23–40. Can be used only in a table.

Defined. Returns 1 if *Value* is evaluated without error; returns 0 (zero) if the result is a zerodivide or other error.

Syntax	Field code	Remarks
Defined (*Value*)	`{=Defined (x/0)}`	Result is 0.
	`{=Defined (gross_income)}`	Result is 1 if `gross_income` exists and it evaluates without error.

Int. Truncates the value of the *Expression* to the largest integer less than the value.

Syntax	Field code	Remarks
Int (*Expression*)	`{=Int (98.6)}`	Result is 98.
	`{=Int (-9.6)}`	Result is –10.

Max. Returns the largest *Expression* in the list of arguments.

Syntax	Field code	Remarks
Max (*Expression1, Expression2,,...*)	`{=Max (4, 5, 99, 3, 2, 1)}`	Result is 99.
	`{=Max ([R2C5], [R4C4], [R9C1])}`	If the values are 12, 19, and 40, result is 40. Can be used only in a table.

Min. Returns the smallest *Expression* in the list of arguments.

Syntax	Field code	Remarks
Min (*Expression1, Expression2,,...*)	`{=Min (4, 5, 99, 3, 2, 1)}`	Result is 1.
	`{=Min ([R2C5], [R4C4], [R9C1])}`	If the values are 12, 19, and 40, result is 12. Can be used only in a table.

Mod. Returns the remainder (modulus) after the division of *Expression1* by *Expression2*; the result has the same sign as *Expression2*.

Syntax	Field code	Remarks
Mod (*Expression1, Expression2*)	`{=Mod (3, 2)}`	Result is 1.
	`{=Mod (-3, 2)}`	Result is 1.
	`{=Mod (3, -2)}`	Result is -1.
	`{=Mod (-3, -2)}`	Result is -1.

Not. Reverses the value of *Logical;* returns 1 if *Logical* is False; returns 0 (zero) if *Logical* is True.

Syntax	Field code	Remarks
Not (*Logical*)	`{=Not (1 + 1 = 2)}`	Result is 0.
	`{=Not (1 + 44 = 67)}`	Result is 1.

Or. Returns 1 if any of the values in the list of arguments is True; returns 0 (zero) if all values in the list of arguments are False.

Syntax	Field code	Remarks
Or (*Logical1*, *Logical2*)	`{=Or (5 + 6 = 10, 8 + 8 = 9)}`	Result is 0.
	`{=Or (2 + 2 = 4, 3 - 2 = 0)}`	Result is 1.

Product. Multiplies all the numbers given as arguments and returns the product.

Syntax	Field code	Remarks
Product (*Expression1*, *Expression2*,...)	`{=Product (5, 4, 2)}`	Result is 40.
	`{=Product([R5C3: R6C3])}`	If R5C3 contains –17.35 and R6C3 contains 3.1415926, the result is –54.5066316. This field must be in a table.

Round. If the specified *NumberOfDigits* is a positive whole number, Word rounds *Expression* to that number of places to the right of the decimal. If *NumberOfDigits* is 0 (zero), Word rounds *Expression* to the nearest integer. (If *Expression* ends in .5, Word rounds up.) If *NumberOfDigits* is negative, Word rounds *Expression* to that number of places to the left of the decimal. If *Expression* has a fractional part, the result of the rounding operation includes a decimal point, even if the result is an integer.

Syntax	Field code	Remarks
Round (*Expression*, *NumberOfDigits*)	`{=Round (2.163, 1)}`	Result is 2.1.
	`{=Round (2.163, 0)}`	Result is 2.
	`{=Round (2.163, -1)}`	Result is 0.
	`{=Round (6.163, -1)}`	Result is 10.
	`{=Round (6, -1)}`	Result is 10.

Sign. Returns 1 if *Expression* is a positive number, 0 if *Expression* is zero, and –1 if *Expression* is a negative number.

Syntax	Field code	Remarks
Sign (*Expression*)	{=Sign (10)}	Result is 1.
	{=Sign (10 - 10)}	Result is 0.
	{=Sign (-44.1)}	Result is –1.

Sum. Adds all the numbers given as arguments and returns the sum.

Syntax	Field code	Remarks
Sum (*Expression1, Expression2,,...*)	{=Sum (43, 27)}	Result is 70.
	{=Sum ([R1C3:R5C3])}	If column 3 in the table that includes this field contains 18, 19, 23, 7, and 10, the result is 77.

ASK Field

{ask *Bookmark Prompt***}**

Field category: Action

Updated by: UPDATE FIELD key (F9); File Print Merge command

Exceptions: Cannot be used in footnotes, headers and footers, annotations, or macros

When Word updates an ASK field, the program prompts you for the text to associate with the specified *Bookmark.* Word displays a dialog box with *Prompt* in it each time the field is updated.

After Word has named the text with the *Bookmark* name you specify, you can refer to the text in result fields, expressions, and so on by using the bookmark name.

You can use the following switches with the ASK field:

Switch	Effect
\o	Prompts you only before printing the first document during File Print Merge.
\d	Specifies the default text to which the bookmark is assigned. This text appears as the proposed response in the dialog box.

AUTHOR Field

{author *[NewName]***}**

Field category: Result

Updated by: UPDATE FIELD key (F9); File Print Merge command. If in header or footer, updated once per printed copy.

When you use an AUTHOR field without the *NewName* argument, Word inserts the author entry from the Edit Summary Info dialog box. You can use the *NewName* argument to change the author entry in the summary information.

Both uses of the field are shown in the following examples:

Field code	Field result	Remarks
`{author} is responsible for this document.`	`John Peak is responsible for this document.`	Inserts the author's name from the summary information into the document.
`{author "\"William Blake\""} is a pseudonym for the author of this paper.`	`"William Blake" is a pseudonym for the author of this paper.`	Changes the author's name in the summary information to `William Blake` and inserts the name in the document. Note that backslashes are needed to insert quotation marks.

AUTONUM Field

{autonum}

Field category: Result

You use the AUTONUM field to insert an automatic numbering field whose results are displayed in arabic format followed by a period. When numbering, Word counts all paragraphs at the current outline level that contain the AUTONUM field. Numbering restarts with each new outline heading level. Word automatically updates numbering when you insert, delete, or rearrange paragraphs.

The following example shows lines numbered with the AUTONUM field:

Field code	Field result
`{autonum} What Is Entropy?`	`1. What Is Entropy?`
`{autonum} Entropy Defined`	`2. Entropy Defined`
`{autonum} The Effects of Entropy`	`3. The Effects of Entropy`

AUTONUMLGL Field

{autonumlgl}

Field category: Result

You use the AUTONUMLGL field to insert an automatic numbering field whose results are displayed in legal format. When numbering, Word counts all paragraphs at the current outline level that contain the AUTONUMLGL field. Numbering restarts with each new outline heading level. Word automatically updates numbering when you insert, delete, or rearrange paragraphs.

The following example shows outline headings that have been numbered with the AUTONUMLGL field (*Introduction* and *Defined Actions vs. Defined Intent* are level-1 headings; *Terms* and *Conditions* are level-2 headings):

Field code	Field result
`{autonumlgl} Introduction`	`1. Introduction`
`{autonumlgl} Terms`	`1.1. Terms`
`{autonumlgl} Conditions`	`1.2. Conditions`
`{autonumlgl} Defined Actions vs. Defined Intent`	`2. Defined Actions vs. Defined Intent`

AUTONUMOUT field

{autonumout}

Field category: Result

You use the AUTONUMOUT field to insert an automatic numbering field whose results are displayed in outline format. When numbering, Word counts all paragraphs at the current outline level that contain the AUTONUMOUT field. Numbering restarts with each new outline heading level. Word automatically updates numbering when you insert, delete, or rearrange paragraphs.

The following example shows outline headings that have been numbered with the AUTO-NUMOUT field (*Introduction* and *Health Care Delivery in Preliterate Societies* are level-1 headings; *Scope of This Paper* and *Terms Used* are level-2 headings; *Disclaimer* is a level-3 heading; *copyrights* is a level-4 heading):

Field code	Field result
{autonumout} Introduction	I. Introduction
{autonumout} Scope of This Paper	A. Scope of This Paper
{autonumout} Disclaimer	1. Disclaimer
{autonumout} Copyrights	a) Copyrights
{autonumout} Terms Used	B. Terms Used
{autonumout} Health Care Delivery in Preliterate Societies	II. Health Care Delivery in Preliterate Societies

COMMENTS Field

{comments *[NewComments]***}**

Field category: Result

Updated by: UPDATE FIELD key (F9); File Print Merge command. If in header or footer, updated once per printed copy.

When you use a COMMENTS field without the optional *NewComments* argument, Word inserts comments from the Edit Summary Info dialog box. You can use the *NewComments* argument to change the comments in the summary information.

Both uses of the field are shown in the following examples:

Field code	Field result
`You can find this document on the server by searching for these words: {comments}.`	`You can find this document on the server by searching for these words: Fiscal 90, foreign exchange, rate of return.`
`The summary information comments for this document have been changed to the following: {comments Fiscal 90}.`	`The summary information comments for this document have been changed to the following: Fiscal 90.`

CREATEDATE Field

{createdate}

Field category: Result

Updated by: UPDATE FIELD key (F9); File Print Merge command. If in header or footer, updated once per printed copy.

You can use the CREATEDATE field to insert the date the document was created, as shown in the first example below. You can use the date-time picture switch to change the format, as shown in the second example.

Field code	Field result
`I started this document on {createdate}.`	`I started this document on 8/2/90.`
`I started this document on {createdate \@ "d MMMM, yyyy, 'at' h:mm AM/PM"}.`	`I started this document on 2 August, 1990, at 4:05 PM.`

DATA Field

{data ***DataFile [HeaderFile]*****}**

Field category: Result

Updated by: File Print Merge command

Exceptions: Cannot be used in footnotes, headers and footers, annotations, data documents, or nested fields.

You use the DATA field to identify the source file for contents Word should insert into each copy of the document when you print merge. The DATA field must precede the first bookmark (REF) field that needs information from the data file. A good practice is to insert the DATA as the first text in the document.

The *DataFile* argument specifies the name of the file that contains the data to be merged. A data file consists of columns of information separated by commas, tabs, or into table cells. If you do not use the optional header file, the first row of the data file must contain the bookmark names you've used in the document you're merging into. These bookmark names identify their columns as the appropriate ones for the bookmark (REF) fields in the main document.

The optional *HeaderFile* contains data field labels. If you decide to use an optional header file (appropriate if the data records come from another program, such as a database), it contains only the bookmark names separated into columns by commas, tabs, or in table cells. Be sure the names are in the same order as the columns of information in the data file.

An example follows. (For more information on the format of the *DataFile* and *HeaderFile*, see "Merging Documents" in the *Word User's Reference*.)

Field code	Remarks
`{data phone.doc}`	Uses field names from the header-file CUST.DOC with the data-file LATE.DOC.
`{data late cust}`	Merges data from PHONE.DOC. This file contains its own header record.

DATA Field

{date ***[date-format-picture]*****}**

Field category: Result

Updated by: UPDATE FIELD key (F9); File Print command

You use the DATE field to insert the date the field was last updated, as shown in the following examples. The default display format is that selected in the Control Panel. For other formats, use the date-time picture switch.

Field code	Field result
`Today's date is {date \@ "MMMM d, yyyy"}.`	`Today's date is July 2, 1990.`
`Today's date is {date \@ "h:mm AM/PM 'on' MMMM d"}.`	`Today's date is 3:00 AM on July 2.`

DDE and DDEAUTO Fields

{**dde** *AppName Filename [PlaceReference]*}

{**ddeauto** *AppName Filename [PlaceReference]*}

Field category: Result

Updated by: UPDATE FIELD key (F9)—DDE; automatic—DDEAUTO

Dynamic Data Exchange (DDE) is a method of linking Windows or OS/2 applications. Both the DDE and DDEAUTO fields control the transfer of information among applications. Word updates a DDE field when you press the UPDATE FIELD key (F9). Word updates a DDEAUTO field as changes occur.

When you want to insert in your document data from another application that is unlikely to change, you can use the INCLUDE field. If the data is likely to change or is updated frequently, however, using DDE ensures that your document includes the most uptodate information. The type of data you want to import determines which field to use. If the data is continually being updated, as with stock quotes, insert a DDEAUTO field. If the data changes less frequently or if you want to be able to "freeze" the data at a point in time, insert a DDE field.

To use DDE, Word needs the following elements:

Element	Meaning
AppName	The name of the application
Filename	A file name or other structure meaningful to the application
PlaceReference	The specific data within *Filename*

The first of the following examples shows a DDE field linked to a Microsoft Excel worksheet. The second example shows a DDEAUTO field linked to a second Microsoft Excel worksheet.

Field code	Field result
The following chart illustrates the reported absorption rates: {dde excel absr.xlc}	The following chart illustrates the reported absorption rates: 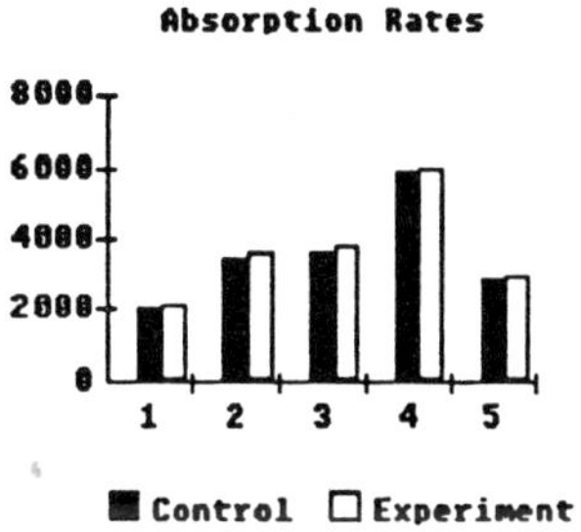
At the time this document was printed, Trey Research common stock was selling for {ddeauto excel stock quo1}.	At the time this document was printed, Trey Research common stock was selling for $101.50.

If you insert a file in metafile format that contains text (such as a Microsoft Excel chart), some of the text may not appear on the screen. If the information is scaled, some of the text may not print. You can usually correct the problem by scaling to a larger size and cropping the resulting image to the desired size.

EDITTIME Field

{edittime}

Field category: Result

Updated by: UPDATE FIELD key (F9); File Print Merge command. If in header or footer, updated once per printed copy.

You use the EDITTIME field to insert the number of minutes the document has been open since its creation, as shown in the following example:

Field code	Field result
It took {edittime} minutes to write this document.	It took 2042 minutes to write this document.

EQ (Formula) Field

{eq *Instructions***}**

Field category: Action

Inserting a Formula field in a document produces a mathematical formula on the screen and in the printed document. Equations can be printed only on PostScript and HP LaserJet printers and any printer that has the Symbol font. Here is an example.

Field code	Field result
`average={eq \f(sum,,count)}`	average = $\frac{\text{sum}}{\text{count}}$

The Formula field has a number of special formatting switches. These switches and their arguments control the formatting of the formula display.

Array (\a)

This switch formats and displays a two-dimensional array, filling the array from left to right and from top to bottom.

Switch and arguments	Effect
\al	Aligns left in column.
\ac	Aligns center in column.
\ar	Aligns right in column.
\co*n*	Specifies number of columns.
\vs*n*	Specifies vertical spacing, in points.
\hs*n*	Specifies horizontal spacing, in points.

The following example demonstrates the Array switch:

Field code	Field result
`The array is {eq \a\ac\co3` `(4,,3,,2,,1,,1,,5,,6,,6,,9)}`	The array is $\begin{matrix}4&3&2\\1&1&5\\6&6&9\end{matrix}$

Bracket (\b)

This switch brackets a single element. By default, Word uses parentheses as the brackets. You can specify any other characters instead.

Argument	Effect
\lc*c*	The *c* argument specifies the left bracket character.
\rc*c*	The *c* argument specifies the right bracket character.
\bc*c*	The *c* argument specifies both bracket characters. If you specify (, [, or {, Word uses the mirror characters.

The following examples show the use of the bracket switch:

Field code	Field result
`{eq \b(A)}`	`(A)`
`Use the following formula: a{eq \b(b+c)}`	`Use the following formula: a(b+c)`
`Solve{eq \b\bc\[(\a\co3 (1,2,3,3,2,1,2,1,3)) {eq x\f\(1,y)}}`	Solve $\begin{bmatrix} 123 \\ 321 \\ 213 \end{bmatrix} x\frac{1}{y}$

Displace (\d)

Use this switch to control horizontal placement of the next character.

Argument	Effect
\fo*n*	Specifies forward space, in points.
\ba*n*	Specifies backward space, in points.
\li	Draws a line from the displaced character to the beginning of the next character.

The displace switch has parentheses, but nothing is ever placed inside them. Displace affects the first element following the parentheses. The following example demonstrates the use of the displace switch:

Field code	Field result
`{eq I\d\ba8()\s\up9(2)\d\ba1()G}`	^{2}G

Fraction (\f)

This switch formats a fraction, as shown in the following example:

Field code	Field result
`If x equals 3 and y equals 12, find {eq \f(x,,y) - z²}`	If x equals 3 and y equals 12, find $\frac{x}{y} = z^2$

Integral (\i)

This switch creates an integral from three elements.

Argument	Effect
\su	Displays a capital sigma and creates a summation.
\pr	Displays a capital pi and creates a product.
\in	Displays the in-line format with the limits to the right of the symbol.
\fc*c*	Substitutes a fixed-height character specified by *c*.
\vc*c*	Substitutes a variable-height character specified by *c*.

The following example demonstrates the use of the integral switch:

Field code	Field result
`{eq \i\su(i=0,n\s(2),\r(i))}`	$\sum_{i=0}^{n^2}\sqrt{i}$

List (\l)

This switch uses a number of elements to create a list of values separated by commas, as shown in the following example:

Field code	Field result
`{eq e\s\up2(\l(1,,2,,...n))}`	$e^{1,2,...n}$

Overstrike (\o)

Use this switch to print an element on top of the previous element. The following arguments can be used:

Argument	Effect
\al	Aligns left edge of character box.
\ac	Aligns center of character box (default).
\ar	Aligns right edge of character box.

The following example demonstrates the use of the overstrike switch:

Field code	Field result
`For the sake of clarity, zero is represented by {eq \o(0,,/)}.`	For the sake of clarity, zero is represented by Ø.

Radical (\r)

This switch displays a radical using one or two elements, as shown in the following examples:

Field code	Field result
`What is the result of this equation? {eq \r(16)}`	What is the result of this equation? $\sqrt{16}$
`What is the result of this equation? {eq \r(3,1)}`	$\sqrt[3]{1}$

Superscript and subscript (\s)

Use this switch to set the position of the elements as superscript or subscript. If there is more than one element, Word stacks the elements, left aligning them, and ignoring any **\up** or **\do** switches.

Argument	Effect
\up*n*	Moves an element up the specified number of points.
\do*n*	Moves an element down the specified number of points.
\ai*n*	Adds the specified number of points of white space to the top of the element box.
\di*n*	Adds the specified number of points of white space to the bottom of the element box.

The following example shows the use of the superscript/subscript switch:

Field code	Field result
`{eq a\s(n,m)}`	a^{n}_{m}

Box (\x)

This switch draws a box around a single element. The following arguments can be used to modify the box:

Argument	Effect
\to	Draws top border only.
\bo	Draws bottom border only.
\le	Draws border on left only.
\ri	Draws border on right only.

The following example shows the use of the box switch:

Field code	Field result
`{eq \x (AC)}`	$\boxed{AC}$
`{eq \x(\a\ac\co3(1,2,3,2,3,1,3,1,2))}`	$\boxed{\begin{matrix}123\\231\\312\end{matrix}}$

FILENAME Field

{filename}

Field category: Result

Updated by: UPDATE FIELD key (F9); File Print Merge command. If in header or footer, updated once per printed copy.

You use the FILENAME field to insert the file name of the document, as shown in the following example:

Field code	Field result
`If you need a copy of this file, it has been named {filename}.`	`If you need a copy of this file, it has been named MTL.DOC.`

FILLIN Field

{fillin *[Prompt]***}**

Field category: Action

Updated by: UPDATE FIELD key (F9); File Print Merge command. If in header or footer, updated once per printed copy.

When you insert this field in a document, Word displays a dialog box prompting you for the text to insert. If the *Prompt* consists of more than one word, surround the prompt text with quotation marks. Word does not check the information for accuracy. It merely inserts the text you type into the document.

You can use the **\d** switch with this field to specify a default response to the prompt. If you want the default response to always be blank, use the **\d** switch alone, without any text following it. Otherwise, the current field result becomes the proposed response for the next update.

FTNREF Field

{ftnref *Bookmark***}**

Field category: Result

Updated by: UPDATE FIELD key (F9); File Print command

When Word updates this field, the program displays the footnote reference number of the footnote specified by the *Bookmark*. The field result takes the formatting of the character following the first field character.

You can use this field to make multiple references to the same footnote or to cross reference footnotes.

Field code	Field result
[2] This process is discussed in Brown's new book (see note {ftnref Brown}).	[2] This process is discussed in Brown's new book (see note 1).

GLOSSARY Field

{glossary *GlossaryName***}**

Field category: result

Updated by: UPDATE FIELD key (F9). If in header or footer, updated once per printed copy.

You use a GLOSSARY field to insert the current contents of the glossary. If you change the contents, Word inserts the new contents when the it updates the field.

GOTOBUTTON Field

{gotobutton *GoToInstruction DisplayText***}**

Field category: Action

For more information: See Chapter 7, "WordBASIC Command Reference."

Double-clicking on this field's codes or selecting the field's results and pressing the DO FIELD CLICK key (Alt+Shift+F9) or executing the **DoFieldClick** statement moves the insertion point as specified by the *GoToInstruction.*

The button area is the *DisplayText* following the bookmark or destination designation. This *DisplayText* can be text, a graphic, or a combination of the two. Do not enclose a multiword *DisplayText* string in quotation marks, unless you want the quotation marks to apppear in the result.

The following example demonstrates the use of the GOTOBUTTON field:

Field code	Field result
Though expensive, alpha-interferon is successful in many treatment *{gotobutton MORE protocols}*.	Though expensive, alpha-interferon is successful in many treatment *protocols*.

If you double-click on `protocols`, you jump to the bookmark `MORE`, which could be an entry that might have a list of references or other information. By defining the *DisplayText* as a single word or short phrase, you can direct the document's readers to information that enhances their understanding of a subject and provides more information without disturbing the flow of the document. You can apply special formatting to the button text, which is italic in this example, to distinguish it from regular text.

IF Field

{**if** *Exp Op Exp IfTrueText IfFalseText*}

Field category: Result

Updated by: UPDATE FIELD key (F9); File Print Merge command. If in header or footer, updated once per printed copy.

You use an IF field to test an expression (*Exp*) and display appropriate text for the result.

Expressions can be bookmarks, text strings, or numbers. You can make the comparison using any of the following operators (*Op*): >, =, <, <>, <=, >=, AND, OR, and NOT.

You can use wildcard characters in = and <> comparisons. Use a question mark (?) to represent any single character and an asterisk (*) to represent a string of characters. For example, `?other` will match with `mother`, `bother`, and so on; `*other` will match with `another`, `brother`, `bother`, and so on. If you use * in the second expression in an IF field, Word checks only 128 characters after that point in the first expression.

The following example demonstrates the use of the IF field:

Field code	Remarks

`Your account is {if {account_status}`
`>= 90 "PAST DUE! PLEASE REMIT!"`
`"Paid in full. Thank you!"}`
	If the bookmark `account_status` is equal to or greater than 90, Word inserts and prints the *IfTrueText* "PAST DUE! PLEASE REMIT!" If `account_status` is less than 90, Word inserts and prints the *IfFalseText* "Paid in Full. Thank you!"

IMPORT Field

{import *Filename***}**
Field category: Result
Updated by: UPDATE FIELD key (F9)

You use an IMPORT field to import a TIFF (Tagged Image File Format) or other supported graphic format file. (The supported formats are installed by Word's installation program in the form of graphic filters.) Word displays the file on screen. If draft view is active, Word displays a blank box. Word prints the picture at full resolution. If Word cannot find the file when updating or printing this field, Word displays and prints a message to that effect.

Field code	Field result
The Tennessee Walking Horse (shown below) is one of the most interesting American breeds. {import c:\\GRAPHICS\\WALKER.TIF}	The Tennessee Walking Horse (shown below) is one of the most interesting American breeds. 

INCLUDE Field

{include *Filename [PlaceReference]***}**
Field category: Result
Updated by: UPDATE FIELD key (F9); File Print Merge command

When Word updates an INCLUDE field, the program inserts the contents of a document or the contents associated with a bookmark in another document. If the document is in a spreadsheet format or RTF format, it is converted to Word format. If the file is not Word file format, use the \c switch followed by the name of the conversion program. This name must match the name specified in the WIN.INI file. To insert a file as plain text without conversion, use **\c Text**.

The following examples show the INCLUDE field used to insert a document, a bookmark, and a document in another file format, respectively:

Field code	Remarks
`{include stocks.doc}`	Includes at the location of this field the entire STOCKS.DOC file.
`{include stocks.doc blue_chips}`	Includes only those stocks specified by the bookmark `blue_chips` in the STOCKS.DOC file.
`{include stocks.doc \c "Multimate Adv 3.6"}`	Converts the MultiMate-formatted STOCKS.DOC file.

The UPDATE SOURCE key (Ctrl+Shift+F7) and the **UpdateSource** statement copies any changes you make to the field result back to the source file. For more information on this statement, see Chapter 7, "WordBASIC Command Reference."

INDEX Field

{index *[Switches]***}**

Field category: Result

Updated by: UPDATE FIELD key (F9)

When Word encounters an INDEX field, the program collects the text and page numbers from the Index Entry (XE) fields and generates an index.

You can use the following switches with this field:

Switch	Effect
\b	Limits the index to the area specified by a bookmark.
\e	Specifies a maximum of three contiguous characters to be used to separate index and page numbers; default is a blank space.
\g	Specifies a page-range separator of up to three contiguous characters; default is a hyphen.

(continued)

Continued

Switch	Effect
\h	Inserts the characters in quotation marks following the switch between the index groups; the options are "AAA", which inserts the specified number of letters (in this case, three) before each group; " " (a blank space), which inserts a blank line; and "~", which indicates that there should be no separator between groups.
\l	Specifies a page-number separator of up to three characters; default is a comma.
\p	Limits index to entries beginning with the specified characters; useful when memory is low.
\r	Runs sublevels on a single line, wrapping text if necessary; topics are separated from subtopics by colons; subtopics are separated by semicolons.
\s	Indicates a sequence name (as used in the SEQ field) following the switch; for more information, see "SEQ Field," later in this section.

The following examples demonstrate the use of these switches:

Field code	Remarks
`{index \b Journal_refs}`	Index is limited to text identified by the bookmark `Journal_refs`.
`{index \e "→"}`	Index entries and page numbers are separated by a Tab character.
`{index}`	Page ranges are indicated by the default character, a hyphen.
`{index \g:}`	Page ranges are indicated by a colon.
`{index \h "-A-"}`	The characters within the quotation marks are inserted in front of each index entry that starts with a new letter. (If the quoted text is a letter, Word advances through the alphabet, inserting the appropriate letter.
`{index \h " "}`	A blank line is inserted in front of the first index entry that starts with a new letter.
`{index \h ""}`	No character is inserted in front of each index entry that starts with a new letter.

(continued)

Continued

Field code	Remarks
`{index \h A}`	The appropriate letter is inserted in front of each index entry that starts with a new letter.
`{index \l ; }`	Semicolons are inserted between page numbers or page ranges.
`{index \p a-ch}`	The index is limited to those index entries that begin with a through those beginning with `ch`.
`{index \s chapter}`	The current number for the sequence name is inserted with the page number of the index entry.
`{index \s chapter \d ":"}`	The specified character (colon) is inserted between the sequence name and the rest of the page number.

Index Entry (XE) Field

{xe *Text [Switches]***}**

Field category: Marker

You use the Index Entry field to mark an entry for collection by the INDEX field. Subentries are created by separating them with colons. For example, `{xe "Absorption:rates"}` creates a two-level index entry. You can create entries with up to six sublevels.

Four field-specific switches can be used with the Index Entry field. All four control the display of text following the index entry text.

Switch	Effect
\r	Text following this switch is a bookmark identifying a range of pages covered by the entry.
\t	Text following this switch is printed instead of a page number.
\b	The page number is printed in bold.
\i	The page number is printed in italic.

The following examples demonstrate the use of these switches:

Field code	Field result
`{xe "Absorption:rates" \r absr}`	`Absorption rates, 12-15`
`{xe "Drug Efficacy" \t "see Absorption rates"}`	`Drug Efficacy see Absorption rates`
`{xe "Absorption rates" \i}`	`Absorption rates, 12`
`{xe "Absorption rates" \i\r absr}`	`Absorption rates, 12-15`

INFO Field

{[info] *InfoType [NewValue]***}**

Field category: Result

Updated by: UPDATE FIELD key (F9); File Print Merge command. If in header or footer, updated once per printed copy.

When Word encounters an INFO field, the program inserts information from the Edit Summary Info dialog box, as shown in the following examples. This field is optional, because you can always use the appropriate field type to change specific summary information data, as shown in the second example.

Field code	Field result
`I've changed the title from "{info title}" to "{info title "Trey Research Employee Benefits"}."`	`I've changed the title from "Employee Benefits at Trey" to "Trey Research Employee Benefits."`
`"I've changed the title from "{title}" to "{title "Trey Research Employee Benefits"}."`	`"I've changed the title from "Employee Benefits at Trey" to "Trey Research Employee Benefits."`

In the following example, the INFO field enables you to supply the summary information item you want to change, as well as the new value:

```
{info {fillin "Info item to change:"} "{fillin "New value for info
item:"}"}
```

KEYWORDS Field

{keywords *[NewKeywords]***}**

Field category: Result

Updated by: UPDATE FIELD key (F9); File Print Merge command. If in header or footer, updated once per printed copy.

You use the KEYWORDS field to insert keywords from the Edit Summary Info dialog box in a document or to change the keywords.

Field code	Field result
`The keywords "{keywords}" are not as descriptive as "{keywords "Cost of Living"}."`	`The keywords "Living Expenses" are not as descriptive as "Cost of Living."`

LASTSAVEDBY Field

{lastsavedby}

Field category: Result

Updated by: UPDATE FIELD key (F9); File Print Merge command. If in header or footer, updated once per printed copy.

You use this field to insert the name of the last person who saved the document. Unlike other information fields, this field cannot alter the document's summary-information sheet because the Last Saved By information is read-only.

Field code	Field result
`This document was last saved by {lastsavedby}.`	`This document was last saved by William Douglas.`

MACROBUTTON Field

{macrobutton *MacroName DisplayText***}**

Field category: Action

For more information: See Chapter 7, "WordBASIC Command Reference."

Clicking this field or selecting the field and pressing the DO FIELD CLICK key (Alt+Shift+F9) or executing the **DoFieldClick** statement runs the selected macro.The button area is the *DisplayText* following the macro name. This *DisplayText* can be text, a graphic, or a combination of the two. Do not enclose a multiword *DisplayText* string in quotation marks, unless you want the quotation marks to appear in the result. You can apply special formatting to the button text or to its paragraph to distinguish the field from regular text.

The following example demonstrates the use of the MACROBUTTON field:

Field code	Field result
`{Macrobutton FilePrint To print this document, click here.}`	`To print this document, click here.`

MERGEREC Field

{mergerec}

Field category: Result

Updated by: File Print Merge command

When Word updates the MERGEREC field, the program inserts the next record number of the current print merge pass. This number corresponds to the paragraph (record) number in the data file and is incremented by the DATA, NEXT, and True NEXTIF fields. The following is an example:

Field code	Field result
`This is record number {mergerec}.`	`This is record number 9.`

NEXT Field

{next}

Field category: Result

Updated by: File Print Merge command

You use the NEXT field to tell Word to move to the next record in the data file and use that record's data in the current document rather than starting another document for the next record. This field is useful when you want to insert lists in one document. Insert one NEXT field for each record to be included. If you want to include a list of 200 records, insert 199 NEXT fields along with 200 instances of the text that uses this data. An example follows:

Field code	Field result	Remarks
{date \@ "dddd"}'s purchases are: {data client list}{name} {p}units{next}{name}{p} units{next}{name} {p}units	Tuesday's purchases are: Jonson 400 units Wilson 300 units Tamkin 500 units	The data file name is `client`; the header file name is `list`. The `name` bookmark represents the name of the client, and the `p` bookmark represents the number of purchases. Note the use of the DATE field.

NEXTIF Field

{nextif ***Exp Op Exp*}**

Field category: Result

Updated by: File Print Merge command

The NEXTIF field is equivalent to the NEXT field, except that Word performs the NEXT operation only when the comparison is True. If the comparison is False, Word does not perform the operation. The expressions and comparison for this field are the same as for the IF field. If one of the *Exp* is a bookmark (REF) field used to check the contents of a data file record, be aware that the comparison checks the current record and only if the comparison is true, uses the next record.

NUMCHARS Field

{numchars}

Field category: Result

Updated by: UPDATE FIELD key (F9); File Print Merge command

When Word updates the NUMCHARS field, the program inserts the number of characters contained in the document. Word gets this number from the Edit Summary Info Statistics dialog box. The number is computed after each printing or when you choose Update in the Statistics box.

NUMPAGES Field

{numpages}

Field category: Result

Updated by: UPDATE FIELD key (F9); File Print Merge command

When Word updates the NUMPAGES field, the program inserts the total number of pages contained in the document. Word gets this number from the Edit Summary Info Statistics dialog box. The number is computed after each printing or when you choose Update in the Statistics box. If you have set up the document in discrete sections with page numbering restarted at the beginning of each section, Word ignores your numbering and counts the total number of pages.

NUMWORDS Field

{numwords}

Field category: Result

Updated by: UPDATE FIELD key (F9); File Print Merge command

When Word updates the NUMWORDS field, the program inserts the number of words contained in the document. Word gets this number from the Edit Summary Info Statistics dialog box. The number is computed after each printing or when you choose Update in the Statistics box. Word defines a word as alphanumeric characters surrounded by white space, a tab, or punctuation.

PAGE Field

{page ***Page-Format-Picture*****}**

Field category: Result

Updated by: UPDATE FIELD key (F9); File Print command

You can use the PAGE field to insert the page number on which the field occurs. This field can be used in headers and footers, as the following examples illustrate:

Field code	Field result
`Page {page}`	`Page 18`
`Page {page \* roman}`	`Page xviii`

PAGEREF Field

{pageref *Bookmark*}

Field category: Result

Updated by: UPDATE FIELD key (F9); File Print command

You can use the PAGEREF field to insert a page number for a cross reference, as shown in the following examples:

Field code	Field result
`See page {pageref macros} for more information.`	`See page 128 for more information.`
`The conventions are listed on page {pageref conventions \* roman}.`	`The conventions are listed on page xii.`

PRINT Field

{print *"PrinterInstructions"*}

Field category: Action

When Word updates the PRINT field, the program sends the *Printer-Instructions* to the printer without translation or formatting. Word treats the entire string as literal text and can include control codes and PostScript programming strings.

Word doesn't check the syntax of the instructions before sending them to the printer. If you send PostScript instructions to a non-PostScript printer, they are ignored and printed as plain text. Consult your printer manual for information on sending PostScript and control codes to your printer.

PostScript

Word provides an environment for using PostScript commands with any Post-Script laser printer. You can intersperse PostScript commands with the text in your documents. Word sends the commands to the printer as native PostScript. Post-Script commands embedded in your document are executed in the order in which they are found.

You can send PostScript programming strings to your printer with the PRINT field and the **\p** switch. The syntax is:

{print \p *Size "Code"***}**

The y-coordinate space used for PostScript commands in Word is the same as normal PostScript. The graphics origin (0,0) is the lower left corner of the page, and the positive directions are right and up.

Drawing takes place within a clipping rectangle, referred to as the ***drawing rectangle***. The graphics origin is translated to the lower left corner of the drawing rectangle.

Size. The *Size* argument defines the coordinate system for your program (that is, where the origin is located on the page). The *Size* argument refers to one of the following groups:

Group	Meaning
page	Current page (default).
para	Current paragraph (the paragraph containing the PRINT field must be at least 1½ inches tall for **para** to produce a result).
pic	Next picture in the current paragraph (the next picture after the PRINT field but before the end of the paragraph).
row	Current table row.
cell	Current table cell.
dict	Contains definitions and procedures for one page.

Use the **dict** group with care. It is intended to be used for defining procedures that will be carried out later on the same page. Word does not define any of the **wp$** variables (described later) for **dict** groups and does not change the drawing environment (the origin, clipping, axes, and so on), so you should not actually draw using this group.

Each of the groups takes certain variables. These variables are shown in the following tables. All measurements are in points, the standard PostScript unit.

Variable (all groups)	Meaning
wp$y	Drawing rectangle height of **page**.
wp$x	Drawing rectangle width of **page.**
wp$page	Current page number.
wp$fpage	Formatted page number (string).
wp$date	Current date (formatted).
wp$time	Current time (formatted).
wp$box	Path containing the drawing rectangle.

Variable (para, page)	Meaning
wp$top	Top margin (**page**); space before (**para**).
wp$bottom	Bottom margin (**page**); space after (**para**).
wp$left	Left margin (**page**); left indent (**para**).
wp$right	Right margin (**page**); right indent (**para**).

Variable (para)	Meaning
wp$first	First-line indent.
wp$style	Style.

Variable (page)	Meaning
wp$col	Number of columns on **page**; the number can vary, depending on the section in which the PostScript appears.
wp$colx	Width of each column.
wp$colxb	Space between columns.

Code. The *Code* argument is the PostScript programming instructions. You must enclose the instructions in quotation marks if they are more than one word.

The following example shows PostScript programming instructions and the resulting text:

Field code	Field result
{print \p page "/phrase { (Word) } def /left 144 def /bottom {wp$y 2 div 30 sub} def /Times-Bold findfont 30 scalefont setfont /say { left bottom moveto phrase show} def /retreat { gsave .02 .02 .98 { setgray say dx dy translate } for grestore } def /dx -1 def /dy .5 def retreat /dx 1 def /dy -.5 def retreat /dx -1 def /dy -.5 def retreat /dx 1 def /dy .5 def retreat 1 setgray say" }	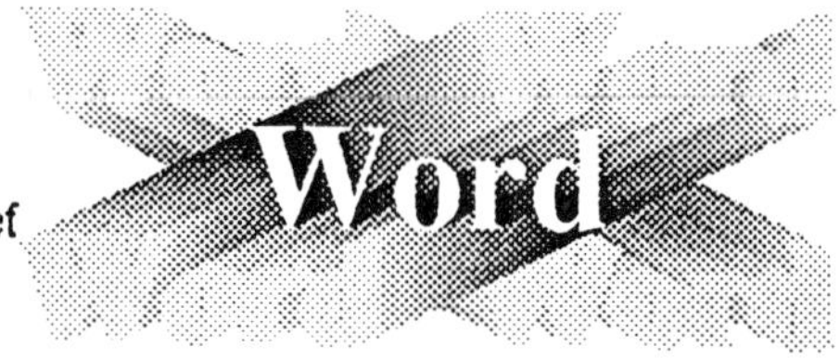

Because Word's text and graphics will be printed on the same PostScript page as your PostScript commands, do not use operators that reset the PostScript environment. The following is a list of operators you should avoid when using PostScript with Word:

- **banddevice**
- **initmatrix**
- **copypage**
- **nulldevice**
- **ramedevice**
- **enderbands**
- **restoreall**
- **howpage**
- **nitgraphics**

For information on using PostScript, see Adobe Systems Incorporated, *PostScript Language Reference Manual* (Reading, MA, 1985) and Adobe Systems Incorporated, *PostScript Language Tutorial and Cookbook* (Reading, MA, 1985).

PRINTDATE Field

{printdate}

Field category: Result

Updated by: UPDATE FIELD key (F9); File Print and Print Merge commands. If in header or footer, updated once per printed copy.

When Word updates the PRINTDATE field, the program inserts the date the document was last printed, as shown in the following example. For the first printing on any particular date, this field will display an earlier date. Beginning with the second printing on any particular date, this field's result will be the current date. To assure that the date in the document is current, use the DATE field instead. To change the date format, use the date-time picture switch.

Field code	Field result
`The {title} was printed on {printdate}.`	`The Trey Research Annual Report was printed on 7/29/90.`

QUOTE Field

{quote *"LiteralText"*}

Field category: Result

Updated by: UPDATE FIELD key (F9); File Print Merge command. If in header or footer, updated once per printed copy.

You use the QUOTE field to insert literal text into a document. Include format switches if you want to change the formatting.

Field code	Field result
`{quote "Trey Research Sets the Pace!"}`	`Trey Research Sets the Pace!`
`{quote \* upper "Trey Research Sets the Pace!"}`	`TREY RESEARCH SETS THE PACE!`

If you want to include ANSI characters that are not readily available from the keyboard in the *LiteralText*, enter them in hexadecimal or decimal format. Precede the hexadecimal number with *0x*, as shown in the following example:

Field code	Field result
`{quote "Microsoft"0xae} is a registered trademark of Microsoft Corporation.`	`Microsoft® is a registered trademark of Microsoft Corporation.`

REF Field

{[ref] ***Bookmark*****}**

Field category: Result

Updated by: UPDATE FIELD key (F9); File Print Merge command. If in header or footer, updated once per printed copy.

When Word updates the REF field, the program links and pastes the *Bookmark* text, as shown in the following example. All formatting is preserved.

Field code	Field result
`More information is available in "{ref Chapter3}."`	`More information is available in "Using Windows."`

In this example, `Chapter3` is the bookmark that marks the text `Using Windows` elsewhere in the document. The reference does not have to occur before the REF field. REF is optional. Only a valid bookmark name is needed unless the bookmark name matches a field type name. In that case, REF is required, as shown in the following example:

Field code	Field result
`{subject}`	`Varieties of Song Birds` (This result is taken from the Subject box in the Edit Summary Info dialog box.)
`{ref subject}`	`Current Dress Code` (This result is taken from a bookmark—subject—in the document text.)

Referenced Document (RD) Field

{rd *Filename*}

Field category: Marker

You use the RD field to have Word generate tables of contents and indexes from multiple files. You should use this field instead of the INCLUDE field when memory is low or anytime you do not want to create a large document to generate a table of contents or index. Pagination in the document containing this field is not affected. Set the page numbers and sequence numbers manually in the individual files before updating the index or table of contents.

You can have as many Referenced Document fields as needed. Set them up in chronological order; for example:

```
{rd Chapter2}
{rd C:\\CHAPTERS\\CHAPTER3.DOC}
```

REVNUM Field

{revnum}

Field category: Result

Updated by: UPDATE FIELD key (F9); File Print Merge command. If in header or footer, updated once per printed copy.

When Word updates the REVNUM field, the program inserts the number of times the document has been saved. Each time you save the document, the revision number changes. Here's an example:

Field code	Field result
`The Annual Report went through many drafts. We finally decided to release draft {revnum}.`	`The Annual Report went through many drafts. We finally decided to release draft 14.`

SAVEDATE Field

{savedate}

Field category: Result

Updated by: UPDATE FIELD key (F9); File Print Merge command. If in header or footer, updated once per printed copy.

You use the SAVEDATE field to insert the date the document was last saved. To change the date format, use the date-time picture switch, as shown in the following example.

Field code	Field result
`The last time anyone worked on this Fiscal '90 file was {savedate \@ dddd}.`	`The last time anyone worked on this Fiscal '90 file was Wednesday.`

SEQ Field

{seq *Identifier [Bookmark]*}

Field category: Result

Updated by: UPDATE FIELD key (F9); File Print Merge command

You use the SEQ field to insert a number in a sequence. For example, you might use SEQ fields to consecutively number tables, illustrations, captions, and so on. The format of the numbers is the same as the format of the field codes. The following example uses the SEQ field to number an illustration:

Field code	Field result
`Illustration {seq illus}. The Reunion of the Soul with the Body (Wm. Blake)`	`Illustration 21. The Reunion of the Soul with the Body (Wm. Blake)`

In the preceding example, `illus` is the identifier. You can have multiple running sequences in a document. Word tracks them by their identifiers. To determine the result of a particular SEQ field, Word counts only the preceding SEQ with the same identifier.

The \c switch repeats the current number in the sequence (the result of the preceding SEQ field). For example, to refer to the same photograph twice, you can set up the field as follows:

Field code	Field result
`Photograph {seq photos} is an example of the solarization technique. Compare the photo below with number {seq photos \c}.`	`Photograph 10 is an example of the solarization technique. Compare the photo below with number 10.`

Another switch, **\r**, resets the sequence number to the number you specify. For example, `{seq illus \r 18}` sets the number to 18, regardless of where the number actually falls in the sequence. Subsequent elements in the sequence are numbered from the specified number (so the next number is 19).

You can also use bookmark names in a SEQ field to set up a cross reference. However, when you use a bookmark, you cannot use the special switches, because the bookmark and the switch would contradict each other. The following example shows the SEQ field used with a bookmark:

Field code	Field result
`The information is summarized in Table {seq tables Accident_Rate}.`	`The information is summarized in Table 14.`

SET Field

{set *Bookmark Data***}**

Field category: Result

Updated by: UPDATE FIELD key (F9); File Print Merge command

You use the SET field to assign a bookmark name to specified text. You can then use the bookmark as "shorthand" for the text. For example:

```
{set Chapter3 "Using Windows"}
```

sets the `Chapter3` bookmark to the text `Using Windows`.

The SET field accepts any legal bookmark name. If the *Bookmark* is illegal or omitted, no error results, but no bookmark is defined. No error results if you define but do not use a bookmark.

SKIPIF Field

{skipif *Exp Op Exp***}**
Field category: Result
Updated by: File Print Merge command

You use the SKIPIF field when you want Word to perform a conditional skip during print merge. If the expression comparison is True, Word cancels the current print merge operation, selects the next record, and starts over from the next record. If the comparison is False, Word continues the current operation. In the following example, Word does not print the letter if the overdue amount is less than $1:

```
{skipif amt <1}
Dear {name}:

   Your account is overdue. Please pay {amt} by the end of the month.
```

STYLEREF Field

{styleref *StyleIdentifier [Switch]***}**
Field category: Result
Updated by: UPDATE FIELD key (F9); File Print Merge command

When Word updates the STYLEREF field, the program inserts the nearest paragraph of text that has the specified style, using the following rules:

Field code	Search action
In text	Backward from the field toward the beginning of the document; if not found, forward from the end of the field toward the end of the document.
In footnotes and annotations	Backward and forward from the footnote reference mark.
In headers and footers when printing without the \l switch	From the beginning of the current page to the end of the current page; if not found, from the beginning of the page to the beginning of the document; if still not found, from the end of the page to the end of the document.

(continued)

Continued

Field code	Search action
In headers and footers when printing with the \l switch	From the end of the current page to the beginning of the document; if not found, from the end of the page to the end of the document.
In headers and footers when not printing	From the beginning of the current section to the end of the document.

The *StyleIdentifier* can be any style name you define in your document or a heading level style. For example, `{styleref blbo}` could mean "bulleted list, bold". The field `{styleref 3}` refers to heading level style 3.

The \l switch works in headers and footers. It indicates that you want to insert the last paragraph on the current page with the specified style. The \l switch is ignored when the STYLEREF appears in text.

SUBJECT Field

{subject *[NewSubject]***}**

Field category: Result

Updated by: UPDATE FIELD key (F9); File Print Merge command. If in header or footer, updated once per printed copy.

You use the SUBJECT field to insert the subject from the Edit Summary Info dialog box. Use the *NewSubject* argument to change the subject.

Table of Contents (TOC) Field

{toc *[Switches]***}**

Field category: Result

Updated by: UPDATE FIELD key (F9)

When Word updates the TOC field, the program creates and formats a table of contents or other type of table (table of charts, illustrations, and so on) from heading levels or the TOC Entry (TC) fields. The following switches can be used with this field:

Switch	Effect
\b	Limits the table of contents to the area specified by a bookmark.
\f	Creates a table of all TC fields that have the specified table ID, which follows the switch; when no *TableID* is specified, creates a table of all TC fields that have no table ID or that have C as their table ID.
\o	Creates a table of contents from the specified outline levels.
\s	Text following this switch is a sequence name; often used in documents that number pages in the chapter-number/page-number style (for example, page 1-2).
\d	Changes the default separator (the hyphen) to another character; up to three characters can be defined as the new separator.

The following examples show the various uses of the Table of Contents field:

Field code	Remarks
`{toc \b chapter1}`	Collects entries from heading levels and generates a table of contents from Chapter 1 (where `chapter1` is a bookmark associated with all of Chapter 1).
`{toc \f}`	Generates a table of contents from all TC fields that have no table ID or that have a table ID of C.
`{toc \o 1-4}`	Generates a table of contents from headings formatted with outline levels 1 through 4.
`{toc \s Chapter}`	Collects entries from heading levels and generates a table of contents, listing the pages for the entries with the chapter number separated from the page number by a hyphen (for example, 1-1).
`{toc \s Chapter \d ":"}`	Collects entries from heading levels and generates a table of contents, listing the pages for the entries with the chapter number separated from the page number by a colon (for example, 1:1).

Table of Contents Entry (TC) Field

{tc *Text [Switches]*}

Field category: Marker

You use the TC field to provide text and page numbers for the table of contents. Two switches control the display of table of contents entries:

Switch	Effect
\f	Identifies the following letter as the table ID, an identifier for the list in which you want this entry to be included; this switch is linked to the \f switch in the Table of Contents (TOC) field.
\l	Identifies the following number as a level number for this entry. These levels are associated with the toc 1 through toc 9 styles for table of contents entries.

The following examples show the uses of the TC field:

Field code	Field result
`{tc "Illustration 9" \f I}`	`Illustration 9      23` (Collected into a table generated by a `{TOC \f I}` field.)
`{tc "Treatment Options" \l 2}`	`Treatment Options      24` (Formatted with style toc 2.)

TEMPLATE Field

{template}

Field category: Result

Updated by: UPDATE FIELD key (F9); File Print Merge command. If in header or footer, updated once per printed copy.

You use the TEMPLATE field to insert the name of the document's template, as shown in the following example:

Field code	Field result
`This document was created from the {template} document template.`	`This document was created from the MEMO.DOT document template.`

If the document is based on NORMAL.DOT, the field has no result.

TIME Field

{time *[Time-Format-Picture]***}**

Field category: Result

Updated by: UPDATE FIELD key (F9); File Print command

You use the TIME field to insert the time the field was last updated. You can place this field in a header or footer. Word uses the display format that is selected in the Control Panel or your WIN.INI or OS2.INI file. To change the format, use the date-time picture switch, as shown in the second of the following examples:

Field code	Field result
`{time}`	`4:03 PM`
`{time \@ HH:mm}`	`16:03`

TITLE Field

{title *[NewTitle]***}**

Field category: Result

Updated by: UPDATE FIELD key (F9); File Print Merge command. If in header or footer, updated once per printed copy.

You use the TITLE field to insert the title from the Edit Summary Info dialog box or to change the title, as shown in the following examples:

Field code	Field result
`What does {title} have to do with Trey's future?`	`What does Keeping the Promise have to do with Trey's future?`
`{title "Seventy Ways to Laugh"}`	`Seventy Ways to Laugh` (Also, Subject box in Edit Summary Info dialog box changed to this text.)

Chapter 10

Rich Text Format

The Rich Text Format (RTF) standard is a method of encoding formatted text and graphics for easy transfer between applications. Currently, users depend on special translation software to move word-processing documents between different DOS and OS/2 applications, and between DOS or OS/2 applications and Apple Macintosh applications.

The RTF standard provides a format for text and graphics interchange that can be used with different output devices, operating environments, and operating systems. RTF uses the ANSI, PC-8, Macintosh, or IBM PC character set to control the representation and formatting of a document, both on the screen and in print. With the RTF standard, documents created under different operating systems and with different software applications can be transferred among those operating systems and applications.

Software that takes a formatted file and turns it into an RTF file is called a *writer*. Software that translates an RTF file into a formatted file is called a *reader*. An RTF writer separates the application's control information from the actual text and writes a new file containing the text and the RTF groups associated with that text. An RTF reader does the converse of this procedure.

RTF SYNTAX

An RTF file consists of unformatted text, control words, control symbols, and groups. For ease of transport, a standard RTF file consists of only 7-bit ASCII characters.

A *control word* is a specially formatted command that RTF uses to mark printer control codes and information that applications use to manage documents. A control word takes the following form:

LetterSequence<Delimiter>

as shown in the following example:

A *Backslash begins each control word*

B *Alphabetic string*

C *Numeric delimiter*

The *Delimiter* can be one of the following:

- A space. In this case, the space is part of the control word.
- A digit or a minus sign (–), which indicates that a numeric parameter follows. The subsequent digit sequence is then delimited by a space or any character other than a letter or a digit. In other words, the parameter can be a positive or negative number. The range of the values for the number is –32767 through 32767. However, Microsoft Word for Windows, Word for OS/2, and Word for the Macintosh restrict the range to –31680 through 31680. If a numeric parameter immediately follows the control word, this parameter becomes part of the control word. The control word is then delimited by a space or a nonalphabetic or non-numeric character in the same manner as any control word.
- Any character other than a letter or a digit. In this case, the delimiting character terminates the control word but is not actually part of the control word.

In the preceding discussion, a letter is an upper- or lowercase ASCII letter.

If a space delimits the control word, space does not appear in the document. Any characters following the delimiter, including spaces, will appear in the document. For this reason, you should use spaces only where necessary; do not use spaces merely to break up RTF code.

A *control symbol* consists of a backslash followed by a single, nonalphabetic character. For example, \~ represents a nonbreaking space. Control symbols take no delimiters.

A *group* consists of text and control words or control symbols enclosed in braces ({ }). The opening { indicates the start of the group and the closing } indicates the end of the group. Each group specifies the text affected by the group and the different attributes of that text. The RTF file can also include groups for fonts, styles, screen color, pictures, footnotes, annotations, headers and footers, summary information, fields, and bookmarks, as well as document-, section-, paragraph-, and character-formatting properties. If the font, style, screen-color, and summary-information groups and document-formatting properties are included, they must precede the first plain-text character in the document. These groups form the RTF file header. If the group for fonts is included, it should precede the group for styles. If any group is not used, it can be omitted. The groups are discussed in the following sections.

Certain control words control properties (such as bold, italic, keep together, and so forth) that have only two states. When such a control word has no parameter or has a nonzero parameter, it is assumed that the control word turns on the property. When such a control word has a parameter of 0 (zero), it is assumed that the control word turns off the property. For example, **\b** turns on bold, whereas **\b0** turns off bold.

Certain control words, referred to as *destinations*, mark the beginning of a collection of related text. An example of a destination is the **\footnote** group, where the footnote text follows the control word. Destination control words and their following text must be enclosed in braces. Destinations added after the RTF specification published in the March 1987 *Microsoft Systems Journal* may be preceded by the control symbol *. This control symbol identifies destinations whose related text should be ignored if the RTF reader does not recognize the destination. (RTF writers should follow the convention of using this control symbol when adding new control words.) Destinations whose related text should be inserted into the document even if the RTF reader does not recognize the destination should not use *. In this chapter, all destinations that were not included in the March 1987 RTF specification are shown with * as part of the control word.

Formatting specified within a group affects only the text within that group. Generally, text within a group inherits the formatting of the text in the preceding group. However, Microsoft implementations of RTF assume that the footnote, header and footer, and annotation groups (described later in this chapter) do not inherit the formatting of the preceding text. Therefore, to ensure that these groups are always formatted correctly, you should set the formatting within these groups to the default with the **\sectd**, **\pard**, and **\plain** control words, and then add any desired formatting.

The control words, control symbols, and braces constitute control information. All other characters in the file are plain text. Here is an example of plain text that does not exist within a group:

```
{\rtf1\ansi \deff0{\fonttbl{\f0\froman Tms Rmn;}{\f1\fdecor Symbol;}{\f2\fswiss
Helv;}}{\colortbl;\red0\green0\blue0;\red0\green0\blue255;\red0\green255\blue255;
\red0\green255\blue0;\red255\green0\blue255;\red255\green0\blue0;
\red255\green255\blue0;\red255\green255\blue255;}{\stylesheet{\fs20 \snext0
Normal;}}{\info{\author Kenn
Wilkinson}{\creatim\yr1990\mo7\dy30\hr10\min48}{\version1}{\edmins0}{\nofpages1}{
\nofwords0}{\nofchars0}{\vern8351}}\widowctrl\ftnbj \sectd
\linex0\endnhere \pard\plain \fs20 This is plain text.
\par }
```

The phrase *This is plain text* is not part of a group.

As previously mentioned, the backslash (\) and braces ({ }) have special meaning in RTF. To use these characters as text, precede them with a backslash, as in \\, \{, and \}.

SEMANTICS OF AN RTF READER

The reader of an RTF stream is concerned with the following:

- Separating control information from plain text.
- Acting on control information.
- Collecting and properly disposing of the plain text, as directed by the current group state.

Acting on control information is designed to be a relatively simple process. Some control information simply contributes special characters to the plain text stream. Other information serves to change the *program state*, which includes properties of the document as a whole, or to change any of a collection of *group states*, which apply to parts of the document.

As previously mentioned, a group state can specify the following:

- The *destination*, or part of the document that the plain text is constructing.
- Character-formatting properties, such as bold or italic.
- Paragraph-formatting properties, such as justified or centered.

- Section-formatting properties, such as the number of columns.
- Table-formatting properties, which define the number of cells and dimensions of a table row.

In practice, an RTF reader will proceed as follows:

1. The reader reads the next character.
2. If the character is an opening {, the reader stores the current state on the stack.

   If the character is a closing }, the reader retrieves the current state from the stack.

   If the character is a backslash, the reader collects the control word or control symbol and its parameter, if any, and looks up the control word or control symbol in a table. It then carries out the action prescribed in the table. (The possible actions are discussed below.) The read pointer is left before or after a control-word delimiter, as appropriate.

   If the character is anything other than {, }, or \, the reader assumes that the character is plain text and writes the character to the current destination using current formatting properties.
3. The reader then reads the next character.

If the RTF reader cannot find a particular control word or control symbol in the look-up table, the control word or control symbol should be ignored. If a control word or control symbol is preceded by an opening {, it is part of a group. The current state should be saved on the stack, but no state change should occur. When a closing } is encountered, the current state should be retrieved from the stack, thereby resetting the current state. If the * control symbol precedes a control word, then it defines a destination group and was itself preceded by an opening {. The RTF reader should discard all text up to and including the } that closes this group.

For control words or control symbols that the RTF reader can find in the look-up table, the possible actions are as follows.

Change destination

The RTF reader changes the destination to the destination described in the table entry. Destination changes are legal only immediately after an opening {. (Other restrictions may also apply; for example, footnotes cannot be nested.) Many destination changes imply that the current property settings will be reset to their default settings. Examples of control words that change destination are **\footnote**, **\header**, **\footer**, **\pic**, **\info**, **\fonttbl**, **\stylesheet**, and **\colortbl**.

Change formatting property

The RTF reader changes the property as described in the table entry. The entry will specify whether a parameter is required.

Insert special character

The reader inserts into the document the character code or codes described in the table entry.

Insert special character and perform action

The reader inserts into the document the character code or codes described in the table entry and performs whatever other action the entry specifies. For example, when Microsoft Word interprets **\par**, a paragraph mark is inserted in the document and special code is run to record the paragraph properties belonging to that paragraph mark.

CONTENTS OF AN RTF FILE

An RTF file can contain combinations of the following elements.

The RTF Version

An entire RTF file is considered a group and must be enclosed in braces. The control word **\rtf*n*** must follow the opening brace. The numeric parameter *n* identifies the version of the RTF standard used. The RTF standard described in this chapter corresponds to version 1.

The Character Set

After specifying the RTF version, you must declare the character set. The control word for the character set must precede any plain text or any table control words. The RTF specification currently supports the following character sets:

Control word	Character set
\ansi	ANSI (default)
\mac	Apple Macintosh
\pc	IBM PC
\pca	IBM PC page 850, used by IBM Personal System/2 (not implemented in version 1 of Word for OS/2)

The Font Table

This group begins with the control word **\fonttbl** and contains descriptions of fonts. All fonts available to the RTF writer can be included in the font table, even if the document doesn't use all the fonts.

A font is defined by a font number, a font family, and a font name as shown in the following example:

```
   A  B  C      D
{\fonttbl\f0\froman Tms Rmn;}. .
```

A *Control word* C *Font family*

B *Font number* D *Font name*

Semicolons separate one font from the next. The font numbers represent the full font definitions in the group and vary with each document. The font families are listed below:

Control word	Font family
\fnil	Unknown or default fonts (default)
\froman	Roman, proportionally spaced serif fonts (Tms Rmn, Palatino, etc.)
\fswiss	Swiss, proportionally spaced sans serif fonts (Swiss, etc.)
\fmodern	Fixed-pitch serif and sans serif fonts (Courier, Pica, etc.)
\fscript	Script fonts (Cursive, etc.)
\fdecor	Decorative fonts (Old English, ITC Zapf Chancery, etc.)
\ftech	Technical, symbol, and mathematical fonts (Symbol, etc.)

If an RTF file uses a default font, the default font number is specified with the **\deff***n* control word, which must precede the font-table group. The RTF writer supplies the default font number used in the creation of the document as the numeric argument *n*. The RTF reader then translates this number through the font table into the most similar font available on the reader's system.

The Style Sheet

The style-sheet group begins with the control word **\stylesheet**. This group contains definitions and descriptions of the various styles used in the document. The style sheet is declared only once, before any document text. All styles in the document's style sheet can be included, even if not all the styles are used.

In some applications, styles are based on, or are the basis for, other styles. In these cases, two other control words can be used:

Control word	Meaning
\sbasedon*n*	Defines the number of the style on which the current style is based (default is 222–no style).
\snext*n*	Defines the next style associated with the current style; if omitted, the next style is the current style.

An example of an RTF style sheet and styles follows:

```
    ...
    {\stylesheet{\fs20 \sbasedon222\snext0 Normal;}{\s1\qr \fs20
A — \sbasedon0\snext1 FLUSHRIGHT;}{\s2\fi-720\li720\fs20\ri2880 \fs20
    \sbasedon0\snext2 IND;}}
    ...
    \widowctrl\ftnbj\ftnrestart \sectd \linex0\endnhere
    \pard\plain \fs20 This is Normal style.
    \par \pard\plain \s1
B — This is right justified. I call this style FLUSHRIGHT.
    \par \pard\plain \s2
    This is an indented paragraph. I call this style IND. It produces a hanging indent.

    \par }
    ...
```

```
This is Normal style.
    This is right justified. I call this style FLUSHRIGHT.
This is an indented paragraph. I call this style IND.
        It produces a hanging indent.
```

A *Style sheet*

B *Styles applied to text*

In this example, PostScript is declared but not used. Some of the control words in this example are discussed in the following sections.

The Color Table

Screen colors, character colors, and other color information are contained in the color-table group. The control word **\colortbl** begins this group. Additional control words for red, green, and blue and the foreground and background colors then use parameter values (0–255) corresponding to the color indexes used by Microsoft Windows to define the amount of red, green, and blue that makes up a color. For more information on color setup, see your Windows documentation.

The following are valid control words for this group:

Control word	Meaning
\red*n*	Red index
\green*n*	Green index
\blue*n*	Blue index
\cf*n*	Foreground color (default is 0)
\cb*n*	Background color (default is 0)

Each definition must be delimited by a semicolon, even if the definition is omitted. If a color definition is omitted, the RTF reader uses its default color. In the example below, three colors are defined. The first color is omitted, as shown by the semicolon following the **\colortbl** control word.

```
...
{\colortbl;\red0\green0\blue0;\red0\green0\blue255;}
...
```

The following example defines a block of text in color (where supported). Note that the **cf/cb** index is the index of an entry in the color table, which represents a red/green/blue color combination.

```
...
{\f1\cb1\cf2 This is colored text. The background is color
1 and the foreground is color 2.}
...
```

If the file is translated for software that does not display color, the reader ignores the color-table group.

Pictures

An RTF file can include picture files created with other applications. These files are in hexadecimal (default) or binary format. The control word **\pict** begins this group. Control words that define and describe the picture parameters follow the **\pict** control word. These control words are listed in the following table (some measurements in this table are in twips; a twip is one-twentieth of a point):

Control word	Meaning
\brdrs	Single picture border.
\brdrdb	Double picture border.
\brdrth	Thick picture border.
\brdrsh	Shadow picture border.
\brdrdot	Dotted picture border.
\brdrhair	Hairline picture border.
\macpict	Source of the picture is QuickDraw.
\pmmetafile*n*	Source of the picture is an OS/2 metafile; the *n* argument identifies the metafile type.
\wmetafile*n*	Source of the picture is a Windows metafile; the *n* argument identifies the metafile type (default is 1–MM_TEXT).
\dibitmap*n*	Source of the picture is a Device Independent bitmap; the *n* argument identifies the bitmap type (default is 0).
\wbitmap*n*	Source of the picture is a bitmap; the *n* argument identifies the bitmap type (default is 0–logical bitmap).
\picw*n*	*xExt* field if the picture is a metafile; picture width in pixels if the picture is a bitmap or from QuickDraw.
\pich*n*	*yExt* field if the picture is a metafile; picture height in pixels if the picture is a bitmap or from QuickDraw.
\picwgoal*n*	Desired width of the picture in twips.
\pichgoal*n*	Desired height of the picture in twips.
\picscalex*n*	Horizontal scaling value; the *n* argument is a value representing a percentage (default is 100).
\picscaley*n*	Vertical scaling value; the *n* argument is a value representing a percentage (default is 100).
\picscaled	Scales the picture to fit within the specified frame; used only with **\macpict** pictures.

(continued)

Continued

Control word	Meaning
\piccropt*n*	Top cropping value in twips; a positive value crops toward the center of the picture; a negative value crops away from the center, adding a space border around picture (default is 0).
\piccropb*n*	Bottom cropping value in twips; a positive value crops toward the center of the picture; a negative value crops away from the center, adding a space border around picture (default is 0).
\piccropl*n*	Left cropping value in twips; a positive value crops toward the center of the picture; a negative value crops away from the center, adding a space border around picture (default is 0).
\piccropr*n*	Right cropping value in twips; a positive value crops toward the center of the picture; a negative value crops away from the center, adding a space border around picture (default is 0).
\wbmbitspixel*n*	Number of bitmap bits/pixel (default is 1).
\wbmplanes*n*	Number of bitmap planes (default is 1).
\wbmwidthbytes*n*	Bitmap width in bytes.
\bin*n*	Picture is in binary format; the numeric parameter *n* is the number of bytes that follow.

The control words for picture border patterns (**\brdrs**, **\brdrdb**, **\brdrth**, **\brdrsh**, **\brdrdot**, and **\brdrhair**) are ignored when translating into Microsoft Word for the Macintosh, which uses character properties to make borders.

The **\wbitmap** control word is optional; if neither **\wmetafile** nor **\macpict** is specified, the picture is assumed to be a Windows bitmap. If **\wmetafile** is specified, the *n* argument can be one of the following types:

Type	*n* argument
MM_TEXT	1
MM_LOMETRIC	2
MM_HIMETRIC	3
MM_LOENGLISH	4
MM_HIENGLISH	5
MM_TWIPS	6
MM_ISOTROPIC	7
MM_ANISOTROPIC	8

If **\pmmetafile** is specified, the *n* argument can be one of the following types:

Type	*n* argument
PU_ARBITRARY	0x0004L
PU_PELS	0x0008L
PU_LOMETRIC	0x000CL
PU_HIMETRIC	0x0010L
PU_LOENGLISH	0x0014L
PU_HIENGLISH	0x0018L
PU_TWIPS	0x001CL

Be careful with spaces following control words when dealing with pictures in binary format. When reading files, RTF considers the first space after a control word the delimiter and subsequent spaces part of the document text. Therefore, any extra spaces are attached to the picture, with unpredictable results.

RTF writers should not use the carriage-return/line-feed (CRLF) combination to break up pictures in binary format. If they do, the CRLF is treated as literal text and considered part of the picture data.

The picture in hexadecimal or binary format follows the picture-group control words. The following example illustrates the group format:

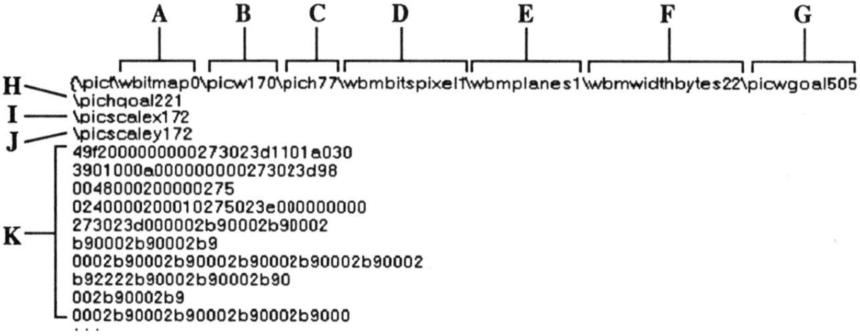

A	*Source*	**G**	*Desired picture width*
B	*Width*	**H**	*Desired picture height*
C	*Height*	**I**	*Horizontal scaling value*
D	*Bits per pixel*	**J**	*Vertical scaling value*
E	*Bitmap planes*	**K**	*Hexadecimal data*
F	*Width of picture in bytes*		

And here's the result:

Footnotes

The group containing footnote text begins with the control word ***\footnote**. Footnotes are anchored to the character that immediately precedes the footnote group. If automatic footnoting is defined, the group can be preceded by a footnote reference character, identified by the control word **\chftn**.

On the next page is an example of a group containing footnotes.

```
    ...
    \ftnbj\ftnrestart \seotd \linemod0\linex0\endnhere \pard\plain
    \ri1170 \fs20 {\up6 Mead's landmark study has been amply annotated.\chftn
A ─┌ {footnote \pard\plain \s246 \fs20 {\up6\chftn }See Sahlins, Bateson, and
   └ Geertz for a complete bibliography.}
    It was her work in America during the Second World War, however, that forms
    the basis for this paper.  As others have noted, \chftn
A ─┌ {\footnote \pard\plain \s246 \fs20 {\up6\chftn}
   └ A complete bibliography will be found at the end of this chapter.}
    this period was a turning point for Margaret Mead.}
    \par
    ...
```

Mead's landmark study has been amply annotated.[1] It was her work in America during the Second World War, however, that forms the basis for this paper. As others have noted,[2] this period was a turning point for Margaret Mead.

---

[1]See Sahlins, Bateson, and Geertz for a complete bibliography.
[2]A complete bibliography will be found at the end of this chapter.

A *Footnotes*

For other control words relating to footnotes, see the sections entitled "Document-Formatting Properties," "Section-Formatting Properties," and "Special Characters," later in this chapter.

Annotations

The group containing annotation text begins with the control word ***\annotation**. Annotations are anchored to the character that immediately precedes the annotation group. The group must be preceded by an annotation reference character identified by the control word **\chatn**. The annotation reference character must in turn be preceded by a group that begins with the control word ***\atnid** and that contains the identification text for the author of the annotation. An example of annotation text follows:

```
...
An example of a paradigm might be Newtonian physics or
Darwinian biology.{\v\fs16 {\atnid bz}\chatn{\annotation
\pard\plain \s224 \fs20 {\field{\fldinst page \\#"'Page:
'#'\line'"}{\fldrslt}}{\fs16 \chatn }
How about some examples that deal with social science?
That's what this paper is about.}}
...
```

Headers and Footers

Headers and footers are treated as separate groups in RTF. Different headers and footers can be defined for different sections in the document. If none is defined for a given section, the headers and footers from the previous section (if any) are used. These groups must precede the first plain-text character in the document section to which they apply.

The control words **\header** and **\footer** begin these groups. These control words can be replaced by the following control words, as appropriate:

Control word	Meaning
\headerl	Header on left pages only
\headerr	Header on right pages only
\headerf	Header on first page only
\footerl	Footer on left pages only
\footerr	Footer on right pages only
\footerf	Footer on first page only

The **\headerl** and **\headerr** and **\footerl** and **\footerr** control words are used in conjunction with the **\facingp** control word, and the **\headerf** and **\footerf** control words are used in conjunction with the **\titlepg** control word. For more information, see "Document-Formatting Properties," later in this chapter.

Information

The RTF file can also contain an information group, which is translated but not displayed with the text. This information can include the title, author, keywords, comments, and other information specific to the file. This information is for use by a document-management utility, if available.

This group begins with the control word **\info**. Some applications, such as Word, ask a user to type this information when saving the document in its native format. If the document is then saved as an RTF file or translated into RTF, the RTF writer specifies this information using the following control words. These control words are destinations and both the control words and the text should be enclosed in braces ({ }).

Control word	Meaning
\title	Title of the document
\subject	Subject of the document
\author	Author of the document
\operator	Person who last made changes to the document
\keywords	Selected keywords for the document
\comment	Comments; text is ignored
\version*n*	Version number of the document
\doccomm	Comments displayed in Word's Edit Summary Info dialog box

The RTF writer may automatically enter other control words, including:

Control word	Meaning
\vern*n*	Internal version number
\creatim	Creation time
\revtim	Revision time
\printim	Last print time
\buptim	Backup time
\edmins*n*	Total editing time (in minutes)
\yr*n*	Year
\mo*n*	Month
\dy*n*	Day
\hr*n*	Hour
\min*n*	Minute
\nofpages*n*	Number of pages
\nofwords*n*	Number of words
\nofchars*n*	Number of characters
\id*n*	Internal ID number

Entries without the *n* parameter have the **\yr \mo \dy \hr \min** format. An example of an information group follows:

```
...
{\info{\title The Panda's Thumb}{\author Stephen J. Gould}{\keywords
science natural history }}
```

Fields

The field group contains the text of Word fields. For more detailed information on fields, see Chapter 9, "Fields."

The field group begins with the control word **\field**. These control words can follow the **\field** control word:

Control word	Meaning
\flddirty	Formatting change has been made to the field result since the field was last updated.
\fldedit	Text has been added to, or removed from, the field result since the field was last updated.
\fldlock	Field is locked and cannot be updated.
\fldpriv	Result is not in a form suitable for display (for example, binary data used by fields whose result is a picture).

Two subgroups are available within the **\field** group. They must be enclosed in braces ({ }) and begin with the following control words:

Control word	Meaning
***\fldinst**	Field instructions
\fldrslt	Most recent calculated result of the field

The **\fldrslt** control word should be included even if no result has been calculated, because even readers that do not recognize fields can generally include the value of the **\fldrslt** group in the document.

An example of some field text follows:

```
 A              B               C
{\field\fldedit{\fldinst author}{\fldrslt Joe Smith}}\par \pard
{\field{\fldinst time \\@ "h:mm AM/PM"}{\fldrslt 8:12 AM}}
 A              B                          C
```

A *Begins field group*

B *Field instructions*

C *Field result*

Index Entries

The index entry group begins with the control word **\xe**. Following this control word is the text of the index entry and other optional control words that further define the index entry.

If the text of the index entry is not formatted as hidden text with the \v control word, the text is put into the document as well as into the index. For more information on the \v control word, see "Character-Formatting Properties," later in this chapter. Similarly, the text of the **\txe** subgroup, described later in this section, becomes part of the document if it is not formatted as hidden text.

The following control words may also be used:

Control word	Meaning
\bxe	Formats the page number or cross-reference in bold.
\ixe	Formats the page number or cross-reference in italic.

The following control words are destinations within the **\xe** group and are followed by text arguments. These control words and their arguments must be enclosed in braces ({ }).

Control word	Meaning
\txe *Text*	Text argument to be used instead of a page number.
\rxe *BookmarkName*	Text argument is a bookmark for the range of page numbers.

Table-of-Contents Entries

The table-of-contents entry group begins with the control word **\tc**. It is followed by the text of the table-of-contents entry and other optional control words that further define the group.

As with index entries, text that is not formatted as hidden with the \v character-formatting control word is put into the document. The following control words can also be used in this group:

Control word	Meaning
\tcf*n*	Type of table being compiled; ***n*** is mapped by existing Microsoft software to a letter between A and Z (default is 67, which maps to C, used for tables of contents).
\tcl*n*	Level number (default is 1).

Bookmarks

This group contains two control words: ***\bkmkstart**, which indicates the start of the specified bookmark, and ***\bkmkend**, which indicates the end of the specified bookmark. A bookmark is shown in the following example:

```
...
\pard\plain \fs20 Kuhn believes that science, rather than
discovering in experience certain structured
relationships, actually creates (or already participates in)
a presupposed structure to which it fits the data.
{\bkmkstart paradigm}Kuhn calls such a presupposed
structure a paradigm.{\bkmkend paradigm}
...
```

Document-Formatting Properties

This section specifies the attributes of the document, such as margins and footnote placement. These attributes must precede the first plain-text character in the document.

The control words that specify document formatting are listed in the following table (measurements are in twips). For omitted control words, RTF uses the default values:

Control word	Meaning
\paperw*n*	Paper width (default is 12,240).
\paperh*n*	Paper height (default is 15,840).
\margl*n*	Left margin (default is 1,800).
\margr*n*	Right margin (default is 1,800).
\margt*n*	Top margin (default is 1,440).
\margb*n*	Bottom margin (default is 1,440).
\facingp	Facing pages (activates odd/even headers and gutters).
\gutter*n*	Gutter width (default is 0).
\deftab*n*	Default tab width (default is 720).

(continued)

Continued

Control word	Meaning
\widowctrl	Widow control.
\hyphhotz	Hyphenation hot zone (amount of space at the right margin in which words are hyphenated).
\ftnsep	Text argument separates footnotes from the document.
\ftnsepc	Text argument separates continued footnotes from the document.
\ftncn	Text argument is a notice for continued footnotes.
\endnotes	Footnotes at the end of the section (default).
\enddoc	Footnotes at the end of the document.
\ftntj	Footnotes beneath text.
\ftnbj	Footnotes at the bottom of the page.
\ftnstart*n*	Beginning footnote number (default is 1).
\ftnrestart	Footnote numbers restart at each section.
\pgnstart*n*	Beginning page number (default is 1).
\linestart*n*	Beginning line number (default is 1).
\landscape	Landscape format.
\fracwidth	Uses fractional character widths when printing (QuickDraw only).
***\nextfile**	Destination; the argument is the name of the file to print or index next; must be enclosed in braces.
***\template**	Destination; the argument is the name of a related template file; must be enclosed in braces.
\makebackup	Backup copy is made automatically when the document is saved.
\defformat	Tells the RTF reader that the document should be saved in RTF format.
\revisions	Turns on revision marking.
\margmirror	Switches margin definitions on left and right pages.
\revprop*n*	Argument indicates how revised text will be displayed: 0 for no properties shown; 1 for bold; 2 for italic; 3 for underline (default); 4 for double underline.
\revbar*n*	Vertical lines mark altered text, based on the argument: 0 for no marking; 1 for left margin; 2 for right margin; 3 for outside (left on left pages, right on right pages; default).
\psover	Prints PostScript over the text.

Section-Formatting Properties

This group specifies section-formatting properties, which apply to the text *following* the control word, with the exception of the section-break control words (those beginning with **\sbk**). Section-break control words describe the break *preceding* the text.

The section-formatting control words are listed in the following table:

Control word	Meaning
\sectd	Reset to default section properties.
\sbknone	No section break.
\sbkcol	Section break starts a new column.
\sbkpage	Section break starts a new page (default).
\sbkeven	Section break starts at an even page.
\sbkodd	Section break starts at an odd page.
\pgnstarts*n*	Beginning page number (default is 1).
\pgncont	Continuous page numbering (default).
\pgnrestart	Page numbers restart at **\pgnstarts** value.
\pgndec	Page-number format is decimal.
\pgnucrm	Page-number format is uppercase roman numeral.
\pgnlcrm	Page-number format is lowercase roman numeral.
\pgnucltr	Page-number format is uppercase letter.
\pgnlcltr	Page-number format is lowercase letter.
\pgnx*n*	Page-number is *n* twips from the right margin (default is 720).
\pgny*n*	Page-number is *n* twips from the top margin (default is 720).
\headery*n*	Header is *n* twips from the top of the page (default is 720).
\footery*n*	Footer is *n* twips from the bottom of the page (default is 720).
\linemod*n*	Line-number modulus–amount to increase each line number (default is 1).
\linex*n*	Distance from the line number to the left text margin in twips (default is 360). The automatic distance is 0.
\linestarts*n*	Beginning line number (default is 1).
\linerestart	Line numbers restart at **\linestarts** value.
\lineppage	Line numbers restart on each page.
\linecont	Line numbers continue from the preceding section.
\vertalt	Text is top-aligned (default).

(continued)

Continued

Control word	Meaning
\vertal	Text is bottom-aligned.
\vertalc	Text is centered vertically.
\vertalj	Text is justified vertically.
\cols*n*	Number of columns for "snaking" (default is 1).
\colsx*n*	Space between columns in twips (default is 720).
\linebetcol	Line between columns.
\endnhere	Endnotes included in the section.
\titlepg	Title page has a special format.

Paragraph-Formatting Properties

This group specifies paragraph-formatting properties. To ensure compatibility with previous versions of RTF, if border properties are specified, the border-segment control word (**\brdrt**,**\brdrb**,**\brdrl**, **\brdrr**, or **\box**) must precede the control word(s) that specify the pattern for the border.

The paragraph-formatting control words are listed in the following table:

Control word	Meaning
\pard	Resets to default paragraph properties.
\s*n*	Designates style; if a style is specified, style properties must be specified with the paragraph.
\ql	Left-aligned (default).
\qr	Right-aligned.
\qj	Justified.
\qc	Centered.
\fi*n*	First-line indent (default is 0).
\li*n*	Left indent (default is 0).
\ri*n*	Right indent (default is 0).
\sb*n*	Space before (default is 0).
\sa*n*	Space after (default is 0).

(continued)

Continued

Control word	Meaning
\sl*n*	Space between lines: if this control word is missing or if **\s1000** is used, the line spacing is automatically determined by the tallest character in the line; if *n* is a positive value, uses this size only if it is taller than the tallest character (otherwise uses the tallest character); if *n* is a negative value, uses the absolute value of *n*, even if it is shorter than the tallest character.
\intbl	Paragraph is part of a table.
\keep	Keep paragraph intact.
\keepn	Keep paragraph with the next paragraph.
\sbys	Side-by-side paragraphs.
\pagebb	Break page before the paragraph.
\noline	No line numbering.
\tx*n*	Tab position in twips from the left margin.
\tqr	Flush-right tab.
\tqc	Centered tab.
\tqdec	Decimal tab.
\tb*n*	Bar tab position in twips from the left margin.
\brdrt	Border top.
\brdrb	Border bottom.
\brdrl	Border left.
\brdrr	Border right.
\brdrbar	Border outside (right side of odd-numbered pages, left side of even-numbered pages).
\box	Border around the paragraph (box paragraph).
\brdrs	Single-thickness border.
\brdrth	Thick border.
\brdrsh	Shadowed border.
\brdrdb	Double border.
\brdrdot	Dotted border.
\brdrhair	Hairline border.

(continued)

Continued

Control word	Meaning
\brsp*n*	Space in twips between borders and an object.
\tldot	Leader dots.
\tlhyph	Leader hyphens.
\tlul	Leader underline.
\tlth	Leader thick line.

Absolute-Positioned Objects

The following paragraph-formatting control words specify the location of the paragraph on the page:

Control word	Meaning
\posx*n*	Positions the paragraph *n* twips from the left edge of the reference frame.
\posxc	Centers the paragraph horizontally within the reference frame.
\posxi	Positions the paragraph horizontally inside the reference frame.
\posxl	Positions the paragraph to the left within the reference frame.
\posxo	Positions the paragraph horizontally outside the reference frame.
\posxr	Positions the paragraph to the right within the reference frame.
\posy*n*	Positions the paragraph *n* twips from the top edge of the reference frame.
\posyil	Positions the paragraph vertically to be in-line.
\posyt	Positions the paragraph at the top of the reference frame.
\posyc	Centers the paragraph vertically within the reference frame.
\posyb	Positions the paragraph at the bottom of the reference frame.
\absw*n*	Absolute width of the paragraph text in twips.
\dxfrtext*n*	Horizontal distance in twips of an absolute-positioned paragraph from text in the main text flow.

(continued)

Continued

Control word	Meaning
\pvmrg	Positions the paragraph vertically relative to the margin.
\pvpg	Positions the paragraph vertically relative to the page.
\phmrg	Positions the paragraph horizontally relative to the margin.
\phpg	Positions the paragraph horizontally relative to the page.
\phcol	Positions the paragraph horizontally relative to the column.

The following is an example of absolute-positioned text in a document:

```
...
\par \pard \pvpg\phpg\posxc\posyt\absw5040\dxfrtext173 abs pos para1
\par \pard \phmrg\posxo\posyc\dxfrtext1152 abs pos para2
...
```

A *Text to be positioned*

Tables

There is no RTF table group. A table is a collection of paragraphs and a table row is a continuous sequence of paragraphs partitioned into cells. The **\intbl** paragraph-formatting control word identifies the paragraph as part of a table. The last paragraph of a cell is terminated by a cell mark (the **\cell** control word), and the row is terminated by a row mark (the **\row** control word). The following control words further define the table:

Control word	Meaning
\clbrdrb	Bottom table cell border.
\clbrdrt	Top table cell border.
\clbrdrl	Left table cell border.
\clbrdrr	Right table cell border.
\trowd	Sets table row defaults.
\trql	Left-justifies a table row with respect to its containing column.
\trqr	Right-justifies a table row with respect to its containing column.
\trqc	Centers a table row with respect to its containing column.
\trgaph*n*	Half the space between the cells of a table row in twips.

(continued)

Continued

Control word	Meaning
\trrh*n*	Height of a table row in twips; when 0, the height is sufficient for all the text in the line; when positive, the height is guaranteed to be at least the specified height; when negative, the absolute value of the height is used, regardless of the height of the text in the line.
\trleft*n*	Position of the leftmost edge of the table with respect to the left edge of its column.
\cellx*n*	Moves the right boundary of a table cell, including its half of the space between cells.
\clmgf	The first cell in a range of table cells to be merged.
\clmrg	Contents of the table cell are merged with those of the preceding cell.

The following example shows some table text:

```
...
\par \trowd \trqc\trgaph108\trrh280\trleft36
\clbrdrt\brdrth \clbrdrl\brdrth \clbrdrb\brdrdb
\clbrdrr\brdrdb \cellx3636\clbrdrt\brdrth
\clbrdrl\brdrdb \clbrdrb\brdrdb \clbrdrr\brdrdb
\cellx7236\clbrdrt\brdrth \clbrdrl\brdrdb
\clbrdrb\brdrdb \clbrdrr\brdrdb \cellx10836\pard \intbl
\cell \pard \intbl \cell \pard \intbl \cell \pard \intbl \row
\trowd \trqc\trgaph108\trrh280\trleft36 \clbrdrt\brdrdb
\clbrdrl\brdrth \clbrdrb \brdrsh\brdrs \clbrdrr\brdrdb
\cellx3636\clbrdrt\brdrdb \clbrdrl\brdrdb
\clbrdrb\brdrsh\brdrs \clbrdrr\brdrdb
\cellx7236\clbrdrt\brdrdb \clbrdr \brdrdb
\clbrdrb\brdrsh\brdrs \clbrdrr\brdrdb \cellx10836\pard
\intbl \cell \pard \intbl \cell \pard \intbl \cell \pard
\intbl \row \pard
...
```

Character-Formatting Properties

The last group controls character-formatting properties. A control word preceding plain text turns on the specified attribute. Some control words (indicated in the following table by an asterisk following the description) can be turned off by the control word followed by 0 (zero). For example, **\b** turns on bold, while **\b0** turns off bold.

The character-formatting control words are listed in the following table:

Control word	Meaning
\plain	Resets application's default character-formatting properties.
\b	Bold*.
\i	Italic*.
\strike	Strikethrough*.
\outl	Outline*.
\shad	Shadow*.
\scaps	Small capitals*.
\caps	All capitals*.
\v	Hidden text*.
\f*n*	Font number.
\fs*n*	Font size in half-points (default is 24).
\expnd*n*	Expansion or compression of the space between characters in quarter-points; a negative value compresses (default is 0).
\ul	Continuous underline*.
\ulw	Word underline*.
\uld	Dotted underline*.
\uldb	Double underline*.
\ulnone	Stops all underlining.
\up*n*	Superscript position in half-points (default is 6).
\dn*n*	Subscript position in half-points (default is 6).
\revised	Text has been added since revision marking was turned on.

To read negative **\expnd** values from Word for the Macintosh, an RTF reader should use only the low-order 6 bits of the value read. Word for the Macintosh does not emit negative values for **\expnd**. Instead, it treats values from 57 through 63 as –7 through –1, respectively (the low-order 6 bits of 57 through 63 are the same as –7 through –1).

Special Characters

The RTF standard includes control words for special characters. If a special-character control word is not recognized by the RTF reader, it is ignored and the text following it is considered plain text. The RTF specification is flexible enough to allow new special characters to be added for interchange with other software.

The special RTF characters are listed in the following table:

Control word	Meaning
\chdate	Current date (as in headers).
\chtime	Current time (as in headers).
\chpgn	Current page number (as in headers).
\chftn	Automatic footnote reference (footnotes follow in a group).
\chatn	Annotation reference (annotation text follows in a group).
\chftnsep	Anchoring character for footnote separator.
\chftnsepc	Anchoring character for footnote continuation.
\cell	End of table cell.
\row	End of table row.
\par	End of paragraph.
\sect	End of section and paragraph.
\page	Required page break.
\column	Required column break.
\line	Required line break (no paragraph break).
\tab	Tab character; same as ASCII 9.
\emdash	Em-dash (long hyphen).
\endash	En-dash (short hyphen).
\bullet	Bullet character.
\lquote	Left single quotation mark.
\rquote	Right single quotation mark.

(continued)

Continued

<table>
<tr><th>Control word</th><th>Meaning</th></tr>
<tr><td>\ldblquote</td><td>Left double quotation mark.</td></tr>
<tr><td>\rdblquote</td><td>Right double quotation mark.</td></tr>
<tr><td>\|</td><td>Formula character.</td></tr>
<tr><td>\~</td><td>Nonbreaking space.</td></tr>
<tr><td>\-</td><td>Optional hyphen.</td></tr>
<tr><td>_</td><td>Nonbreaking hyphen.</td></tr>
<tr><td>\:</td><td>Specifies a subentry in an index entry.</td></tr>
<tr><td>*</td><td>Marks a destination whose text should be ignored if not understood by the RTF reader.</td></tr>
<tr><td>\'hh</td><td>A hexadecimal value, based on the specified character set (may be used to identify 8-bit values).</td></tr>
</table>

Note that an ASCII 9 is accepted as a tab character, and the code word \\<**ASCII10**> (line feed) or \\<**ASCII13**> (carriage return) is treated the same as the control word **\par**. You must include the backslashes or RTF ignores the control word. (You may also want to insert a carriage-return/line-feed pair without backslashes at least every 255 characters for better text transmission over communication lines.)

Here are the code values for the following special characters:

Keyword	ANSI (Word for Windows and OS/2)	Apple Macintosh
\bullet	149	0xA5
\emdash	150	0xD1
\endash	151	0xD0
\lquote	145	0xD4
\rquote	146	0xD5
\ldblquote	147	0xD2
\rdblquote	148	0xD3

Chapter 11

External File Converters

Microsoft Word has built-in file-format converters for many word-processing applications. You can also add your own file-format converters by editing your WIN.INI (Windows) or OS2.INI (OS/2) file.

WIN.INI OR OS2.INI CONVERTER ENTRIES

You can install a converter by modifying the [Microsoft Word] section of your .INI file. In Windows, you can make the modification using Notepad or another text editor. OS2.INI is not a viewable text file, so you must modify it using the Startup Option dialog box available when you select the Utilities Customize command. Converter entries have the following form:

convnum = *n*
conv1 = *"description" drive:\path\filename.dll ^.ex1 ^.ex2...*
conv2 = *"description" drive:\path\filename.dll ^.ex1 ^.ex2...*
...
conv*n* = *"description" drive:\path\filename.dll ^.ex1 ^.ex2...*

The *description* is the name used to refer to this converter. If you install a converter that implements multiple file formats, use a different entry with an appropriate *description* for each format; for example, `WordPerfect 4.1` and `WordPerfect 4.2`.

The *drive:\path\filename.dll* is the full path name and file name of the converter's executable file.

The extensions *.ex1*, *.ex2*, and so on, tell the converter that files with these extensions could have the format this converter recognizes.

WINDOWS ARGUMENTS

Most arguments to and from converter libraries are in the form of global handles. Word allocates global objects for each item before calling the converter. The converter should resize the objects, if necessary, to hold any data it wants to pass to Word. Objects are resized by calling the following Windows function:

```
GlobalRealloc(gh, lcb, GMEM_MOVEABLE);
```

OS/2 ARGUMENTS

Most arguments to and from converter libraries are in the form of global segments. Word allocates global objects for each item before calling the converter. The converter should resize the objects, if necessary, to hold any data it wants to pass to Word. Objects are resized by calling the following OS/2 function:

```
DosReallocSeg(gh, lcb);
```

WINDOWS CALLING CONVENTIONS

Calls out of the converter must use a "call other stack" mechanism. This mechanism requires the Microsoft Co-Routine Manager (CRMGR.W86). To obtain CRMGR.W86 and the test converter used to produce some of the example code in this chapter, in the United States call Microsoft Consumer Response at 800–426–9400 and ask for the Technical Reference disk. Outside the United States contact your local Microsoft representative for more information about available services. If you do not know who your representative is, refer to the list of Microsoft's international addresses included in the Word package.

CRMGR.W86 is a C library whose functions allow a Windows Dynamic Link Library (DLL) called from Word to operate with SS==DS. Without this library, any calls out of a DLL will cause the system to crash.

All calls out of a DLL are made through the following intermediary function:

LCallOtherStack(*pfn, hStack, pwArgs, cwArgs*)
DWORD *(FAR PASCAL *pfn)( );*
WORD *hStack;*
WORD **pwArgs;*
WORD *cwArgs;*

The *pfn* argument is the function to be called, *hStack* is a handle to Word's stack, *pwArgs* is a pointer to the arguments to the function, and *cwArgs* is the count of words of arguments. For example, the following routine is used in place of **GlobalRealloc( )**:

```
PASCAL LibGlobalRealloc(gh, lcb, w)
HANDLE gh;
LONG lcb;
WORD wMode;
{
   return (int)LCallOtherStack(GlobalRealloc, hStackCaller, &w, 4);
}
```

All calls to Word and Windows must go through this mechanism, even though it is not shown in the examples that follow. The *hStack* argument is passed to the converter from Word as an argument to the **InitConverter( )** function, described later in this chapter.

When a converter DLL is linked, the entry points that Word will access are listed following the **EXPORTS** keyword in the .DEF file. Because Word will access these routines by name, it is important to ensure that the names are maintained in the resident name table for the DLL. To do this, do not specify an ordinal value for the function (@1). If ordinal values must be specified, use the **RESIDENTNAME** keyword to keep the name resident.

OS/2 CALLING CONVENTIONS

Some calls out of the converter must use a "call other stack" mechanism. This mechanism requires the Microsoft Co-Routine Manager (CRMGR.OS2). To obtain CRMGR.OS2 and the test converter used to produce some of the example code in this chapter, in the United States call Microsoft Consumer Response at 800–426–9400 and ask for the Technical Reference disk. Outside the United States contact your local Microsoft representative for more information about available services. If you do not know who your representative is, refer to the list of Microsoft's international addresses included in the Word package.

CRMGR.OS2 is a C library whose functions allow an OS/2 Dynamic Link Library (DLL) called from Word to operate with SS==DS. Without this library, some calls out of a DLL will cause the system to crash.

All calls out of a DLL that cause events to be posted to the Presentation Manager message queue must be made through this intermediary function:

LCallOtherStack(*pfn, hStack, pwArgs, cwArgs*)
DWORD *(FAR PASCAL *pfn)( );*
WORD *hStack;*
WORD **pwArgs;*
WORD *cwArgs;*

In general, other calls out of a DLL do not need to use this function. Examples of functions that do need to use this function are **WinMessageBox( )** and **WinDlgBox( )**.

The *pfn* argument is the function to be called, *hStack* is a handle to Word's stack, *pwArgs* is a pointer to the arguments to the function, and *cwArgs* is the count of words of arguments. For example, the following routine is used in place of **WinMessageBox( )**:

```
PASCAL
   LibMsgBox(hwndParent, hwndCaller, lpszTitle, lpszMessage, idWindow,
flStyle)
HWND hwndParent;
HWND hwndCaller;
LPSTR lpszTitle;
LPSTR lpszMessage;
USHORT idWindow;
USHORT flStyle;
{
   return (int)LCallOtherStack(WinMessageBox, hStackCaller, &flStyle, 10);
}
```

All calls to Word and all calls to OS/2 that cause events to be posted to the Presentation Manager message queue must go through this mechanism, even though it is not shown in the examples that follow. The *hStack* argument is passed to the converter from Word as an argument to the **InitConverter( )** function, described later in the chapter.

When a converter DLL is linked, the entry points that Word will access are listed following the **EXPORTS** keyword in the .DEF file. Because Word will access these routines by name, it is important to ensure that the names are maintained in the resident name table for the DLL. To do this, do not specify an ordinal value for the function (@1). If ordinal values must be specified, use the **RESIDENTNAME** keyword to keep the name resident.

INITIALIZING A CONVERTER

To initialize a converter, Word calls the following routine:

InitConverter(*hStackWord, hWndWord*)
WORD *hStackWord;*
HWND *hWndWord;*

The converter should save *hStackWord* for use in **LCallOtherStack( )** calls. At this time the converter should also create its own heap (if it is going to use one) and its stack, by calling **HStackMyData( )** and **CreateStack( )**, both provided by CRMGR.W86 and CRMGR.OS2.

The application window handle of Word is provided in *hWndWord.* Converters that need to display a dialog box to obtain input from the user should pass *hWndWord* to **DialogBox** or **DialogBoxIndirect** (the Windows routine that displays a dialog box) as *hWndParent.* Otherwise, the user might cause the system to crash by activating Word.

If the converter needs to display a Windows message box (to report an error condition, for example), the converter must use the **MB-SYSTEMMODAL** message box style; otherwise, the user will be able to activate Word, causing the system to crash.

FINDING A CONVERTER FOR A FILE

To determine whether a file has a format that a converter can understand, Word calls the following function:

IsFormatCorrect(*ghszFile, ghszDescription*)
HANDLE *ghszFile, ghszDescription;*

The *ghszFile* argument contains a zero-terminated string that gives the full path and file name of the file. The converter opens the file, scans the file as necessary to determine whether it can understand the format, and then closes the file. The **IsFormatCorrect( )** function returns 1 if the converter can convert the file and 0 (zero) if it cannot. If the converter works on multiple file formats and if it can convert this particular file, it should fill *ghszDescription* with the description string for the format from which the file will be converted.

CONVERTING A FILE TO RTF

To convert a file from a "foreign" format into RTF, Word calls this function:

ForeignToRtf(*ghszFile, ghBuff, ghszDescription, ghszSubset, lpfnOut*)
HANDLE *ghszFile, ghBuff, ghszDescription, ghszSubset*;
int *(FAR PASCAL *lpfnOut)( )*;

The name of the file to be converted is in *ghszFile*. The *ghBuff* argument is a handle to the buffer by which RTF is to be transferred between the library and Word. The *ghszDescription* argument is the description for the desired conversion (taken from WIN.INI/OS2.INI or from the return value of **IsFormatCorrect( )**). The *ghszSubset* argument is a string containing the desired subset of the file. For example, in a Microsoft Excel worksheet, the subset could be a named range or an area defined by a cell reference. The meaning of this argument is determined by the converter. The *ghszSubset* argument can be ignored by the converter.

The *lpfnOut* argument is a pointer to a Word function that is called by the converter with each chunk of RTF that has been converted. The Word function is called by:

wReturn = *(*lpfnOut)(cch, nPercentComplete)*;

The *cch* argument is a count of the bytes of RTF data that the converter has placed in *ghBuff*. The *nPercentComplete* argument is a number between 0 and 100, representing the converter's estimate of how much of the conversion process has occurred (for display to the user). If *lpfnOut* returns a negative value, **ForeignToRtf** immediately returns to Word, returning the same negative value.

A converter must not assume that Word verified the file format by calling **IsFormatCorrect**. When **ForeignToRtf** is called, the converter should first open the file to be converted and determine whether it can understand the file's format. Having determined that it can convert the input file, the converter converts it by passing chunks of RTF to Word via *lpfnOut*. If the converter successfully completes the conversion, it returns 0 (zero). If the converter is unable to complete the conversion correctly (due to low memory or because the converter cannot understand the file format), the converter must report to the user errors resulting from its operation, by returning a negative value, as shown in the following table:

Return value	Meaning
0	Successful conversion
–1	Could not open user file
–2	Error during read
–3	Error opening conversion file
–4	Error during write
–5	Invalid data in conversion file
–6	Error opening exception file
–7	Error writing exception file
–8	Out of memory
–9	Invalid document
–10	Out of space on output
–11	Conversion file too large for target
–12	Not used
–13	Conversion canceled by user

CONVERTING A FILE TO A FOREIGN FORMAT

To convert a Word document into a foreign format, Word calls this function:

RtfToForeign(*ghszFile, ghBuff, ghszDescription, lpfnIn*)
HANDLE *ghszFile, ghBuff, ghszDescription*;
int *(FAR PASCAL *lpfnIn)( )*;

The name of the file to be converted is in *ghszFile*. The *ghBuff* argument is a handle to the buffer by which RTF is to be transferred between the library and Word. The *ghszDescription* argument is the description for the desired conversion (taken from WIN.INI or OS2.INI).

The *lpfnIn* argument is a pointer to a Word function called by the converter to obtain more RTF to convert. The Word function is called by the following:

wReturn = *(*lpfnIn)(fPicture, 0)*;

If the *fPicture* argument is 1, pictures are sent to the converter in RTF. If *fPicture* is 0 (zero), the converter cannot convert graphic objects, and Word strips them out. The second argument is an unused word. If there is no more RTF (conversion is complete), the return value is 0 (zero). If RTF has been placed in *ghBuff*, the return value is a positive number equal to the number of characters placed in the buffer). If the operation results in an error, the return value is a negative number (see the preceding table for these return values).

The converter repeatedly calls Word to obtain RTF text and converts that RTF text into the destination file format until one of the following happens: Word returns 0 (zero), indicating successful completion; Word returns a negative number, indicating an error; or the converter encounters a situation making it unable to continue successfully. The converter then returns 0 (zero) if the conversion was successfully completed; the value returned by Word if *lpfnIn* returned an error value; or an error value listed in the preceding table if for some other reason the converter could not complete the operation. The converter must report to the user errors resulting from its operation.

INSTALLING A CONVERTER AUTOMATICALLY

The following routine allows Word to dynamically install converters without user interaction:

PASCAL GetIniEntry(*ghIniName, ghIniExt*)
HANDLE *ghIniName, ghIniExt*;

The converter reallocates *ghIniName* and fills it with the correct description strings that should be placed in the WIN.INI or OS2.INI file for the converter.

The converter reallocates *ghIniExt* and fills it with the corresponding extensions to be placed in the WIN.INI or OS2.INI file.

The two buffers are filled with a sequence of zero-terminated strings, the last of which is empty. The two buffers must contain the same number of strings.

GetIniEntry has no return value.

In the *ghIniName* strings, do not include the quotation marks that will be included in the WIN.INI or OS2.INI entry. You should, however, include the ^. portion of the entries in the *ghIniExt* strings.

For example, the test converter returns the following sequences, where `\000` represents an embedded NULL (chr 0) in the string:

```
ghIniName:
Test Converter 1.0\000Test Converter 1.5\000Test Converter 2.0\000\000
ghIniName:
^.foo\000^.foo ^.bar\000^.foo\000\000
```

This results in the following WIN.INI or OS2.INI entries:

```
"Test Converter 1.0" <path>\CONV-TST.DLL ^.foo
"Test Converter 1.5" <path>\CONV-TST.DLL ^.foo ^.bar
"Test Converter 2.0" <path>\CONV-TST.DLL ^.foo
```

The buffers passed to the DLL are initialized with a single empty string in each. If the converter cannot reallocate the buffers, it should return to Word. If either buffer does not have a non-empty string on return, the call is considered to have "failed" and no entry is made in WIN.INI (Windows) or OS2.INI (OS/2).

Appendix A

Programming Style

Just as good writing style can improve the readability and clarity of documents, so programming style can contribute to the readability and clarity of WordBASIC programs. You might think that programs should be written to run and not to be read. A program is useful only if it runs, but it is more useful if, in addition, it is written so that it can be read and understood, for the following reasons:

- A WordBASIC program may need to be modified or expanded long after its creation, when you no longer remember how the program works.
- A program may become so complex that you can no longer easily visualize how the program functions. A readable programming style makes writing, testing, and debugging of a complex WordBASIC program easier.
- Someone other than you may need to use and modify a WordBASIC program. This is especially true in a business environment, where a useful macro may be shared among many coworkers.

WRITING READABLE PROGRAMS

Writing programs for readability is neither difficult nor complex. For anyone who uses WordBASIC often, a readable programming style should rapidly become a habit. There are no hard rules to good programming style. The methods presented in this section are only suggestions; feel free to adapt them to create a style that you find both readable and easy to write. Your decisions on programming style may also vary with the type of macro you are working on. Style is much less important in a 5-line program than in a 200-line program.

Remarks

You can use the WordBASIC statement **Rem** to insert remarks in a program. You might use remarks to explain what the macro does or to explain the purpose of individual program statements, lines, or subroutines. WordBASIC ignores text to the right of the **Rem** statement when the macro is executed. A single quotation mark serves the same purpose as the **Rem** statement, and its use results in a less cluttered appearance.

Here are some typical examples of the use of remarks in WordBASIC programs:

```
Sub CheckOpen
Rem *****************************************************
Rem ***  This subroutine searches for the file Newfile$      ***
Rem ***  and opens it. If the file does not exist, a new     ***
Rem ***  file with the name NewFile$ is created.             ***
Rem *****************************************************
.
.
.
For Count - 1 To CountWindows()        'Loop number of times that there
                                       'are windows
   Name$(Count) - WindowName$(Count)   'Load Window names into Name$ array
Next Count                             'End Count loop
.
.
.
```

Indents

WordBASIC ignores tabs inserted before program lines, so you can use the Tab key to indent program lines. The proper use of indents can make the structure of a program apparent at a glance. Here are some suggested places to use indents.

Inside subroutines or function definitions.

```
Sub BeepMsg(Msg$, type)
   Beep
   MsgBox "Macro", Msg$, type
End Sub
```

Inside loops, such as For...Next and While...Wend.

```
For CL = 1 To 10
   Beep
   Print CL
Next CL
```

In If...ElseIf...Else...EndIf statements.

```
If Target < 10 Then
      Print "Entry is too long":EnterTarget
   ElseIf Target = 10
      Goto Exit
   Else
      Print "Entry is too small":EnterTarget
EndIf
```

In Select Case statements.

```
Select Case TWX = 0
      MsgBox "Link", "Channel Not Found", 0
   Case TWX = 1
      MsgBox "Link", "Channel Open", 0
   Case Else
      MsgBox "Link", "Unable to Open", 0
End Select
```

In dialog-box definitions.

```
Begin Dialog UserDialog 180, 50
   Text 7, 10, 90, 9, &Name of File to Edit:"
   TextBox 95, 8, 80, 12, .TB
   OKButton 70, 28, 34, 14
End Dialog
```

The following example shows a combination of indented items that occur one inside the other, to create a series of nested indents:

```
Sub TooManyWindows
   For Count = 1 To CountWindows()
      Select Case Count = 1
            Window1
         Case Count = 2
            Window 2
         Case Count = 3
            Window 3
         Case Else
            For CL = 1 To 3
               Beep
               Print "Too many windows"
            Next CL
      End Select
   Next Count
End Sub
```

Descriptive Naming

WordBASIC variable names, subroutine names, function names, and labels can be up to 40 characters long and can be a mixture of uppercase and lowercase letters. You should take advantage of this flexibility by making names in WordBASIC programs descriptive of their function. Here are some examples of obscure and readily understandable names:

Poor	Better
TL	TimeLoop
C$	CompanyName$
MK2CL	MakeTwoColumn
TOTOROORTOTAL	ToToroOrTotal

Blank Lines

WordBASIC ignores blank lines. You can use blank lines to group lines of code that belong together. For instance, you might put a blank line before each subroutine and function definition to clearly set them off from the rest of the program.

Some programmers also prefer to identify functions and subroutines with a banner (see the **Sub CheckOpen** example earlier in this section). A banner not only distinguishes the function or subroutine from the body of the program but also provides information about what the function or subroutine does, what variables are used, what they are used for, and other useful information.

MAINTAINING PROGRAMS

Remember that remarks are only useful as long as they accurately reflect the way the program works. If you make changes in the way the program operates, it is important to also make changes in the remarks to reflect these modifications. The remarks should be adjusted even when the changes are small, because programs have a way of evolving in small increments. Over a period of time, a series of tiny changes can leave the remarks seriously out of sync with the program.

It is possible for a program to change in such a way that a variable, function, or subroutine name no longer reflects its use in the program. If you decide to modify a name, use Word's Edit Replace function to make the change, rather than doing it manually. Not only is this technique easier and quicker, but it avoids the difficult-to-find bugs that can plague a program should you miss changing an occurrence of the name.

Appendix B

Program Examples

STRINGSEARCH

The following macro searches a text file for a given string. The search is case sensitive. Some significant points to notice in this macro are:

- Use of a **FileOpen** dialog equivalent and the loading of a default filename string into that dialog.
- Use of a **While...Wend** loop.
- Use of an **Open** statement to open a sequential file. Also notice how the file name from the **FileOpen** dialog is used.
- Use of an **Eof** function to detect the end of a file.
- Use of **Line Input** to read an unformatted text file.
- Use of an **If...Then** statement to control the search process. An **InStr( )** function tests for the target string in each line of text as it is read.
- Use of a **Close** statement to close the sequential file.

```
Sub MAIN
   DisableInput
   REM Sets up a dialog record
   Dim dlgrec As FileOpen
   REM Fills the dialog record with the defaults
   GetCurValues dlgrec
   dlgrec.Name = "*.TXT"
   REM Allows the user to change the values
   On Error Goto bye
   Dialog dlgrec
   On Error Goto 0
   Search$ = InputBox$("Search for what string?")
   REM Connects the specific file to stream 1
   Open dlgrec.Name For Input As #1
   Print "Searching..."
      REM While not at the end of file 1
      REM Reads one line of the file into Text$
      REM and exits from the search loop
      REM otherwise loops again
      While Not(Eof(1))
         Line Input #1, Text$
         If Instr(Text$, Search$) Then
            MsgBox Search$ + " was found in file: " + dlgrec.Name
            Goto Found
         End If
      Wend
   REM Beeps at the end of the file
   Beep
   MsgBox Search$ + " was not found in file: " + dlgrec.Name
Found:
   REM Closes the file
   Close
bye:
End Sub
```

LISTMANAGER

The ListManager macro maintains a list of text items. This list is stored in a string array variable when the macro is running and in a sequential disk file when it is not. When you run the ListManager macro, you are presented with an initial dialog box. If you select the File Open option button, the **FileOpen** dialog is used to open a file. Note that the default name is **.LST*. Use the file extension LST for all ListManager files. You can then select an existing ListManager file, and it is loaded into the array. If you select New File, you are prompted (using the **InputBox$( )** function) for a file name. Be sure you use a legal file name and that the extension is LST. After you have selected a list to load or have created a new list, you are presented with a dialog box that allows you to manipulate the list. The list appears

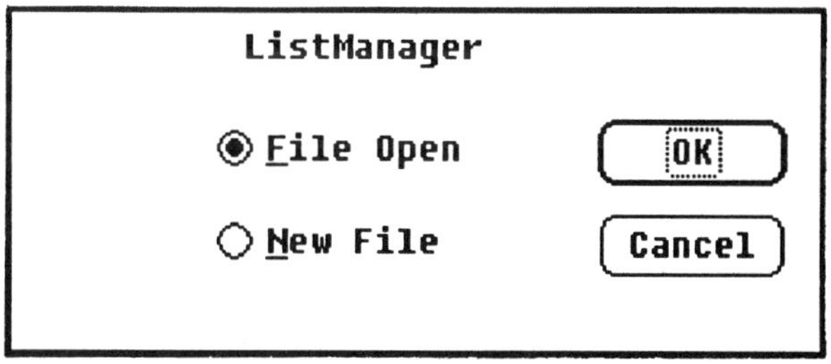

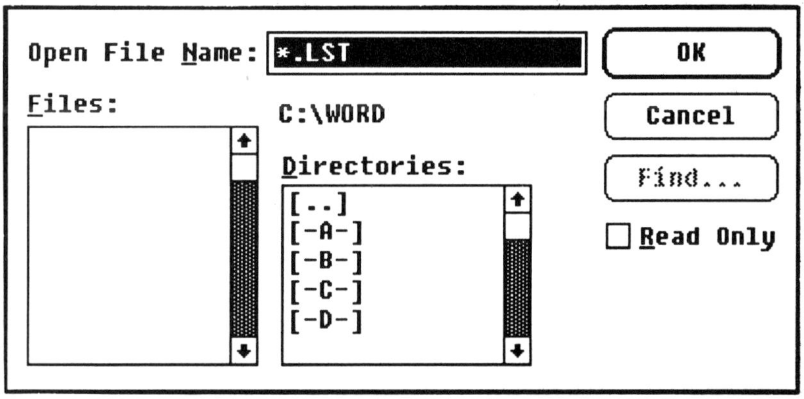

in the combination box at the left (use Alt+L to select the combination box from the keyboard). You can select an item from the list or type new text into the text area at the top of the combination box. There are two ways to add items to the list. First, you can type text into the combination-box text area, select the Add to List option button, and select OK. The text appears at the end of the list. Second, if you selected text before running the macro, you can add the text to the list by selecting first Selection to Item and then OK.

The Item to Insertion option places the text in the text area of the combination box at the insertion point. The List to Document option dumps the entire contents of the current list into the document, starting at the insertion point. The Remove from List option looks for the combination-box text in the list. If the item is found, it is deleted, and the size of the list is reduced by one. The Find Item option looks for an exact match between the combination-box text and a list item. If one is found, you are alerted as to its position in the list. The Move to Top option also looks for the combination-box text in the list. If the text is found, it is moved to the top of the list. If it is not found, the text is inserted as the first item in the list.

If you select Cancel, the current list is saved to a disk file and the macro ends.

The ListManager macro demonstrates array manipulation and sequential file methods. You could use it as the starting point for dozens of programs that need to manipulate lists of information (file names, phone numbers, department names, addresses, and so forth).

You could modify ListManager in a number of ways as a means of developing your programming skills. You might want to try one or more of the following exercises:

- Currently the file name entered in the input box when you select the New File option is not checked. Add lines that check to see whether the file name is legal. One approach is to **Open File$**, using the SaveList and LoadList subroutines as your guide. If the name is illegal, you can use **On Error** (see Chapter 6, "More WordBASIC Programming Concepts") to trap the error that is generated and then prompt the user for a legal name. Remember that the **CancelButton** in the dialog box can also create an error.
- ListManager as presented here creates a list of up to 500 items. When you add items to the list, there is no checking to ensure that the list is not already 500 items long. Attempting to add more than 500 items to the list creates an error. One approach to checking is to find all locations in the program where the list is expanded and to add an **If...Then** statement to make sure the *ListSize* variable is not 500. You could also use an **On Error** statement to trap the error when it happens and take corrective action.
- No default text is provided in the combination box. Add statements so that the text that previously appeared in the combination-box appears as the default.

NOTE: *The text in the combination box is stored in the variable Item$. For information on providing a default value to a combination box, see Chapter 6, "More WordBASIC Programming Concepts."*

- An unused subroutine, FindItemLike, is included in the program. FindItemLike looks for any occurrence of *Item$* in a list item. For instance, if *Item$* contains the text `Ball`, FindItemLike finds an item containing the text `ball`, `balloon`, or `baseball`. Add the FindItemLike subroutine as a new option on the main ListManager dialog box. Remember that you will have to change the dialog-box definition and add a new item to the **Select Case** statement that handles the dialog results.

```
'+++++++++++++++++++++++++++++++++++++++++++++++++++++
'ListManager - Maintains list files. List items or whole lists can be
'inserted in documents. Selected text can be copied into lists.
'+++++++++++++++++++++++++++++++++++++++++++++++++++++
'Global variables
'+++++++++++++++++++++++++++++++++++++++++++++++++++++
Dim Shared List$(500)          '*** Dim List array
Dim Shared Item$               '*** Dim Item passing string
Dim Shared ListSize            '*** Dim List Size
Dim Shared File$               '*** List file name
'+++++++++++++++++++++++++++++++++++++++++++++++++++++
'Main program line
'+++++++++++++++++++++++++++++++++++++++++++++++++++++
Sub MAIN                                    'Main line
DisableInput

REM Checks for macro window
   If InStr(WindowName$(),":")<>0 Then
      MsgBox "Command not available in a macro window"
   End If

fPreview = FilePrintPreview()
FilePrintPreview 0

   Begin Dialog UserDialog 300, 100         'Begin FileDlg
      OKButton 216, 32, 70, 20              'OK
      CancelButton 216, 58, 70, 20          'Cancel
      Text 85, 5, 150, 9, "ListManager"     'Title

                     'Option group: Open file or new file
      OptionGroup .FileOption
         OptionButton 75, 32, 120, 18, "&File Open"
         OptionButton 75, 58, 100, 18, "&New File"
   End Dialog          'End FileDlg
   Dim FileBox As Dialog UserDialog
   On Error Goto restore
   Dialog FileBox      'Do the defined dialog
   On Error Goto 0
                     'Check option button status and
                     'Call subroutine accordingly
```

(continued)

```
   If FileBox.FileOption = 0 Then
      Dim dlgrec As FileOpen   'Dim as FileOpen
      GetCurValues dlgrec      'Get current FileOpen
                               'default values
      dlgrec.Name = "*.LST"    'Set file name mask to
                               'find *.LST files
      On Error Goto restore
      Dialog dlgrec            'Do FileOpen dialog
      On Error Goto 0      File$ = dlgrec.Name      'Pass filename to load
                               'list subroutine
      LoadList
   Else
      File$ = InputBox$("File name for new list (filename.LST)", "ListManager")
   End If
Start:                 'Return point for main loop
On Error Goto Exit     'Responds to error created by choosing
                       'Cancel button.

Begin Dialog UserDialog 400, 220   'Begin Edit dialog definition
   OptionGroup .EditOption         'Select command
      OptionButton 185, 25, 200, 18, "&Item To Insertion"
                       'Copy .Item to insertion point
      OptionButton 185, 42, 200, 18, "&Selection to Item"
                       'Add selection to list
      OptionButton 185, 59, 200, 18, "List to &Document"
                       'Dump the entire list to the document
      OptionButton 185, 76, 200, 18, "&Add to List"
                       'Add .Item to list
      OptionButton 185, 93, 200, 18, "&Remove from List"
                       'Delete item matching .Item from list
      OptionButton 185, 110, 200, 18, "&Find Item"
                       'Search for string in list matching .Item
      OptionButton 185, 127, 200, 18, "&Move to Top"
                       'Sort list in alphabetical order
   OKButton 220, 180, 90, 20
   Text 185, 185, 40, 20, "Go:"          'For OK
   CancelButton 320, 180, 70, 20
   Text 150, 5, 200, 18, "&List Manager"   'Dialog title
   ComboBox 10, 25, 165, 180, List$(), .Item
   End Dialog                            'End Edit dialog definition
   Dim EditBox As Dialog UserDialog
   On Error Goto restore
   Dialog EditBox
   On Error Goto 0
   Item$ = EditBox.Item
                       'Process commands and branch accordingly
```

(continued)

```
  Select Case EditBox.EditOption
      Case 0
         Insert Item$
                     'Copy .Item to insertion point
      Case 1
         Item$ = Selection$( )
         AddToList
                     'Add selection to list
      Case 2
         ListToDoc
                     'Dump the entire list to the document
      Case 3
         AddToList
                     'Add .Item to list
      Case 4
         DeleteFmList
                     'Delete item matching .Item from list
      Case 5
         Search
                     'Search for string in list matching .Item

      Case 6
         ItemToTop
                     'Move item matching .Item to top of list
      Case Else
         Print "Whoops, fix that program!"
                     'Detects illegal commands
   End Select
Goto Start
Exit:
SaveList             'Save and close list

restore:
FilePrintReview fPreview
bye:
End Sub              'End Main line

'++++++++++++++++++++++++++++++++++++++++++++++++++++
'Subroutines
'++++++++++++++++++++++++++++++++++++++++++++++++++++

'____________________________________________________
'ListToDoc - Place list into document, paragraph delimited,
'starting at the insertion point.
'____________________________________________________
Sub ListToDoc
   For Count = 0 To ListSize - 1        'Loop through the list
      Insert List$(Count)               'Insert the item
      Insert Chr$(11)                   'Insert a return
   Next                                 'End of loop
End Sub                                 'ListToDoc
```

(continued)

```
'________________________________________________________
'Search - Search list for exact match to Item$. Notify user
'of result.
'________________________________________________________
Sub Search
Pointer = FindItem(Item$)
   Select Case Pointer
      Case - 1
         MsgBox Item$ + " not found", "List Manager", 64
      Case Else
MsgBox Item$ + " is item #" + Str$(Pointer + 1) + " in the list", "List Manager", 64
   End Select
End Sub                                    'Search

'________________________________________________________
'AddToList - Append Item$ to end of list.
'________________________________________________________
Sub AddToList
   ListSize = ListSize + 1                 'Enlarge list by one
   List$(ListSize - 1) = Item$             'Set last item in list as List$
End Sub

'________________________________________________________
'DeleteFmList - Delete item matching Item$ from list.
'________________________________________________________
Sub DeleteFmList
   Pointer = FindItem(Item$)          'Find item to delete
   Select Case Pointer
      Case - 1                        'Item not found
         MsgBox "Not Found", "List Manager"
      Case Else                       'Item found
         For Count = Pointer To ListSize
                                      'Overwrite item to delete and
                                      'shrink list to take up space
            List$(Count) = List$(Count + 1)
         Next                         'Count
         ListSize = ListSize - 1
                                      'List is one smaller now
   End Select
End Sub                               'DeleteFmList


'________________________________________________________
'ItemToTop - Make Item$ the first item in list.
'________________________________________________________
Sub ItemToTop
   Pointer = FindItem(Item$)          'Is Item$ in list?
```

(continued)

```
  Select Case Pointer
     Case - 1                       'Item$ doesn't exist in list
                                    'Enlarge list by one before inserting
                                    'Item$ at top
        ListSize = ListSize + 1
     Case Else                      'Item$ already exists, delete before
                                    'inserting at top
        For Count = Pointer To ListSize
           List$(Count) = List$(Count + 1)
        Next
   End Select

     For Counter = ListSize To 0 Step - 1
        List$(Counter + 1) = List$(Counter)
     Next                           'Move the entire list down
                                    'one item, opening room at the top
   List$(0) = Item$                 'Make Item$ the first item in list
End Sub
'_____________________________________________________
' End Edit Subroutines
'_____________________________________________________

'_____________________________________________________
' Utility Subroutines and Functions
'_____________________________________________________

'_____________________________________________________
'FindItem - Find exact match to Search$ in list and return
'location. If not found, return -1.
'_____________________________________________________
Function FindItem(Search$)
   Count = 0
   While Count <= ListSize And List$(Count) <> Search$
      Count = Count + 1
   Wend
   If List$(Count) <> Search$ Then FindItem = - 1 Else FindItem = Count
End Function

'_____________________________________________________
'FindItemLike - Find first occurance of Search$ in any list
'string. If not found, return -1.
'_____________________________________________________
Function FindItemLike(Search$)
   Count = 0
   While Count <= ListSize And InStr(List$(Count), Search$) = 0
      Count = Count + 1
   Wend
   If InStr(List$(Count), Search$) = 0 Then FindItem = - 1
Else FindItem = Count
End Function
```

(continued)

```
'________________________________________________________
'SaveList - Save list into sequential files.
'________________________________________________________

Sub SaveList
   Open File$ For Output As #1        'Open file
   For Count = 0 To ListSize - 1
      Print "Writing file: " ; File$ ; ", Record: " ; Count + 1
      Write #1, List$(Count)
   Next
   Close #1
End Sub                               'End SaveList

'________________________________________________________
'LoadList - Read list from sequential files.
'________________________________________________________

Sub LoadList
   Open File$ For Input As #1         'Open File
      While Not(Eof(1))               'Loop until end of file
         Read #1, List$(ListSize)
                                      'Read a record into an item
         ListSize = ListSize + 1
                                      'Increase the list size by one
         Print "Reading Item: " ; ListSize
      Wend                            'End loop
   Close #1                           'Close file
End Sub                               'End LoadList
```

Appendix C

Using Windows Dynamic Link Libraries

> **NOTE:** *WordBASIC supports calls to Dynamic Link Libraries only under Windows. WordBASIC does not currently support OS/2 Dynamic Link Libraries. Using Dynamic Link Libraries requires experience with Windows programming. Be careful when working with these features. You may accidentally reset the computer or damage software. Always work with copies of your software and documents (including your NORMAL.DOT file); never work with the originals.*

You can access the Windows Dynamic Link Libraries from your WordBASIC macros. To use an external library function, declare it as a subroutine or function in your macro. Use a **Declare** statement to tell Word the name of the new subroutine or function, its parameters, and the type of value returned. The syntax for this statement is:

Declare Sub *SubName* **Lib** *LibName* [*ParameterList*] [**Alias** *ModuleName*]

Declare Function *FunctionName* **Lib** *LibName* [*ParameterList*] [**Alias** *ModuleName*]

Lib *LibName* specifies the Dynamic Link Library containing the subroutine or function. The *LibName* for Word is MSWORD. If you want to rename the subroutine or function module, use the **Alias** keyword followed by the *ModuleName*.

You define return-value types by using the keyword **As** followed by the type (Integer, Long, Double, or String) at the end of the statement. You define argument types by using the same keyword and types after the given argument. You can define the argument type as String by appending a dollar sign ($) to the argument name. For example, in the statement

```
Declare MySub Lib "mylib" (foo As Integer, bar$) As String
```

the `foo` argument is an integer, the `bar` argument is a string, and the return value is a string.

The following example declares an external function for use within Word for Windows:

```
Declare Function IsAppLoaded Lib "kernel" (name$) As Integer Alias
      "GetModuleHandle"
Sub MAIN
   AppName$ = InputBox$("Enter an application name (e.g., Excel)")
   If IsAppLoaded(AppName$) Then Print "The application is loaded"
End Sub
```

Appendix D

Translating Fonts

Because a word processor's fonts are dependent on its printer drivers, fonts may not translate perfectly to and from Microsoft Word for Windows or Word for OS/2 and other word-processing programs. To overcome this problem, you can customize font translation of some file formats by creating your own font-mapping file. This file overrides some or all of the translations made by the Word file-format converters. You can create a font-mapping file for the following file formats:

- Microsoft Word for DOS
- Microsoft Works for DOS
- DisplayWrite

All files transferred to and from Word for Windows or Word for OS/2 are translated using Rich Text Format (RTF) as an intermediate format. For example, a Word for DOS file is transferred first into RTF, and then into Word for Windows or Word for OS/2 format. For more information on RTF, see Chapter 10, "Rich Text Format."

CREATING A FONT-MAPPING FILE

The information necessary to map fonts from one word processor to another is contained in an ASCII file, named with the following format:

AAA-BBB.DAT

The three characters preceding the hyphen in the ASCII file name represent the file's original format, shown here as *AAA*. The three characters following the hyphen represent the file's translated format, shown here as *BBB*. So, for example, a file translating RTF fonts into Word for DOS fonts would be called RTF-PCW.DAT. The following table shows the ASCII font-mapping file names. The content of the files is described later in this appendix.

To convert this format	Into this format	Create this file
Word for DOS	Word for Windows or Word for OS/2	PCW-RTF.DAT
Word for Windows or Word for OS/2	Word for DOS	RTF-PCW.DAT
Works (word processor)	Word for Windows	WWP-RTF.DAT
Word for Windows or Word for OS/2	Works (word processor)	RTF-WWP.DAT
DisplayWrite	Word for Windows or Word for OS/2	DCA-RTF.DAT
Word for Windows or Word for OS/2	DisplayWrite	RTF-DCA.DAT

When creating a font-mapping file, bear in mind the following rules:

- RTF fonts are specified in half-points.
- The names of fonts are not case sensitive.
- The lines in the file must be arranged in alphabetical order, based on the first character of each line (a–z, 0–9).
- Comment lines can be inserted by preceding the comment with a number sign (#). The number sign must be the first character in the line.

TRANSLATING BETWEEN WORD FOR WINDOWS OR WORD FOR OS/2 AND WORD FOR DOS

Entries in the PCW-RTF.DAT file must be in the following format:

DOSWordFontNumber;RTFFontName[,RTFFontFamily]

For example,

```
8;courier,modern
```

converts all Word for DOS characters in font 8 (Helvetica) into Courier RTF characters, while

```
16;tms rmn,roman
```

converts Word for DOS characters in font 16 (Roman a) into Tms Rmn RTF characters.

For a list of all the Word for DOS font numbers, see *Printer Information for Microsoft Word*, which came in your Word for DOS package.

Entries in the RTF-PCW.DAT file must be in the following format:

RTFFontName;DOSWordFontNumber

For example,

```
courier;8
```

converts all Courier RTF characters into Word for DOS characters in font 8 (Helvetica), while

```
tms rmn;16
```

converts Tms Rmn RTF characters into Word for DOS characters in font 16 (Roman a).

TRANSLATING BETWEEN WORD FOR WINDOWS OR WORD FOR OS/2 AND WORKS

Works and Word for Windows or Word for OS/2 font translations can be customized in the same way as those for Word for DOS; the only difference is in the name of the ASCII file (WWP replaces PCW in the file name designation).

TRANSLATING BETWEEN WORD FOR WINDOWS OR WORD FOR OS/2 AND DISPLAYWRITE

Entries in the RTF-DCA.DAT file must be in the following format:

RTFFontName,RTFPointSize[,RTFPointSize];GFID[,[Width][,Attribute]]

For example,

```
tms rmn,0-20;25
```

converts all Tms Rmn RTF characters between 0 and 10 points to GFID 25 characters, while

```
tms rmn,24;26
```

converts all 12-point Tms Rmn RTF characters into GFID 26 characters.

Entries in the DCA-RTF.DAT file must be in the following format:

GFID[-GFID];RTFFontName,[RTFFontFamily],RTFPointSize

For example,

```
25;tms rmn,roman,20
```

converts all GFID 25 characters into 10-point Tms Rmn RTF characters, while

```
26;tms rmn,,24
```

converts all GFID 26 characters into 12-point Tms Rmn RTF characters.

NOTE: *Although the RTFFontFamily parameter is optional, the comma preceding it is not (as in the second line of the preceding example).*

Index

C

D

E

F

G

H

I

J

K

L

M

V

W

The manuscript for this book was prepared and submitted to Microsoft Press in electronic form. Text files were processed and formatted using Microsoft Word.

Principal word processor: Joan Anderson
Principal proofreader: Laura Mathews
Principal typographer: Byron Canfield
Cover color separator: Wescan Color Corporation

Text composition by Microsoft Press in Times Roman with display type in Times Bold, using Ventura Publisher and the Apple LaserWriter IInt.

Printed on recycled paper stock.